Friends and Exiles
A Memoir of the Nutmeg Isles and the Indonesian Nationalist Movement

 Cornell University

Des Alwi
edited by Barbara S. Harvey

Friends and Exiles
A Memoir of the Nutmeg Isles and the Indonesian Nationalist Movement

SOUTHEAST ASIA PROGRAM PUBLICATIONS
Southeast Asia Program
Cornell University
Ithaca, New York
2008

Cornell Southeast Asia Program Publications
640 Stewart Avenue, Ithaca, NY 14850-3857

Studies on Southeast Asia No. 44

Printed in the United States of America

ISBN: hc 978-0-87727-774-3
ISBN: pb 978-0-87727-744-6

Cover Design: Maureen Viele

TABLE OF CONTENTS

LIST OF ILLUSTRATIONS

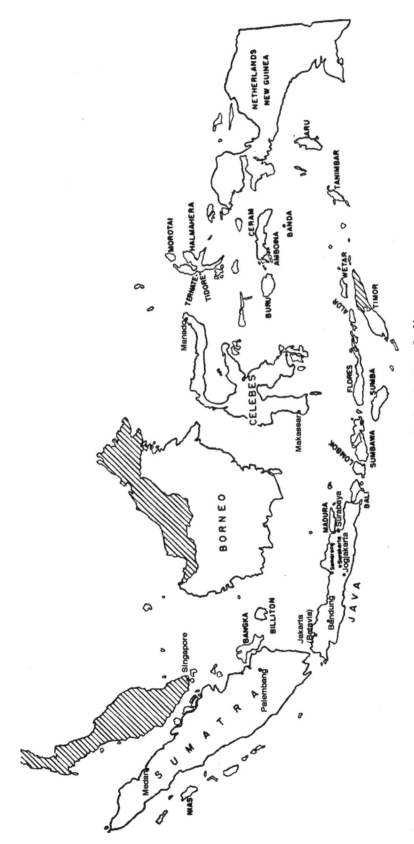

The Netherlands East Indies.

INTRODUCTION

Des Alwi was born and grew up in the Banda Islands, the fabled spice islands, where nutmeg originated. These seven islands are tiny specks in the vast Indonesian archipelago that stretches some three thousand miles along the equator in Southeast Asia. Indonesia is the world's fourth largest country, with an estimated population of 220 million. Indonesia comprises an estimated three hundred distinct ethnic groups, each with its own language. Most of these groups are indigenous, but people of Arab descent and sizeable communities of Chinese descent are found, especially in the major cities, where they often dominate commerce and are well-represented in the professions. The Javanese are the largest ethnic group, comprising nearly half the population, and traditionally staff the government bureaucracy. Indonesia's two largest cities, the capital, Jakarta, and the commercial center, Surabaya, are located on the politically and culturally dominant island of Java.

The Banda Islands are located more than a thousand miles to the east of Java, in the center of the Molucca Islands. Ambon, long-time capital of the Moluccas, lies about 120 miles to the northwest of Banda. With the sea providing easy communication, the Molucca islands are ethnically mixed, a tendency enhanced by various policies of the Dutch colonial rulers.

Indonesia, or parts of it, came under Dutch rule starting in the seventeenth century with the involvement of the Dutch United East India Company (Vereenigde Oost-Indische Compagnie, or VOC) in governance as well as trade as it sought to establish monopolies over valuable tropical produce. The spices that drew European adventurers and traders to Asia, and Christopher Columbus to what is now the Americas, were indigenous to the Moluccan islands.

The forts, or remains of forts, still to be found in the islands of the Banda group bear mute testimony to the struggles of the Portuguese in the sixteenth century, and the Dutch and British in the seventeenth century, to control the trade in nutmeg, a highly desirable spice of incredible value. In a 1667 treaty between the Dutch and the British, the British ceded their claim to the small nutmeg-producing island of Run, their only foothold in the Bandas, and in turn the Dutch ceded the island of Manhattan to the British.

The indigenous people of the Banda Islands were not mere bystanders in this competition. In a brutal suppression of Bandanese opposition in 1621, at the direction of the Dutch East India Company governor general, Jan Pieterszoon Coen, leaders of the Bandanese community were executed, and many inhabitants of the islands were exiled to Java, to be sold into slavery. The role of Japanese mercenaries in the employ of the Dutch in these tragic events has not been forgotten in Banda. The historian Willard Hanna has estimated that, of an original population of about fifteen thousand, only one thousand remained in the Bandas after this suppression. In order to cultivate the valuable nutmeg trees, the VOC made grants of land, known as *perken*, mostly to one-time employees of the Company, and provided each with twenty-five slaves to do the actual work. As the number of surviving Bandanese was insufficient various indigenous people were brought from other islands of the Moluccas, Timor, Borneo (now Kalimantan), and also Java.

Thus, it is not unusual for Banda that Des Alwi's ancestors include Arabs, Chinese, Javanese, Manadonese, and Sumatrans, but the mixture does make him truly Indonesian. Des Alwi was born while the Dutch still ruled the Netherlands East Indies, and his family was impoverished by the Great Depression (1930s), which hit this richest of Dutch colonies hard. His grandfather, Said Tjong Baadilla, the "Pearl King" of the East Indies, was declared bankrupt in 1933 and died soon thereafter.

By the 1930s, a nationalist movement opposed to Dutch colonial rule and looking toward an independent Indonesian state had gained enough traction to appear threatening to the Dutch. Many of the young leaders were Dutch educated, having been schooled either in Indonesia itself, or in the Netherlands. There were only three institutions of higher learning in the Indies during the colonial period—the Medical and Law Faculties in Jakarta (then Batavia) and the Institute of Technology in Bandung—a circumstance that helps to explain the preponderance of doctors, lawyers, and engineers in the nationalist movement, as well as in the colonial civil service.

Education at all levels for the native population was very limited during the colonial period. Between 1921, when the first tertiary education became available, and 1940, there were only 230 Indonesian graduates of government institutions. Most elementary education in the local language provided for only three years of schooling, and most secondary education was reserved for those categorized as "European." This government educational system was supplemented by special schools for children of native soldiers and for those categorized as "foreign Orientals," mainly ethnic Chinese. Particularly in areas where Christian missionaries were active, church-supported schools provided an alternative source of education, as did the many Islamic schools, both traditional, associated with rural religious teachers, and modern, primarily associated with the Modernist Islamic organization Muhammadiyah, which had been founded in 1912 in Jogjakarta. A secular nationalist school system, the Taman Siswa, was established in 1921, also in Jogjakarta, and many of its graduates were prominent in the nationalist movement.

Sukarno, later to be the first president of independent Indonesia, was a graduate of the Institute of Technology in Bandung. He founded the Indonesian Nationalist Party (Partai Nasional Indonesia, or PNI) in 1927, was arrested by the colonial authorities in 1929, and in 1933 was exiled to the island of Flores in eastern Indonesia, and then to Bengkulu in southern Sumatra. Mohammad Hatta, the first vice president of Indonesia, was a graduate of the Rotterdam School of Economics. While in the Netherlands he chaired the Perhimpunan Indonesia (Indonesian Union), of which Sutan Sjahrir, a law student in Leiden, was a member. When these men, both Minangkabau of West Sumatra, returned to Indonesia in 1931 and 1932, they decided to emphasize the education of political cadre rather than political mobilization, which had been Sukarno's forté. The colonial authorities were quick to recognize that this new emphasis posed as much threat to their rule as did political activism, and banned their Indonesian National Education Club (Pendidikan Nasional Indonesia, or PNI-Baru).

In 1934, the Dutch exiled Hatta and Sjahrir, first to the notorious prison camp Boven Digul (in what was then New Guinea) and then, just over a year later (in early 1936), to Banda, an easier incarceration, but still isolated from political developments.

These two men soon became important and beloved members of the Bandanese community. They established a free afternoon school for the local children, and Sjahrir informally adopted several, including Des, his sister Lily, and his cousins Mimi and Ali. Association with the two Dutch-educated nationalists shaped the destiny of these young people. On the outbreak of the Pacific War in 1941, the Dutch authorities returned Hatta and Sjahrir to Java, hoping to enlist them against a prospective Japanese invasion. However, the Dutch forces quickly crumbled in the face of the Japanese army, and many of the Dutch in the Indies were interned for the duration of the war. A number of Netherlands East Indies officials escaped to Australia, where they formed a colonial government in exile.

Hatta, together with Sukarno, who had also been returned to Java from exile, did cooperate with the Japanese administration of the Indies. Like many Indonesians, they initially welcomed the Japanese as liberators from the Dutch; neither abandoned hope for eventual independence. The exigencies of wartime rule, and the frequent brutality of the Japanese military, led most Indonesians to believe that no foreign rule could be accepted.

Sjahrir, who had taken three of the adopted Bandanese children with him to Java, led what has been described as an "underground" during the Japanese Occupation. It was an "underground" in that it was secret and illegal, but it was not a "resistance" that committed sabotage or other active, overt opposition to Japanese rule. Together with other anti-fascist nationalists, Sjahrir maintained a network that exchanged news of the progress of the war, and he educated and trained nationalist cadre to fight for independence when that became possible. Japanese control during the Occupation was so efficient that virtually no overt opposition was possible.

Unable to accompany Hatta and Sjahrir on the American Catalina that came to Banda in January 1942 to take the two nationalist leaders to Java, Des Alwi made his way to Java in succeeding months. As a lad of fourteen, he drew on a network of relatives and family friends—and his own ingenuity—to obtain ship's passage first to Ambon, then to Makassar, a major port in South Sulawesi for inter-island shipping, and finally to Java, where he remained for the duration of the Japanese Occupation. Living with Sjahrir and the other Bandanese children, but with his school fees provided by Hatta, Des first enrolled in a technical school in Jakarta. There he learned radio electronics, a helpful skill for the underground network seeking uncensored news from foreign broadcasts.

As a member of the Sjahrir household in Jakarta, Des became acquainted with members of the underground nationalist movement, who were frequent visitors, but as a boy Des remained on the fringes. Some members of the Sjahrir circle had been members of the PNI-Baru that Sjahrir and Hatta established after their return from the Netherlands in the early 1930s. A significant number were associated with the Taman Siswa school system. Many were graduates of, or students at, the Medical and Law Faculties in Jakarta. The Japanese closed all tertiary institutions in 1942, but subsequently reopened the Medical Faculty, which remained the only functioning higher educational institute for the duration of the Occupation.

Many of the younger nationalists were associated with three *asrama*—dormitories, but dormitories that served as spiritual homes, as implied in the root word, *ashram*, meaning a Hindu-Buddhist spiritual center for study and meditation. Residence at one of these *asrama* provided an institutional locus to youth in the capital, and those who lived, studied, and argued together formed long-lasting personal and political ties. All these *asrama* were located in the heart of Jakarta's elite residential area.

Closest to the Sjahrir circle was the *asrama* of the Medical Faculty, usually identified by its location at Prapatan 10. As tertiary-level education was so limited, these students inevitably came from the elite of native society, and perhaps because the content of their study was Western, they tended to be Western in their orientation.

The Asrama Angkatan Baru Indonesia (Indonesian New Generation Asrama), located at Menteng 31, was sponsored by the Japanese army's propaganda department. The youth associated with this *asrama* tended to have been at least somewhat involved in anti-colonial activities before the war, and to have come from somewhat lower levels of native society. Established nationalists, such as Sukarno and Hatta, were among those who lectured on nationalist themes in the training sessions, and the youth in this *asrama* also had links to Indonesians who were working at the Japanese news agency and the city newspaper.

The third of these *asrama*, Asrama Indonesia Merdeka (Independent Indonesia Asrama), at Kebon Sirih 80, was established only in October 1944, after Japan had promised to grant independence to Indonesia. It was run under the auspices of Rear Admiral Tadashi Maeda, who was the liaison officer between the Japanese Army in Java, and the naval administration, based in Makassar, responsible for eastern Indonesia. The roster of older nationalists who lectured to the trainees at Kebon Sirih 80 was virtually identical to those who addressed students at Menteng 31, and both conservative and leftist nationalists were associated with the *asrama*.

In early 1944, as the situation in Jakarta became more tense, with arrests of a number of those thought to be anti-Japanese, Des went to Surabaya. He continued his technical education there and linked up with an East Javanese anti-Japanese network established by Sjahrir's nephew Johan Sjahruzah.

With an instinct for being where the action was, Des returned to Jakarta before Sukarno and Hatta's proclamation of Indonesian independence on August 17, 1945, two days after the Japanese surrender to the Allies, which ended the Second World War. A decision by the Allies shortly before the Japanese surrender designated British forces under Lord Louis Mountbatten to accept the surrender of the Japanese forces in the Indies. Apparently convinced by their Dutch allies that the Netherlands would be welcomed back after the brutal Japanese Occupation, the British were unprepared for the strength of the pro-independence sentiment among the Indonesian population.

Another trip across Java brought Des to Surabaya in time for the heaviest fighting of the Revolution—the battle of Surabaya, against British Indian troops. During the three weeks of clashes in November 1945, Des served as a radio officer with a prominent local youth organization, which encompassed many of his underground associates.

Under pressure from the British, eager to extricate themselves from this misadventure in the Dutch East Indies, and with the willingness of progressive Dutch politicians, the Netherlands reached an agreement with the nascent Republic of Indonesia in November 1946 that provided, among other elements, for recognition of *de facto* Republican control over parts of Java and Sumatra. Believing that this Linggadjati Agreement meant that Indonesia was about to receive its independence, Des left for Europe in 1947 to study abroad. When the first Dutch military action against Indonesia started in July 1947, he went to London, where he worked in the information department of an Indonesian office that had been opened in London by the Republic. While in London, Des took a course at the Regent Street Polytechnic, and in 1947 enrolled as a student at the British Institute of Technology. He later worked as a technician and a translator for the BBC.

Because he was absent for most of the Revolution, 1945 to 1949, Des's account of this crucial nation-forming event is quite attenuated. Following the recognition of Indonesia's independence in December 1949, Des returned to Indonesia in July 1950, working initially for Radio Republik Indonesia. He was sent to Ambon, where elements opposed to the new Republic of Indonesia attempted to establish a Republic of the South Moluccas (RMS), an effort that was defeated by the Indonesian armed forces.

In 1952, Des was appointed as an Indonesian delegate to the International Telecommunications Union Conference in Geneva, and in 1953 he joined the Indonesian diplomatic service, with postings in Europe (Switzerland and Austria) and in Manila. He ends his memoir as he embarks on a diplomatic career.

His life subsequent to 1953 was still fraught with challenge, thanks in large part to volatile conditions in Indonesia. Hatta resigned as vice president in 1956 and Sukarno instituted "Guided Democracy" in 1957, effectively ending Indonesia's first attempt at parliamentary democracy. Des was serving as press attache at the Indonesian Embassy in Manila at the time, and became increasingly distressed by these political developments. When Des brought several Philippine correspondents, including Ninoy Aquino of the *Manila Times*, to North Sulawesi to interview a prominent anti-Sukarno colonel, Ventje Sumual, Des was recalled to Jakarta by Foreign Minister Subandrio. However, rather than return to Jakarta, Des instead joined the rebellion, becoming the overseas spokesman for Permesta, the Sulawesi half of the rebel government, PRRI (Pemerintah Revolusioner Republik Indonesia, Revolutionary Government of the Republic of Indonesia), established in Sumatra in February 1958. This experience, and the placing of his adopted father, Sjahrir, under house arrest in 1962, helps to explain the negative views of Sukarno so obvious in Des's memoir.

Based in Hong Kong from 1958 until the surrender of the rebel leaders in 1961, Des, with his wife and children, moved to Malaya in 1961. Following the fall of Sukarno, Des, still resident in Malaya, worked with Indonesian Foreign Minister Adam Malik and Presidential Special Assistant Ali Moertopo as a mediator to end the confrontation, begun in 1963, between Indonesia and the newly formed Malaysia. Des also helped with the formation of ASEAN, the Association of Southeast Asian Nations, in 1967, as mentioned in a speech by then Malaysian Foreign Minister Ghazali Shafie in 1981 when he received the Dag Hammarskjold award.

Des Alwi and his family returned to Indonesia in 1966. Since that time, Des has devoted himself, with considerable success, to rescuing Banda from neglect and decay. He has restored the houses in which Hatta and Sjahrir lived and taught during their years in Banda Neira, and established a small museum. His hotel in Banda Neira is a favorite destination for snorkeling diplomats from Jakarta, and for many foreigners who have heard of the beauty of Banda and its sea gardens. Des founded, and is the chairman of, Banda's Culture and Heritage Foundation.

Deeply distressed by outbreaks of inter-religious violence in Ambon and other Moluccan islands, Des has been an important voice for peace and tolerance, and was personally responsible for protecting the lives of a group of Christian refugees in Banda Neira.

For his service to Indonesia during the Revolution, to Banda, and to promoting religious harmony, in August 2003, Des was awarded the *Maha Putra* medal by Indonesia's then president, Megawati Sukarnoputri, daughter of Sukarno, the president Des had opposed nearly fifty years earlier.

* * *

In an oral culture, such as Indonesia's, history is remembered, often with amazing detail, and is not dependent on the written word. The memories recounted in Des Alwi's memoir are told with the immediacy of a child's remembering significant, or pleasurable, events of his past. Thus, the memoir does not represent the reflections of the adult Des Alwi on his childhood and his association with the nationalist leaders whose presence in his life so changed it. Not much given to introspection, Des does not analyze the influence of Hatta and Sjahrir on him or the impact of this association on his life.

The influence, particularly of Sjahrir, is evident in many of the biases Des shares with his adopted father. In a larger sense, although Des Alwi has remained rooted in Banda, the island of his childhood that he so loves, the fact that he has become a national figure reflects the impact on his life of the two nationalist mentors.

Des's portrayals of Hatta and Sjahrir as seen by a boy in a remote island add a dimension to what we know of these men. We see Hatta as serious, responsible, and respected; Sjahrir as playful, principled, and complex. These insights into their personalities shed light on their later careers.

This memoir of an almost carefree childhood also provides insight into inter-ethnic relations in the colonial period. Friendships crossed ethnic lines, as demonstrated not only in Des's relations with his ethnic Chinese and Eurasian friends, but in Sjahrir's visits to the elderly Dutch woman who had been his teacher in Medan years before. That such friendships, which go beyond tolerance, are possible is important in the Indonesia of today where inter-ethnic and inter-religious strife have torn the social fabric and resulted in so much death and destruction.

Although the 1945–49 Revolution against the Dutch was the seminal event in the history of the Republic of Indonesia, it occupies little space in this memoir. In part this is because, at the time, Des was just beginning to become a conscious nationalist, largely due to his association with Sjahrir and those around him. Still a teenager, Des was not privy to the intricacies of political competition among the nationalists during the Japanese Occupation and Revolution. In addition, because Des includes in this memoir only those events he experienced himself, his departure from Indonesia for study abroad in 1947, when the Revolution was far from over, helps to explain his very limited discussion of this history-making event.

Barbara S. Harvey

NOTES ON FURTHER READING

A version of Des Alwi's memoir that focuses on his childhood in the Banda Islands is being published in Jakarta under the title *A Boy From Banda: A Spice Island Childhood* (also edited by Barbara S. Harvey).

A popular account of the British-Dutch rivalry over the spice islands provides considerable historical information on the Banda Islands: Giles Milton, *Nathaniel's*

Nutmeg (New York: Penguin Books, 2000). A useful history, but possibly more difficult to obtain outside Indonesia, is Willard A. Hanna's *Indonesian Banda: Colonialism and its Aftermath in the Nutmeg Islands* (Banda Neira: Yaysan Warisan dan Budaya Banda Neira, 1991). Hanna is also the principal author of a beautifully illustrated book, *Banda: A Journey Through Indonesia's Fabled Isles of Fire and Spice* (Banda Neira: Yayasan Warisan dan Budaya Banda, 1997).

Des Alwi has written an account of his time with Hatta and Sjahrir: *Bersama Hatta, Syahrir, Dr. Tjipto & Iwa K. Soemantri di Banda Naira* (Jakarta: Penerbit Dian Rakyat, 2002). The Banda Culture and Heritage Foundation published Des Alwi's *Turbulent Times Past in Ternate and Tidore* in 1987, and recently published his *Sejarah Maluku: History of the Moluccas: Banda, Ternate, Tidore, and Ambon.*

Sjahrir's own account of his life, published in English as *Out of Exile* (New York, NY: Greenwood Press, 1949, translated and with an introduction by Charles Wolf, Jr.), includes his stay in Banda and some discussion of his thoughts and activities during the Japanese Occupation. Rudolf Mrázek's biography, *Sjahrir: Politics and Exile in Indonesia* (Ithaca, NY: Cornell Southeast Asia Program Publications, 1994), discusses Sjahrir's period of exile in Banda (based partly on interviews with Des Alwi and his sister Lily), and has a particularly insightful account of the nature of Sjahrir's underground during the Japanese Occupation.

The classic study of Indonesia in the late-colonial period, under the Japanese Occupation, and during the Revolution is: George McT. Kahin, *Nationalism and Revolution in Indonesia* (Ithaca, NY: Cornell University Press, 1952, reprinted 2003, Cornell Southeast Asia Program Publications). Additional insights are provided by Benedict R. O'G. Anderson in: *Java in a Time of Revolution* (Ithaca, NY: Cornell University Press, 1972).

NOTE ON THE SPELLING OF PROPER NAMES

Indonesian spelling conventions have changed twice since Indonesia became independent. In the first change, the Dutch *oe* was changed to *u*. In the second, in 1972 the Indonesian and Malaysian government agreed to adopt uniform spelling for their very similar languages, both based on classical and *pasar* (market) Malay. Because many individuals did not change the spelling of their names, and their preference is followed where known, it is well to be aware of the alternative forms. They are:

"c"	instead of	"tj"
"sy"	instead of	"sj"
"j"	instead of	"dj"
"y"	instead of	"j"

Place names and street names have also changed over the years. To alleviate confusion, the capital of Indonesia, Jakarta, will be used for the same city that was called Batavia when it was capital of the Dutch East Indies. I have used the English Molucca Islands instead of the Indonesian Maluku, because the former is somewhat familiar. However, I have used the Indonesian Sulawesi for the island the Dutch called the Celebes, and Kalimantan for the Indonesian portions of the island of Borneo.

PUNCTUATION AND NOTES

Brackets in the text indicate insertions by the editor; parentheses were in the author's original text. The footnotes were provided by the editor; Des Alwi is credited in instances where he provided the information included in the footnote.

TITLES AND FORMS OF ADDRESS

It is usual in Indonesia to use a courtesy title in addressing someone, rather than an unadorned name. Many of the forms used are based on kinship terms. Some of the most common found in the text are:

Abang	Elder brother
Bung	Brother; used especially in the period of the Revolution, and applied particularly to Sukarno; connotation of friend or comrade.
Drs.	Dutch equivalent of a Master's degree.
Ibu or *Bu*	Mother; used to address an older woman.
Mbakyu or *Yu*	Elder sister
Mr.	Dutch law degree
Nyong	Young man (used in Eastern Indonesia)
Nyonya	Older, respected married woman; Mrs.
Oma	Grandmother
Pak or *oom* (Dutch)	Uncle
Tanta (Dutch)	Aunt
Tuan	Older, respected man, boss, or superior; Mr.

CHAPTER ONE

FAMILY

I was born in Neira, a small island of the Banda group in the Molucca archipelago, on November 17, 1927. The Banda group, although small in comparison to the other islands of the Moluccas, for the past five centuries has been famous for its nutmeg. The quality, and the sweet, pleasant smell of Bandanese nutmeg cannot be compared to nutmeg grown elsewhere. The Banda group comprises seven large islands and several small reef islets. Banda Besar (Great Banda) is banana-shaped and the largest of the group. Its western tip is separated from Gunung Api [Fire Mountain, volcano], a rocky volcano island, at an almost touching distance. Banda Neira, the so-called capital of the group, is again separated by a deep, blue lagoon from Gunung Api at a yelling distance. The two "sister" islands, Ai and Run, lie about three nautical miles from the western side of Gunung Api. Two smaller islands, Rozengain (or Rosengen), and Pulau Pisang (Banana Island), have been renamed Hatta Island and Sjahrir Island. Nutmeg is grown on all the Banda islands except Gunung Api, where only coconuts and tapioca are produced. Banda is also famous for its forts, built by the Portuguese and Dutch in the sixteenth and seventeenth centuries, relics of the time when spices were considered as expensive as gold and things to be fought for. Foreign tourists frequently visit Banda to see these old forts, nutmeg plantations, and the "sea gardens"—colorful coral reefs with cabbage or cauliflower-shaped sea plants surrounded by brightly colored fish.

THE POPULATION OF BANDA

Banda's population was a mixed lot: Dutch, Portuguese, Arabs, Chinese, and people from many other islands in the Indies archipelago. Whether named Schelling, Da Costa, van den Broeke, Barentz, Phillipus, Baadilla, Ong, Tan, Johar, Mahudim—all were considered Bandanese if they followed Bandanese customs and spoke Bandanese-Malay dialect. They all participated in prau races and festivals, fished, grew nutmeg, ate *bakasem*,[1] and, last but not least, believed in the *foe-foe* [black magic, Bandanese Malay].

Even the proud Ambonese who had lived in Banda for more than a decade considered themselves Bandanese. Butonese, who came from the over-populated island of Buton off the southeast coast of Sulawesi, formed Banda's "working class." They were the sailors, divers, plantation workers, vegetable growers, gardeners, and house servants. The Butonese and the people from the island of Sarua were considered "minority" groups as long as they still spoke their own dialect, but were

---

[1] A favorite dish of the Bandanese, Des describes *bakasem* as consisting of "fine chopped tuna intestines, salted, mixed with some coconut wine, then put in a bottle, tightly closed, and put in the sun for several days. Then it can be eaten with young mangoes by adding lots of hot chili peppers or cooked with young papaya leaves." Des adds: "No pure Dutch person would like to taste this dish."

no longer considered a "minority" when they, too, spoke Bandanese-Malay and participated in Bandanese festivals and dances.

Many of the "Europeans" were, in fact, Eurasians, descendants of a *perkenier* (Dutch planter) and a native wife. We children called them *oom*, "uncle" in Dutch. They were often called *burgers*,[2] the equivalent of "citizen" in English. Many could not speak Dutch properly and were assimilated into the Bandanese population, joining in all kinds of native festivals. Some of the *burgers* believed in *guna-guna* (black magic [Indonesian]) and *orang halus* [ghosts], the invisible protectors of Banda.

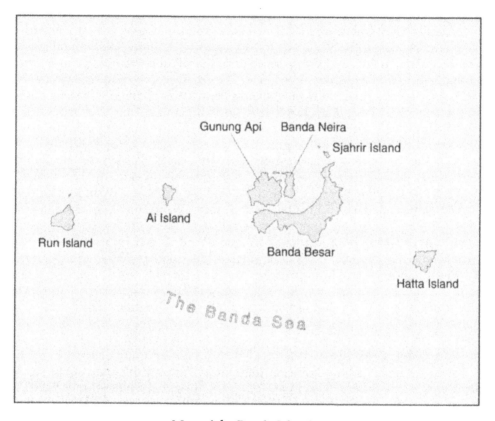

Gunung Api   Banda Neira

Sjahrir Island

Ai Island

Run Island

Banda Besar

Hatta Island

The Banda Sea

Map of the Banda Islands

During my childhood there were three categories of Chinese in Banda. The first were the Banda Chinese, who were already assimilated. They only used Chinese family names, but used Bandanese, Dutch, Muslim, or Christian given (first) names, such as Piet Siu, Hassan Tan, Achmad Lim, and Nochi Kwee. The second were locally born, but still used completely Chinese names, such as: Ho Kok Chai and Tan Eng Teng. The third were the *totok*, China-born and still wearing black trousers and white cotton jackets. The first group did not speak Chinese and did not like to be called *orang China*. They were usually Christian or Muslim, and their families had been in Banda Neira for generations. Some of them were as brown-skinned as any Indonesian. The second group, those who were born in Banda Neira, spoke a little

---

[2] "Burger" means citizen, civilian (in contrast to civil servant or official), middle-class person, bourgeois; in the Indies, *burger* often refers to business people of Dutch origin or status.

Chinese and still followed Chinese customs. The third group were the real Chinese, and most of them were shopkeepers.

GRANDFATHER AND GREAT-GRANDFATHER

My grandfather was named Said Tjong Baadilla. His mother was a member of the Tay family, said to be descendants of Ming Dynasty Chinese who had attacked Batavia [Jakarta] in the mid-seventeenth century and were exiled to Banda. Her father was head of the Chinese community; one daughter married a Montanus of Spanish descent, one married an ethnic Chinese named Nio Chiu, and the third, my great-grandmother, married Abdullah Baadilla. Baadilla is a name found in Spain and the Philippines, and is thought to be of Moroccan origin. The first evidence of a Baadilla in Banda is a gravestone dated 1797 of Said bin Aidit, who was the father of Awad Baadilla. Awad was a friend of Desa Abdullah, the head of the small Arab community of six or seven families in Banda and a mosque official. Desa Abdullah had come to the Moluccas from Malacca, where his younger brother, Munshi Abdullah, had been secretary to Sir Stamford Raffles, founder of Singapore. Desa Abdullah was among a group of Malays of Arab descent who came to Banda to take over the spice trade when the British marines, commanded by Captain Cole of the Royal Marines, occupied Banda during 1810–1817.[3]

Abdullah Baadilla, the son of Awad, had business in his blood. He was an entrepreneur who owned motorized sailing vessels, and was the first to operate a shipping line between Banda and Gresik, in East Java. The Dutch colonial government called this the *post-lijn* [mail line], and favored it because it avoided the port of Makassar, whose waters were full of pirates at that time. He died on one of his voyages to Gresik, leaving his business to his three sons.

The eldest son, my grandfather, Said, was seventeen years old when his father died. With his younger brothers, Abdul Rahim, sixteen, and Salim, fifteen, they formed a company they called Baadilla Brothers. The three boys were usually called by their Chinese names, Tjong, Nana, and Tjotjo. Said Tjong Baadilla took the lead in expanding the shipping firm from carrying post and cargo to carrying passengers. But he didn't stop there. At the age of twenty-four, in 1880, realizing that there was a market in Europe for mother-of-pearl for buttons, he began to search the Moluccas and the waters off Papua, even as far as the Southern Philippines, for mother-of-pearl shells.

While Said Tjong Baadilla was the brains of the enterprise, the younger brothers also played a role. The second brother, Abdul Rahim (Nana), had an eye for the ladies, and made strategic marriages with the daughters of the Raja of Buton in Bau Bau, the Raja of Maros in South Sulawesi, and the Raja of Kokas in Papua. These alliances expanded the area of influence of the firm; perhaps it could be called a kind of *humas* [public relations]. The youngest brother, Salim, or Tjotjo, was in command of the fleet of ships, which by the turn of the century numbered thirty-three schooners and ninety-nine motorized sailing vessels.

---

[3] Willard A. Hanna, *Indonesian Banda: Colonialism and Its Aftermath in the Nutmeg Islands* (Banda Neira: Yayasan Warisan dan Budaya Banda Neira, 1991), p. 98, mentions the settlement of Arab and Chinese merchants in Banda during the British occupation. According to Des Alwi, the British captured three warehouses in Banda full of nutmeg and mace, valued at over one-million British pounds. The amount was enough to cover the cost of the British occupation of Jakarta and the Moluccas.

Said Tjong Baadilla, grandfather of Des Alwi

During the 1880s and 1890s there was fierce competition for pearls and mother-of-pearl in the islands of the Moluccas, especially Banda and Aru, among Australian, Japanese, and Spanish–Filipino divers, which the Dutch authorities attempted to regulate. The Baadilla Brothers had forged agreements with local rulers and independent divers, and came to dominate the pearl-diving business. Most divers were recruited and trained in Banda Neira, and the majority of them were Bandanese. Crew members were usually Butonese long settled in Banda Neira. When Grandfather Tjong Baadilla expanded his pearl-fishing fleet, he recruited some Papuan crew members and some Japanese divers.

The Netherlands East Indies [NEI] government granted the pearl-diving concession to the Baadilla Brothers, initially for the Aru Sea and Banda Islands, but eventually also for Seram, Misol, and Raja Empat Islands off the south coast of Papua. Granting a single concession made it easier for the Dutch to control the area, but the Baadilla Brothers also paid the NEI government handsomely for the rights to the pearls and mother-of-pearl found there.

In addition to the pearl industry, my grandfather owned nutmeg plantations on Banda Besar Island. He was an influential exporter of nutmeg, pearls, and mother-of-pearl. In 1909 the Dutch named him as Kapitein Oranglima, the head of the traditional community [*Kepala Adat*]. However, he was more familiarly called Kapitein der Arabien, although there were only ten families of Arab descent in Banda at the time.[4] My grandfather was known in the Moluccas as "Tuan Besar Said Baadilla" [master, important individual] of Banda, the "Pearl King" of the Netherlands East Indies.

My grandfather went to the Netherlands in 1896 to present Queen Emma, the mother of Queen Wilhelmina, with a pigeon-egg sized pearl that he had brought from the Moluccas. On his second journey to the Netherlands, in 1909, he was made a knight of the Oranje Nassau Order by Queen Wilhelmina, the mother of Queen Juliana. After the ceremony he presented a large pink pearl to Queen Wilhelmina.[5]

A devoted Muslim, my grandfather visited Mecca twice. He annually donated 30 percent of his business profits to charity. He even built his own mosque. In 1880, at the age of twenty-four, my grandfather went on his first pilgrimage to Mecca. There he met a religious leader from Tuban, who invited him to visit East Java. He did, and later married a daughter of the religious leader and took her, my grandmother Salma, to the Moluccas. They had four sons and ten daughters. My mother, Halijah [usually called Ijah], was the tenth of my grandfather's fourteen children.

FOUR UNCLES

My grandfather was probably one of the first non-Dutch persons in the East Indies to send his sons to school in Holland at the beginning of the twentieth century. Two of the sons had reputations as playboys, but the second son, by the name of Achmad, headed the family's pearl-fishing industry.

The eldest son, Abdul, spent most of his time traveling several times a year to Java and Singapore. He kept four wives, one in Java and the rest in the Moluccas. He was not at all interested in pearl fishing since he did not want to stay away from shore too long and was often seasick while at sea. Work in the nutmeg plantation did not suit Abdul either, since it required hard work. Besides hard work, life on the

[4] The *Regeerings Almanak voor Nederlandsch-Indie*, 1896, Vol. 1, appendix FF, p. 391; and *Regeerings Almanak voor Nederlandsch-Indie*, 1909, Vol. 1, appendix OO, p. 675, list the Baadilla Brothers, including Sech Said bin Abdullah Baadilla, Salim bin Abdullah Baadilla, and Abdul Rachman bin Abdullah Baadilla, as owners and managers of the Perken Kelien Noorwegen on Lonthor. Sech Said bin Abdullah Baadilla is listed as the Luitenant der Arabieren in the *Regeerings Almanak*, 1909, Vol. 2, p. 268, which notes that he was appointed to this position on June 28, 1889.

[5] Letter from Queen Wilhelmina to Governor General van Heutz, dated December 7, 1909 (in Des Alwi's possession). The gift of a pearl to the Queen is mentioned by Soetan Sjahrir, *Out of Exile* (New York, NY: Greenwood Press, 1949), p. 171. Queen Emma, the Queen Regent from 1890 to 1898, is said to have "had a great interest in the Indonesian Archipelago," dating from "1883, when she visited the Colonial Exhibition in Amsterdam...." See Rita Wassing-Visser, *Royal Gifts from Indonesia: Historical Bonds with the House of Orange-Nassau (1600–1938)* (The Hague: House of Orange-Nassau Historic Collections Trust, 1995). This volume does not include a complete listing of gifts from Indonesia to the Dutch royal family, and emphasizes gifts from Javanese royalty.

plantation was too quiet and monotonous for Uncle Abdul. According to my mother, the only job that suited him was to go on inspection tours by big KPM [Koninklijk Pakketvaart Maatschappij, Royal Packet Company, the Dutch inter-island shipping line][6] freighters that sailed around the Moluccas, or to go to Java to collect the Baadilla company's earnings there. Mother said that Uncle Abdul often squandered the money he collected in Java for his own personal use.

Uncle Abdul was always neatly dressed. He could often be seen in a white, high-collared jacket with silver buttons worn with long trousers. A pocket watch with a golden chain would be hanging from the upper pocket. During his afternoon walks, he could be seen with a carved, silver-handled walking stick.

The third son, Ali, was studying in Holland when he married a Dutch girl. He returned to Banda with her, bringing along a Dutch cook. The story is told that their arrival caused anxiety among some Dutch residents of Banda; the Dutch colonial officials of the Moluccas were rather embarrassed by the presence of a pure Dutchman working as a cook in one of the Baadilla households. To avoid this, my grandfather appointed the cook, a Mr. Sondagg, as a sort of plantation manager in charge of the transportation of nutmeg from Banda Besar to the harbor at Neira. Several times a month, when there was sufficient nutmeg to be shipped to the central godown (warehouse) of Messrs. Baadilla & Sons, in Neira, Mr. Sondagg would travel along in a big prau. He would be dressed in a white, high-collared uniform, and he would be seated on top of the sacks containing nutmeg. Whenever Ali met Sondagg at the harbor he would shout at him, in the presence of the Dutch harbormaster, "Will you stay with me and cook some pea soup for my wife?"

The Muslim community of Banda Neira wanted to convert Sondagg to Islam by persuading him to marry a Muslim Bandanese girl. However, Sondagg had no intention of remaining in the East for a long time. When he was preparing to return to Holland a tragedy occurred. On one of his usual journeys to transport the nutmeg to Neira, a sudden gale struck the boat and overturned it. Sondagg was a non-swimmer and drowned. His body was found two days later. My grandfather ordered a grand Christian funeral for him.

After this incident Uncle Ali went to Holland. There he divorced his first wife and married a French woman. He brought her to Java and lived there with her. Ali visited Banda Neira occasionally to collect his allowance or sell some of his land.

It was my grandfather's second son, Achmad, who did his best to keep the family business going. He was a hard-working man and commanded a fleet of over thirty motorized pearl-fishing schooners. Most of his time was spent at sea, either pearl fishing or on expeditions to locate new pearl-fishing grounds. He experienced several shipwrecks in the Aru Sea, and once or twice drifted to New Guinea and Australia. When he was a teenager he spent a year in Australia, with William Clark in Brisbane, to gain experience in the pearl-fishing industry. To enable Achmad to go to Australia my grandfather had to put up a bond of fifty pounds.

Uncle Achmad led a simple life. He had only one wife, and only one son, who was my grandfather's first grandson. The other Baadilla children produced a total of about fifty grandchildren for the old man. Uncle Achmad was killed during the Japanese Occupation, not by the Japanese but in an air raid in 1944 by a few

---

[6] The shipping company played a crucial role in inter-island travel and communication—including mail service and trade.

Australian B-25 airplanes that struck Banda Neira. Uncle Achmad's house was near the harbor, and he refused to evacuate to Gunung Api Island.

I do not remember Uncle Ding, my grandfather's fourth son, as he died soon after the Baadilla company went bankrupt in 1933. Some people said that Ding's death was due to his disappointment at the extravagance of Abdul and Ali that contributed to the downfall of the company. By that time my grandfather was too old to take an active interest in the company. He died in 1934 at the age of seventy-eight.

The family. Back row, left to right: Emma (Great Uncle Tjotjo's granddaughter), Aunt Nena, Uncle Ding, Ijah (Des Alwi's mother), Aunt Ili, Aunt Nona, Aunt Non (wife of Uncle Achmad), Aunt Eca, Uncle Ali. Middle row: Uncle Achmad, Grandmother Salma, Aunt Irma (also called Ama), Grandfather Said Tjong Baadilla, Aunt Att, Uncle Abdullah, Ibrahim (first grandson). Seated on ground: Aunt Silva, Aunt Mien (youngest daughter), Cici (also called Caca, Great Uncle Tjotjo's granddaughter).

FATHER

My father, Alwi, was a captain on one of my grandfather's pearl-fishing schooners. Alwi was a descendant of the Sultans of Palembang, in South Sumatra. His father, Pangeran Omar, had been sent to Ternate in 1850 to learn the fate of his grandfather, Sultan Badaruddin, and the Sultan's younger brother, Ibrahim. Badaruddin had been exiled to Ternate by the Dutch because he had been close to

Raffles when the British controlled that part of Sumatra, and he had taken his brother with him. Pangeran Omar learned that Sultan Badaruddin had died. Nevertheless, Omar chose to remain in Ternate as head of the horse guard of the Sultan of Ternate. During one of Omar's horse-buying trips to Manado, he eloped with Ida Tangkau, the Manadonese wife of the Dutch *resident*.[7] They settled in Ternate, where Alwi was born.

When Pangeran Omar died, Alwi joined his brother, who was already working as a captain on one of the Baadilla schooners. Alwi arrived at Banda Neira in 1912, when he was only twelve years old; he joined his brother's schooner as a cabin boy, and later as a mate. At the age of twenty he became the youngest *nakhoda* [ship's captain] in the Baadilla fleet. His first job as captain was to search for new pearl-fishing grounds around the western and southern coasts of New Guinea, since the existing concession areas were getting exhausted after ten years of continuous fishing. Outside these areas there was too much competition from Australian and Japanese companies. Although the Netherlands East Indies government did not allow foreign companies to operate or to dive inside their territorial and inter-island waters, the ban was not very effective since the Dutch only occasionally sent a small patrol ship. My father located some mother-of-pearl beds around the shallow waters off the Tanimbar Islands, and near Port Darwin in Australia. His search for new mother-of-pearl beds around Seram coastal areas was not so successful, but he discovered many areas containing *trocadero* shells near Seram's eastern coast. Although *trocadero* shells were not as valuable as mother-of-pearl shells, they had some market value.

My father married the millionaire Baadilla's daughter in 1923, and went with her to Java to spend their honeymoon. I came to earth four years later, as their second child and the tenth grandson of "the Pearl King" of the East Indies.

IMPACT OF THE DEPRESSION

I did not realize until the age of six that my grandfather, Said Tjong Baadilla, was once the richest man in Banda Neira, and probably one of the richest in the Moluccas. My mother told us that when she was a child she had her own maidservant, and every Baadilla child had one. The servant took her to school, carried her bag, stayed at school with her, and looked after her during break time.

My mother told me that I was born in a large marble-floored house just near the house of my grandfather. When the Baadilla glory crumbled in 1933, we had to leave that house, and move to a non-marble-floored house about a hundred yards from the harbor of Neira. Our former house was then sold to Mr. Ho Kok Chai, a rich Chinese, who was at the time the *Kapitein* [head] of the Chinese community of Banda.

---

[7] In the Dutch colonial administrative system, a *resident* was a senior officer in the European civil service; in the Moluccas, the *resident* was based in Ambon. A *controleur* was a more junior European officer, whose described duties were "inspection and supervision." The *controleur* in Banda was the sole European officer. In Java a *regent* was a hereditary official with the highest rank in the native civil service, while in Banda a *regent* was the head of a village or kampong. See J. S. Furnivall, *Netherlands India: A Study of Plural Economy* (Cambridge: Cambridge University Press, 1939; reprinted 1967), pp. xxi–xxii.

The house where Des Alwi was born

I was three years old when the Baadilla empire began to shake: the price of mother-of-pearl shell slumped drastically,[8] nutmeg prices went down, and copra reached rock bottom—and the Great Depression hit the world. The Baadilla company continued to pay the salaries of the divers, schooners' crews, plantation workers, and other employees of the company, for over two years, despite the low prices of the merchandise. The overhead cost was so large that the company was unable to repay the interest on loans that had been taken out to expand the pearl-fishing industry (new motorized schooners, diving equipment, wharves, warehouses), nutmeg-replanting schemes in Banda, and new nutmeg-planting schemes in western New Guinea, in the Fak-Fak area. Uncle Ding, who had taken over management of the company from grandfather, was the man behind these new ventures. Bad management and the depression were the causes of the downfall of the "Baadilla Empire," the company that was started by Great-Grandfather Abdullah Baadilla in 1860, and expanded by Grandfather Tjong Baadilla in 1880.

The creditors from Amsterdam and Batavia, and the Koks of Banda Neira, began to press for repayment of their loans, and brought court cases. A commission was established to investigate the value of Tjong Baadilla properties in the Moluccas and elsewhere. As a result, Tjong Baadilla was declared bankrupt in 1933. Uncle Ding was jailed for one year. The court blamed him for transferring certain properties, such as company houses, to other owners after the establishment of the investigative commission. Uncle Ding died soon after he finished his jail sentence.

---

[8] Bakelite, a sort of plastic invented in 1926, began to replace mother-of-pearl for use as buttons.

The pearl-fishing fleet, consisting of over thirty schooners, was sold at auction. The nutmeg plantations were taken over by the creditors, and resold to the *perkeniers* [plantation owners] and other firms. A Chinese named Chiu, who used to work as wharf master in Dobo, in charge of the mother-of-pearl shells in the godowns there, bought nearly all the schooners and Dobo godowns at auction for a very low price. He became rich overnight. Chiu had climbed from a deckhand to schooner captain to wharf master during the Baadilla pearl-fishing era.

The Koks of Banda

Kok and Sons of Neira took over Tjong Baadilla's place as the richest family in the Moluccas. The Koks were Bandanese Chinese by birth, but became naturalized Dutch citizens. They continued to use their original Chinese name because it sounded Dutch; Kok is also a Dutch family name. The Koks married Dutch people; the sons married Dutch women and the daughters married Dutchmen. The Koks did not mix much with the local people or other Chinese merchants of Banda. They considered themselves "Europeans" and had nothing to do with the "natives" or the "foreign Orientals" [NEI census classifications] of Banda. When the Bandanese were having their yearly festival and needed some contributions from the locally born rich people, no Kok would contribute. Although the Koks had been in Banda for generations, they did not consider themselves Bandanese.

The Koks owned about half of the total nutmeg plantations, as well as many houses and godowns, in the Banda group. They even had their own pier in front of their office, near the government harbor. The Kok enterprise was run by the eldest son, Theo, since old man Kok was about eighty years old.

The Koks were very strict people. They would not allow us children to swim in their harbor or make use of their pier. The Koks had several motorboats to be used for pleasure and to inspect their plantations. These boats were never loaned to anyone, not even to their own employees who happened to be seriously ill or had an accident, and badly needed a doctor's care at Neira. Although they obtained their riches from the Banda soil, they did not care much about Banda and its people.

My Father and His Friend Ho Kok Chai

When my grandfather went bankrupt, my father was jobless. My father was too proud to work for Chiu, who had purchased most of the Baadilla fleet, and too poor to have his own pearl-fishing schooner. If he had had his own schooner, he could have fished for pearl shells himself and could have made plenty of money. Instead he began to work on a commission basis for the firm of his boyhood friend Ho Kok Chai. Ho exported nutmeg collected from the Bandanese smallholders, who then still had a few nutmeg groves here and there on the islands. The bigger plantations, the so-called *perken*, exported their own nutmeg. Ho was new to the pearl-fishing industry and thus needed my father's advice.

Father would only travel with Ho Kok Chai to locate new shell beds. Later, when Ho established his own pearl-fishing firm with two schooners, my father didn't want to be the captain of one of the schooners. He simply refused to work under his friend, but was willing to help Ho in his business as an adviser on a commission basis. My father did not want to work with Ho on a salary basis; he did not want to be Ho's employee, not just because he was proud of being the son-in-law of *Tuan*

Besar Baadilla, but because he considered Ho his best friend. If he worked for Ho, then Ho would be his boss, which meant he would have to listen to Ho and then they would not be good friends anymore.

Later on Ho abandoned his pearl-fishing firm, but kept the two schooners for business and pleasure trips to Seram and other islands in the Banda group. Ho's new firm, which dealt with nutmeg from smallholders, progressed rapidly, and soon Ho bought some land at Bemo on Seram Island to grow his own nutmeg. But the soil at Seram is not so good for nutmeg, and Ho then turned his plantation into a holiday resort for himself and my father. The two of them would disappear from Banda Neira for a couple of months a year, and send their children a couple of birds and deer every now and then. Every time Father went with Ho to look for adventure at Seram Island, our family received sacks of rice and other foodstuff from Ho's shop, and every time the two were away at Seram, Ho's son, Koon, and I spent our time in Ho's other schooner, looking for adventure in the other Banda islands. We roamed around the nutmeg forest of Banda Besar, shooting *walor* (wild doves) with our air rifles, and went fishing in the bay.

GRANDMOTHER, AND MEMORIES OF GRANDFATHER

After my grandfather's death, my grandmother still helped the now-jobless people of Banda who used to work for her husband, although her gifts were not as large as during the good old days when her husband was still alive and had a rather large pension.

I remember seeing old people who came every Friday morning to visit my grandfather, bringing all sort of presents to the house, such as a bunch of young coconuts, *delima* (pomegranate) fruits, rare sea shells, dried fish, giant sea lobsters, carved walking-sticks, and many other delicious and peculiar things. Some of the old people took their strong sons along to help clean the water tanks in the house and to carry clear water from the well to fill them. They also repaired old broken furniture and made wooden toys for us, the grandchildren. While their sons worked, the fathers sat on the veranda, putting their arms on their knees as a sign of respect, and chatted and joked with Grandfather Tjong until the *warok* flowers dropped from the trees. The five-petaled *warok* flower, the size of a teacup, is yellow and always falls on the ground about noontime when the sun is above one's head in Banda. Old people in Banda judge when it is noon by the falling *warok* flowers. Then it is time for lunch and for the religious Muslims to prepare for the mid-day prayer.

Grandfather Tjong would put on his black *songkok* [rimless cap] and walk with his guests to the *langgar* [small mosque or prayer room], situated inside the compound of the house, to wash and then join the Friday noon prayers. Lunch would be served in the *langgar*, after prayer time.

Some of the edible presents the old people brought were used for the *kenduries* [ritual meals] that were held at the *langgar* every now and then. The rare and peculiar items brought to my grandfather were kept in the Baadilla museum, on the right wing of Grandpa Tjong's private residence. Even after the Baadilla empire crumbled, the museum was still intact and attracted many local and foreign visitors. The governors-general of the former Netherlands East Indies, in their once-in-seven-years inspection tours around the archipelago, stopped at grandfather's residence to look at the priceless collection of rare and peculiar items of the Moluccan Archipelago: stuffed birds of paradise; natural pearls of all sizes and colors—pink, yellow, white, grayish; fine polished mother-of-pearl shells, some with pearls still attached on the shells; all kinds of seashells, some as large as a bathtub; colorful butterflies, large and small; *akar bahar* [black coral plant]; old porcelain and ceramics from China and Japan; skeletons of sea animals, such as the *duyong*, a sea animal that was often mistaken for a mermaid; all sizes of sea turtles, and fans, combs, cigarette cases, and ornaments made from tortoise shell; miniature schooners and models of all kinds of praus that were used in the olden days in inter-island trade and pearl fishing in the Moluccas; species of birds with their nests and eggs of Banda and other Moluccan and New Guinea islands; and many other curiosities of the Moluccas.

The house, *rumah besar*, that belonged to Des Alwi's grandparents. Sutan Sjahrir moved into this house following the death of Des Alwi's grandmother.

After grandfather's death, the house was still frequented by visitors and friends from faraway places, but not as many as during the time he was alive. Some loyal friends (but not the *perkeniers*) occasionally sent some edible presents, and once a week dispatched their sons to work in the house, but they did not send any more rare and peculiar items as they used to do. The private museum was a place the Bandanese were proud of, and they considered it their own showplace.

CHAPTER TWO

FRIENDS AND SCHOOL

The sub-district where we lived was called Kampong[1] China because most big Chinese shops were located there. Large offices and godowns of the nutmeg and mace exporters, Chinese and Arab shops, and tailors and hairdresser shops were situated in this district. It was also the commercial center of Banda Neira, as the harbor was situated there. The Bandanese called the harbor compound *"los,"* a corruption of the Dutch word *loods,* meaning storehouse or shed. We called the wharf *"jembatan,"* the Indonesian word for bridge. The *los* and the *jembatan* were the pride of our district.

Once a week, a KPM ship would arrive, bringing in merchandise, rice, and other foodstuff from Makassar, and taking away the spices that Banda produced, especially nutmeg. In addition to the KPM ships, many praus from Seram, Timor, and other islands came to this harbor to sell their cargoes. Among the commodities they brought were sago, green and mandarin oranges, goats and pigs, small dug-out canoes, clay items, many kinds of parrots, cloves and spices, many varieties of fruit, and other foodstuff.

THE *LOS*—THE HARBOR OF BANDA NEIRA

The harbor was central to my childhood in Neira. We boys swam, fished, and played tag, and even stored our fishing rods and swimming trunks (really old pants) between the wooden planks in the lower parts of the wharf. Most of us "graduated" as swimmers and divers when we were about four or five years old.

The *los,* besides being our playground, was also where we boys could earn some pocket money by selling fish to visitors and guiding tourists who arrived on KPM ships to the nutmeg plantations on Neira, or to the sea gardens (coral reefs) near Gunung Api Island. Some kind-hearted tourists tipped us with silver coins, some only gave us a few cents or took us to the ship where they treated us with cakes and lemonade. When the ships left the wharf, some passengers threw coins in the water for us to dive for.

My weekly earnings in this manner amounted to about twenty-five to fifty cents, and sometimes over two guilders when silver coins were thrown at us. I gave this money to my mother, and in return I received a few cents to enable me to buy sweets or marbles. The other members of the Baadilla family considered it a disgrace to dive for coins, and said that it marred the good name of the Baadillas.

My grandmother occasionally summoned her servant to fetch me from the "operation diving ground," and I would be brought to appear before her. In Bandanese Malay, with a heavy Javanese accent and some Dutch words mixed in, she would reprimand me for behaving like a beggar and would tell me to stop diving for coins. Usually after the audience my grandmother would give me a ten-

---

[1] "Kampong" means village or urban neighborhood.

cent silver piece. When my coin-diving persisted and became too much for the family, I was sent to a Koran-reading class in the afternoons. In spite of this, I still managed to stay away from the reading lessons whenever a ship called at the harbor.

I liked the ships and crews so much that I would not miss boarding a ship every time one stopped at the Neira harbor. Usually when I returned from my regular visits to the ships that came from Makassar, I would have a basket of fruits and vegetables that my crew friends presented to me as gifts for my family. Some crew members also visited our house when they were off-duty.

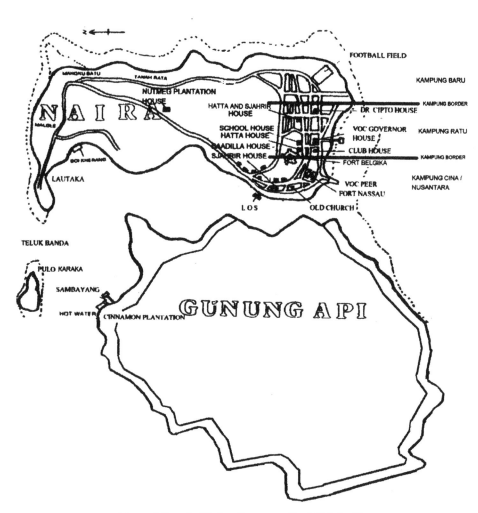

Map of Banda Neira (here spelled "Naira")

RIVALS

We boys of Kampong China and Negreh districts considered the harbor compound and wharf as our "de facto territory." We did not allow boys from other districts to swim there unless they were school friends or related to one of us. We also knew our limits—that we were not allowed to swim in their territorial waters, unless, of course, we were introduced by our friends there.

I remember one occasion, we quarreled with the Negreh boys over the *los*. Negreh was a corruption of the Dutch word *negorij*, meaning settlement or small village. Being only a small settlement, where most Neira *burgers* lived, Negreh was annexed to the district of Kampong China under one district head. Later on, families from the island of Ambon, working in the offices of Neira, came to settle at Negreh. Our two kampongs had always been united, especially when we played soccer against the boys of Ratu or other districts' teams, and we came out together as the Kampong China eleven. The Negreh boys' claims to the *los* were first made after an intra-kampong soccer match when the China boys beat the Negreh boys. Luckily the quarrel was only temporary; the Banda-born Negreh boys used their good offices to reconcile the differences between us and the Ambonese boys of Negreh. When we beat the Kampong Ratu team, we were united again, and the *los* was again accessible to both parties.

The regent who looked after Kampong China and Negreh happened to live in Negreh, and when we won the soccer match against the Ratu team he invited both parties to his house to eat the *jambu* (rose apples) that grew in his garden. Although the head of a district in Banda was called a regent, he was different from the real regents they had in Java.[2] A regent in Java administratively controlled a regency that consisted of several real districts, with an area maybe twenty times larger than the whole of the Banda group put together. Our Bandanese regent was merely a village, or kampong, head, without any administrative or territorial power. To be a regent in Java one had first to come from aristocratic stock. Then, after ten years of elementary and secondary education, one had to be trained at the Higher School for Native Civil Servants, where only the so-called blue-bloods and children of high and loyal civil servants were admitted.

Our Bandanese regents did not need to come from aristocratic stock, as did their colleagues in Java, and they did not need to go to school to become a regent. All these regents needed was to know how to read and write, to be honest and popular, and to possess some assets so that they would not be tempted to cheat the *controleur* when turning over the taxes collected from the poor fishermen, small traders, and harbor workers, who all earned less than five guilders a month.

SCHOOL

The only European Elementary School [Europees Lagere School, ELS] of Banda Neira was in Kampong Ratu, the residential area of Banda Neira, located right in the center of the town of Neira. The three main roads of Neira pass through Kampong Ratu. Most big houses in Neira are in Kampong Ratu, including the large houses belonging to the *perkeniers*. The residence and adjoining office of the *controleur* were there, and nearly all the schoolteachers of the ELS lived there. In fact, most Christian people of Banda lived in Kampong Ratu.

---

[2] It was difficult to become a true regent. When one finally graduated from the three-year course, one would start to work as a trainee in the colonial administrative service. Then, after a long and hard process, one would gradually and step-by-step climb the colonial administrative-service stairs, and only after twenty years' or more climbing (from assistant to deputy to district chief), and at last after hard work and complete loyalty to the Dutch Crown, one would become a regent. Not many succeeded, though, only the blue-bloods and completely loyal ones.

This school was only for Dutch nationals, high colonial government officials, and the like. My mother was the prime mover to have me study at the ELS. When she sought my entry when I was age six years old, I was turned down by the Dutch headmaster because I was not considered European. But my mother did not give up hope, and when I was seven she tried again. This time she registered me as the grandson of Baadilla, who had been an honorary mayor of Banda Neira, a title given to all sub-district heads who had served more than twenty-five years with the colonial government, and who were considered loyal to the Dutch Queen. However, the headmaster still remembered the previous year's attempt, and told my mother that I could not use the name Baadilla since it was she, and not my father, who was a Baadilla. According to the headmaster my father was a native, thus non-European, and for that reason I could not be admitted into the ELS. As far as I was concerned, I was glad that I was not able to go to school, since I was scared of the headmaster, a tall, bald-headed Dutchman with big spectacles.

Thus my mother gave up hope of having me in that school, as I was already seven years old and she could not try again the next year because the same headmaster would still be there. She refused to send me to the native school, which at that time ended at the fifth grade, with no possibility for higher education. So instead of going to school like my friends, I enjoyed my life swimming, fishing, and roaming around in the nutmeg plantations to look for wild mangos, rose apples, and other tropical fruits. And when a tourist ship arrived at the harbor I would dive for silver coins that the tourists threw into the sea.

Later, at the suggestion of some friends, my mother sent me to a private afternoon school, which was run by Aunt Willy. Aunt Willy's school, as we called it, was about a mile's walk from my home. We had to be at school at exactly 2:00 PM; should we be late Aunt Willy would give us a stroke of the rattan on our legs. I was not very happy about the school, but since it was not far from the beach I could go swimming when we finished school at five o'clock in the afternoon. When it was too hot in the classroom I always gazed out of the window looking at the fishing boats that passed by on their way to the fish market, which was nearby. I could recognize every fishing boat, and would sometimes wonder whether they had a good catch or not. I was often caned by Aunt Willy for gazing out of the window.

The first aim of Aunt Willy's school was to make us speak Dutch. In fact, she did not care about other subjects, or probably she was not so good at them. All our reading materials were old and torn Dutch schoolbooks that she received from the *jaga* [watchman] of the European Elementary School.

Aunt Willy, although dark-skinned, spoke Dutch with a real Holland accent because she had lived there for a long time. The story was told that when Aunt Willy was a baby, she was found in the New Guinea jungle by Dutch missionaries, who took care of her and brought her to Holland. When she was a teenager, she was adopted by an Ambonese family, who were visiting the Netherlands during the "once-in-a-lifetime big leave" the East Indies colonial government granted to its employees. When this family returned to the Moluccas, Aunt Willy followed them, but with no special qualifications she found it impossible to secure a government job. So she went to Banda Neira to open an afternoon school for backward children and children whose parents wished them to learn Dutch, but were unable to send them to the European Elementary School.

After I had been a few months at Aunt Willy's school I was able to read, write, and understand a little Dutch, but I was unable to speak the language. Although we were forced to speak Dutch at school I did not feel inclined to speak the language. All I could say when spoken to was to answer Aunt Willy with "Ja" or "Neen."

THE EUROPEAN ELEMENTARY SCHOOL

In July 1935, just before the new school term started, the ELS headmaster was transferred to Java. His successor was a young Dutch schoolteacher who had just come from Holland. Since this temporary schoolmaster had not had any experience with the Indies, he raised no barrier or discrimination, and allowed me to enter the ELS when my mother sought to enroll me using her family name. My mother was satisfied to have me studying at the European school, but she often complained about my being overage, at eight, as a first-grader. She said that if only my grandfather were still alive I would have been in school at least two years earlier. When my grandfather was alive he used to take his grandchildren to enroll in school, no matter whether the grandchildren were the children of his daughters or his sons. No Dutch headmaster would object to the enrollment, as they knew that my grandfather was very popular in the Moluccas.

Des Alwi's European Elementary School

I did not find my first year at school easy. I can still remember how ashamed I felt when I had to line up with my classmates, boys and girls of about six years of age, every morning before entering the classroom. My other playmates would be lined up with the second- and third-grade classes. It was usually after school hours when some boys from other kampongs would tease me for being seated among little children much younger than I was. Dutch children sometimes screamed and jeered at me with taunts such as, "Hey big buffalo, how much is one plus one?" However, being new at school, I did not dare fight against them. Also, I was advised by my mother not to fight in school, especially against the Dutch children, for fear of their parents. If they complained, I could be dismissed, and at that time the European school was considered a good school.

Also, I was not used to wearing shoes, and I especially disliked leather shoes. On my way home from school I would often take off my shoes, tie both laces together, and carry them over my shoulders. My mother found a solution to this, and made me wear white tennis shoes to school. But as white shoes soiled easily, I dyed them with black Chinese ink.

We were already a poor family when I entered the ELS in 1935, and had only one servant at home. The Ho Kok Chai's, who had bought our former home, had about eight servants. Ho Chao Koon, the son of the family, and Ho Chao Bien, the daughter, went to school with one of their many servants. I walked to school with the Ho children, not that I was afraid to go to school alone, but Koon, as we called him, was my playmate, as our fathers had been in their youth.

HALIK, THE BOY PEDDLER

After my grandfather's bankruptcy and my father's loss of his job as schooner captain, we were no longer rich. Our breakfast consisted of a cup of tea with two teaspoons of sugar and fried bananas, which we bought for one cent each from child peddlers who came to our house early in the morning. These child peddlers, mostly under twelve years of age, roamed about the Neira streets every morning selling their fried bananas, sweet potatoes, and rice cakes. Our favorite boy peddler was Halik, who was about ten years old. Halik's fried bananas were usually bigger than those sold by the others, and my mother knew his mother. Halik's father used to work as a diver in my grandfather's pearl-fishing industry at Dobo, a small town on one of the Aru Islands. He lost his life some years ago when a rubber hose that supplied fresh air to the submerged divers failed during a diving operation. The crew pulled him up, but it was too late.

Halik had an elder sister called Atih, who assisted their mother in preparing the fried bananas, and two young twin brothers, Putih and Hitam. Putih means "white" in Indonesian, and Hitam means "black" or "dark." We children found it very hard to tell Putih from Hitam, but Halik gave us a clue: Hitam had a birthmark on his left ear and Putih was more fair-skinned.

Halik's mother was too poor to send him to school. We kids sometimes wondered how Halik could read and write the Roman alphabet without going to school. He only went to Koran-reading classes given by the local imam. For his Koran-reading classes Halik read and wrote the Arabic script, and knew the Koran verses by heart.

Halik was my playmate and one of the best coin divers among our childhood friends. He looked a bit undernourished; he was very thin and had two long arms with a kind of long-shaped face. He was a hard-working boy. If he was not peddling cakes he would stay in his mother's market stall selling peanuts, boiled corn, or other edible items. I often saw him picking up balls at the local tennis court for five cents an hour.

Halik was always present at the harbor when a ship arrived, to sell his fried snacks to the passengers and crew members. If the passengers of a Java-bound KPM steamer, with oil workers from New Guinea aboard, started throwing coins at the swimming children, Halik would leave his basket of cakes under the care of Hitam and Putih, and would join in the adventure of diving. Halik was a really good diver, and could go under water down to twenty-five feet, and could stay just over a minute. He would harvest all the coins lying below twenty feet. He was primarily interested in diving for the silver coins; only after he had harvested them would he look for the copper coins at the sea bottom. His "catch" was always bigger than that of the other children. Occasionally, when his harvest reached over one guilder, he treated us to his fried bananas, which were supposed to be sold, but by now were already cold. If no coins were being tossed, Halik would fetch his dugout canoe and pick up empty beer bottles thrown overboard. He would later sell those empty bottles to Chinese stores for one cent apiece.

Halik was a genius at all kinds of games, such as kite flying, fishing, and climbing trees. He was a daredevil, all right, except for one thing: he was afraid of dogs. As business-like as Halik was, he never entered a house that had a dog. Uncle Barentz, a KNIL [Koninklijk Nederlandsch Indisch Leger, Royal Netherlands Indies Army] pensioner, was very fond of Halik's cakes, but Halik avoided the Barentz house because of the Barentzs' dog. Halik would only come to the house when Uncle Barentz assured him that the dog was in the house and already chained. Halik's grandfather was a haji, and that is why Halik was so religious. His fear of dogs was based on the Islamic teaching that no dog should lick you since a dog's saliva is considered *na'jis* (dirty).

In our boy's world Halik was recognized as a tough boy and a daredevil. Halik never started a fight unless he was provoked or insulted. We seldom saw him fighting anyone, but when he fought, even a bigger boy, you could see Halik's rapid action against the attackers. He would fight like a cock—he would jump, kick, dive, and swing at the attackers with his left and right hooks. Halik always fought without his shirt; he was afraid his shirt might get torn and then he would certainly receive a spanking from his mother when he returned home.

Nolsy Philippus (who was later Indonesia's bantam-weight boxing champion) had a fight with Halik once, and Halik won. Nolsy had a dangerous habit of trying to fight boys he thought were the same or stronger than himself. On one of Halik's fried-banana rounds, Halik happened to pass the Philippus house. Nolsy called Halik, saying he wanted to buy a fried banana. Halik refused to enter the Philippus house because he was afraid of the dogs—and, of course, the pigs, even though the pigs were locked in their cages near the seaside. Nolsy told Halik that he was a customer, and being the customer, Halik, the seller, should enter his house. Halik refused and walked away. Nolsy sent his mean dogs after Halik. Halik was shocked, but when he came out of his shock, he was angry and told Nolsy, "Keep your silly dogs away. I do not like them."

We boys were playing marbles under the shade of the mango trees and stopped to watch the incident. Halik was very angry. He asked us to look after his basket with the fried bananas, then he took his shirt off. We knew that Halik meant business. He dared Nolsy to step out to the street. Nolsy could not refuse or he would lose prestige in front of us boys. But Halik was too quick for him, and avoided Nolsy's blows while raining punches on Nolsy's head. We boys pulled Halik away from Nolsy when we saw Auntie Philippus coming with a rattan stick. Besides receiving Halik's beating, Nolsy also got a spanking from his ma. Nolsy came out of the fight with a sour smile, but he and Halik became friends again after a while.

FRUIT, AND COFFINS, NEXT DOOR

Our house was on Harbor Street, and grandfather's residence, known as the *rumah besar* (big house), was on the next street, called the Middle Street, about a hundred yards by road from our house. However, from our garden door I could get to the kitchen of the *rumah besar* by going through the backyard of the Kok's godown, which was sandwiched between our house and the *rumah besar*. I only used this shortcut in daytime; at night I was scared of several coffins stored on the godown's back veranda.

This godown had been a large, beautiful, marble-floored house. A rich head of the Chinese community [*Kapitein China*] used to live there. When he retired, he and his wife went to Ambon to visit their children, but he died suddenly in Ambon. His wife did not want to go back to Banda Neira, and the house was sold to grandfather, complete with two coffins from Suchow [Xuzhou province, China] that the owners would not be using.

Grandmother, being a *foe-foe* follower and very superstitious, didn't want to remove the coffins from the house or even give them to those who urgently needed them. She only removed them from the special storage room in the house to the back veranda. Because of the coffins nobody dared to rent the house, even when grandma guaranteed that anyone who rented the house could remove the coffins, as long as it was not she who "chased" the coffins away. Still there were no takers, and no caretakers could be found to look after the house with the coffins. The house was then neglected, as were the fruit trees in the yard with big *jambu* and papayas. At the time of my grandfather's bankruptcy this house was taken over by the Koks, who turned it into a godown. The Koks never opened their godown's back doors, and I was really the master of this unwanted territory with its hidden fruit treasures.

None of the other boys discovered this hidden treasure, although later on some boys began to sniff it out, since I usually treated them with big juicy rose apples from the backyard. However, they could not get inside the backyard, as it was blocked by our house, the *rumah besar*, and, of course, the coffins. Occasionally I invited some of my trusted friends to enjoy the fruit in the Kok's godown backyard. I warned them not to try to steal the rose apples by climbing the walls of the yard, because if they did the coffins would get them and turn them stiff.

When a KPM ship was at the harbor and the *jambu* tree bore fruit, I could earn as much as twenty cents a day by selling the fruit to the passengers and sailors through Halik, our favorite boy peddler. Luckily the Koks didn't know that those juicy rose apples that were sold near the harbor, which their servants sometimes bought for their masters' after-dinner fruit, legally belonged to them. Otherwise, coffins or no coffins, superstition or no superstition, money comes first. If they had known that those sweet, large, juicy rose apples belonged to them, they would certainly have opened their godown's back doors to claim the backyard and the fruit.

BIRD AND ANIMAL COLLECTION

We also used the Kok's godown backyard to raise our chickens, and I kept my pet *rusa* (deer) there. The deer was a gift from my father when he returned from his sea journey around Seram Island. A distant uncle brought me a casuari [kind of bird] from the Aru Islands. I also had a collection of many *luries* (small parrots), gifts from KPM sailors or brought by my father from other Moluccan Islands or from New Guinea. In my collection I also had many Banda sea birds and many other colorful birds. However, they didn't last long; I was asked by grandmother to release many of them and some of them died in their cages. I had such a big collection in the illegal backyard zoo that it attracted many children as visitors. They came not only to watch the birds and animals, but also to get *jambu* fruit. Every morning before I went to school I had to make sure that the backyard door near the kitchen of grandma's house was locked properly, just in case some non-school-going kids would wander inside my menagerie to play or to tease the animals.

One day, with the help of La Mono, a mute Butonese servant of grandma's, I moved one empty coffin and placed it vertically in front of the godown's back door. A few weeks later the godown clerk opened the door to spy on what was going on in the backyard, but the coffin blocking the door crashed down, missing him by inches. He was so shocked to see the falling coffin that he closed the door and never opened it again. I had won the game, and was in full control (de facto) of the Kok's godown backyard.

Grandma and her servants at the *rumah besar* also heard the noise of the crashing coffin on the hard marble floor. They really thought that the coffin had moved by itself. Since such mystery was top gossip news in Neira, soon people began to say that the old *Kapitein China* had returned to his old house to claim his coffin. By chance I had picked the captain's coffin—it was the larger of the two unused coffins. Grandma sent some flowers to the *kramat* [sacred place] on Papenberg Hill a few days after the "return" of the *Kapitein China*, whom she had known as a friend and neighbor. After the coffin incident only a few people came to see the animals. Now the animals could live in peace in the abandoned backyard, and the fruit on the *jambu* tree grew undisturbed.

When my father returned from his voyages to Seram Island, and was out of work, he grew some vegetables in the backyard and sold the crop to Chinese people in Neira. In truth, Chinese vegetables, such as *vetchais*, white pumpkins, grew much better than the other kinds of vegetables we had in the garden. It was as if the soil of the old Chinese captain's backyard had some Chinese agricultural deposits in it. While hoeing the soil, my father found some small Chinese ornaments, gold teeth, broken Chinese pots, and marbles of different colors than the ones we used to play with. The vegetables he grew brought some income for the family. The few golden ornaments he found in the ground were sold, and that kept the family going for a few weeks.

CHAPTER THREE

POLITICAL EXILES IN BANDA

In February 1936 two political exiles, Sutan Sjahrir and Mohammad Hatta,[1] arrived at Banda Neira. Before arriving in Neira, they had spent a year in prison in Java, and another year at Digul, a Dutch concentration camp in New Guinea. There were already several exiles in Banda, among whom were Doctor Tjipto Mangunkusumo, Mr. Iwa Kusuma Sumantri, and some members of the Sarekat Islam Indonesia.[2] Dr. Tjipto (we called him Uncle Tjip), one of the pioneers of the Indonesian nationalist movement, was banished to Banda Neira in 1928, after spending a few years in prison in Java. Iwa Kusuma Sumantri came to Banda Neira two years after Uncle Tjip. Two other Sarekat Islam people had been banished to Banda Neira soon after the abortive uprising against the Dutch in 1926,[3] but they were later released and sent back to Java.

I knew Uncle Tjip well because as a boy I used to go with my grandfather to visit him in his house at Kampong Ratu. My grandfather was a friend of the Sarekat Islam exiles; he was interested in Islamic issues, and the two *kiais* (religious leaders) who had been banished to Banda Neira happened to come from the same district in East Java as my grandmother. Through the Sarekat Islam people Grandfather knew Uncle

---

[1] Sutan Sjahrir (1909–1966) was from West Sumatra; he studied law in the Netherlands but did not earn a degree. He was active, with Hatta, in Pendidikan Nasional Indonesia (PNI–Baru), an organization dedicated to the education and training of a nationalist cadre. Sjahrir remained close to Hatta despite their differing roles in the Japanese Occupation and in independent Indonesia. Sjahrir served as first prime minister of Indonesia, 1945–1947. Mohammad Hatta (1902–1980), also from West Sumatra, earned a *docterandus* (or Drs.) degree, the Dutch equivalent of a US master's degree, from the Rotterdam Business School. During the Japanese Occupation, Revolution, and early years of independent Indonesia, Hatta served first as deputy, then as vice president, to Sukarno, Indonesia's first president.

[2] Dr. Tjipto Mangunkusumo was a medical doctor and one of the founders of Budi Utomo, a culturally focused organization important in the awakening of nationalism in the Indies. Critical of traditional Javanese culture, Dr. Tjipto later founded a radical multiracial party, Indische Partij. He was in exile in Banda from 1928 to 1941. Iwa Kusuma Sumantri earned a law degree from Leiden University in 1925. Like Hatta, he had been chairman of the Perhimpunan Indonesia while a student in the Netherlands. A Marxist in his student days, he taught Indonesian history in Moscow before returning to the Indies in 1926, where he was active in labor organizations and as a journalist. Arrested by the Dutch in 1929 on suspicion of being a communist, he was exiled to Banda from 1930 to 1941. It was while he was in Banda that he is said to have become an orthodox Muslim. Sarekat Islam is usually considered to have been the first politically based nationalist organization in the Dutch East Indies. George McTurnan Kahin, *Nationalism and Revolution in Indonesia* (Ithaca, NY: Cornell University Press, 1952), pp. 64–100, and passim, includes a detailed discussion of the nationalist movement and important figures in it.

[3] The uprisings in West Java in November 1926 and West Sumatra in January 1927, communist-led but with significant participation by local Islamic leaders, were easily put down by the Dutch, but nevertheless heightened suspicion and fear of nationalist organizations and activities.

Tjip, who was in Neira with his Eurasian wife and two children, who were her nephews. Uncle Tjip was very much respected in Banda Neira. Being a nationalist leader as well as a medical doctor, he treated his patients for free. Although Banda Neira had a hospital, the Dutch doctor there didn't want to visit the ordinary people's houses, he only visited the houses of patients who could pay.

Left: Dr. Tjipto Mangunkusumo. Right: Dr. Tjipto Mangunkusumo and his wife, whom Des Alwi called Tante (Aunt) Mie

ARRIVAL OF HATTA AND SJAHRIR

The day Hatta and Sjahrir arrived in Banda, February 11, 1936, I was swimming with friends near the pier of Banda Neira. It was raining, just a drizzle, and clouds blanketed half of Gunung Api. We liked to swim in the rain because it made the water feel warmer than the air, and if it were raining the harbormaster, Uncle Koko Latuperisa, would not come out of his office to chase us away. It is impossible for me to forget that afternoon, because that began a change in my life and my future.

Exactly at five o'clock that afternoon the rain stopped. At the same time, *controleur* Kortman, the official responsible for the administration of the Banda Islands, arrived. To avoid him, we hid behind the posts of the pier. From there we saw a white boat, the *Fomalhaut*, approach the harbor, slowly nearing the wooden pier. In the bustle of greeting the ship's arrival, we boys ran to rescue the dry clothes that we had hidden.

All eyes were directed toward two gentlemen in white jackets and ties as they disembarked from the ship. The two gentlemen had brought with them eight large wooden cases and four large leather bags. One of the gentlemen wore eye glasses; the other smiled at me. I paid close attention to them; although I was only eight years old, and a student in the second grade of the ELS, I realized from their pale visages that the two gentlemen had come from internment at Boven Digul. From observing passengers on the white ship each time it neared the harbor, I knew that everyone who came from Digul had a pale face. It seemed that they had suffered from a lack of food or had been ill with malaria. As young as I was, I realized that the two gentlemen who had just arrived had been exiled for opposing the Dutch colonial government.

On several cases was written the name Drs. Mohammad Hatta, but the other name was difficult to read. The younger and thinner gentleman came over to me and asked, in Dutch, "Are you from here?"

"Yes," I replied.

"Do you know where Dr. Tjipto Mangunkusumo's house is located?"

"Yes, but it is far from here," I told him. "But Mr. Iwa Kusuma Sumantri's house is directly across from the harbor."

Fomalhaut—the white ship that brought Mohammad Hatta and Sutan Sjahrir to Banda Neira, 1936

The two new arrivals were finding it difficult to carry their heavy cases. The captain of the *Fomalhaut*, a blonde Dutchman, short and rather plump, asked the *controleur* to have the prisoners, who usually were brought along by the police to accompany the *controleur* when a ship called at Banda Neira, help carry the luggage of the two gentlemen. The *controleur* replied, "Let the reds carry their own belongings."

The first mate of the *Fomalhaut*, M. Pardi, was older than the captain, but hadn't had the opportunity to become a captain because he was an *inlander* [native].[4] Hearing the exchange between the captain and the *controleur*, Mr. M. Pardi told the captain to let the ship's crew carry the belongings of the two gentlemen.

I ran across from the harbor to tell Mrs. Iwa Kusuma Sumantri about the arrival of the two gentlemen, and then I accompanied them to the Sumantri's house. I borrowed a bicycle from a friend and rode to the home of Uncle Tjipto Mangunkusumo to let him know that the two new arrivals from Digul had asked about the location of his house.

Families of exiles in Banda. Standing, from left to right: Mr. Iwa Kusuma Sumantri, Hatta, Dr. Tjipto Mangunkusumo, Donald (Dr. Tjipto's nephew), Mulyadi (a school teacher), Louis (Donald's younger brother), Sjahrir. Adults seated left to right: Mrs. Iwa, Mrs. Tjipto (Tante Mie), Mrs. Mulyadi. Three children of the Iwas and three of the Mulyadis stand among the women.

Every afternoon Uncle Tjipto sat on the veranda in front of his large colonial house, looking toward the open sea. In the distance all that could be seen was the island of Banda Besar, located across the deep, blue Banda Bay. When he saw me coming, Uncle Tjipto immediately asked, "What is it, Des?"

---

[4] In colonial society the *inlander*s ranked at the bottom. Europeans were at the top, followed by Eurasians and foreign Orientals (largely Chinese; Japanese were honorary Europeans).

I replied, "There are two gentlemen asking for you, but I'm not sure of their names. One, if I'm not mistaken, is Mohammad Hatta, but I don't know the name of the other gentleman."

"Why don't you know the name of the other gentleman?"

"I couldn't read his name," I said.

Uncle Tjipto laughed and went into the house to put on his high-collared jacket, with the chain of his watch hanging from his left pocket. Then he accompanied me on foot to the Sumantri's house. There he offered room in his home to the two arrivals, but Mrs. Iwa suggested that they stay first at her home and move the next day to the Tjipto's.

MEETING THE EXILES

I next remember meeting Sjahrir and Hatta at the birthday party of the Sumantri's four-year-old daughter, Tuty. I had to wear shoes on that day, and being an amateur shoe wearer, I had difficulty playing with the children at the party. My shoes were killing me, but I couldn't take them off because my mother said it was most impolite to remove my shoes at a party. I bet my shoes were one size too small; they were secondhand leather shoes that had already been worn by a cousin. Not able to play leapfrog with the other children, I sat under the Sumantri's mango tree and watched them play.

Sjahrir, who was directing the games, recognized me as the boy who had taken him and Hatta to the Sumantri's house on their arrival in Neira. He wondered why a healthy boy sat on the ground, not playing. He came to me, and said in Dutch, "Why aren't you playing?"

I couldn't answer him. My Dutch was not sufficient, and I was too shy to point at the damn shoes. All I could do was shake my head and say "*Neen*" ("no" in Dutch).

Sjahrir said, "I need a strong boy who can assist me by holding the rope for the children to jump." He held my hands and pulled me up. The other children watched me while I limped toward them. Sjahrir then told me that I could take off my shoes; he probably realized they were too small. I was happy to remove them, and now I could tell my mother later that an older man at the party told me to do so. I joined the games, and even won a sack of sweets by skipping ten times over the rope.

We called the two gentlemen from Sumatra Uncle Hatta, or used his nickname, Uncle Kaca Mata, for his dark-rimmed glasses, and Uncle Sjahrir, or Uncle Rir.

Although Sjahrir and Hatta received only a small allowance from the Dutch East Indies government for being in exile, they shared their money with others. At that time the cost of living in Banda Neira was very low. All that people needed to buy was rice and clothing. Hatta occasionally received some extra income from Java or Holland, which he earned from his articles and books published there. He used most of his extra income to support the other political prisoners at Digul, who only received a few Dutch guilders per month from the colonial government.

Sjahrir liked children very much. Every Sunday he stopped at Grandmother's house to talk to the Old Lady, and we kids would be there to go with him afterward for swimming, sailing, or rowing.

School for the Children

Soon Sjahrir and Hatta opened an afternoon school for the children of Banda Neira. Hatta gave lessons to the older children, and Sjahrir the younger ones. Hatta gave lessons to children who didn't have a chance to enroll at the European school, but studied at the Malay language school, which was known during the pre-war days as a second-class school. Hatta's school gave these children extra lessons in Dutch and other subjects that were not given at the Malay school. The two exiles even waived the tuition for the bigger boys whose parents could not afford to send them to the high school on Ambon Island, and for those children who had completed the five-year native school and who were unable to get higher education.

At my father's suggestion, I resigned from Aunt Willy's school and joined the two exiles' free afternoon school. On the back veranda of the large residence of the two lonely bachelors, Sjahrir and Hatta, we were given lessons in reading, writing, and arithmetic. All lessons were given in Dutch.

The house was rented from *perkenier* de Vries for only twelve and a half guilders a month. It had a large backyard with, of course, many fruit trees: *sawo*, *galak* mangoes, papayas, and pomelos. I was sure to be at the school half an hour before the lessons started, entering from the garden door and walking straight into a mango or *sawo* tree. Hatta would be very annoyed when he discovered me in his fruit trees. I don't think he cared much about the fruit, but he was afraid that I might break my neck falling from one of those small trees.

The school organized and run by Hatta

About twenty pupils attended the exiles' afternoon classes. Most of the pupils were the Baadilla grandchildren. The others were Uncle Tjip's adopted children, Donald and Louis; Husein and Tjahtji Maskat, children of an ex-pearl-schooner captain who had eloped with an Australian girl from Darwin, and lived happily ever after with her at Neira; and a few Bandanese who didn't have the chance to continue their studies at high schools in Ambon, Makassar, or Java.

There were also some children of nutmeg plantation administrators, but they came very irregularly. Their fathers didn't like them to mix with the political exiles, afraid that the colonial government might not like their association with the anti-colonial exiles. These children only came to the afternoon classes when they thought they needed some extra lessons because they were behind at the Dutch school, or when they were too naughty at their own homes and their mothers, to get rid of them for a few hours, sent them to the free afternoon lessons. However, when their fathers came to Neira from the other islands to collect the plantation's payroll, or to bring nutmeg to the head office, those children would automatically disappear from the afternoon school. They would join again some days later, as soon as their fathers departed for their plantations.

Hatta would become angry when a boy didn't know his lessons. His class was separated from Sjahrir's by a blackboard that faced our class. I could hear his shouting and calling names at one Bandanese boy who was not so bright. Hatta's favorite word when he was angry was *monyet* (monkey). At first we didn't know what *monyet* meant, because the Bandanese slang for monkey was *yaki*. We were amused when Uncle Sjahrir told us what it meant. I was glad that I wasn't in Hatta's class as he would certainly have called me *monyet* for climbing his fruit trees.

From studying in the afternoon school I became adopted by Hatta and Sjahrir, or rather Sjahrir. Because I was very unruly and naughty at home, my mother was happy to send me to live with the exiles. I stayed with them in their residence, only one block away from the European primary school. I occupied a large room, and was a little scared to sleep there. Uncle Rir taught me not to be afraid of ghosts—he said they didn't exist.

As the school was so close, I would often rush to school when the bell rang for lessons to begin. At school I made rapid progress because of the extra lessons given by Sjahrir and Hatta.

THE UNCLES' DAILY ROUTINES

During his time in Banda, Uncle Kaca Mata was always neatly dressed in a clean, long-sleeved white shirt and long white trousers. He woke up around six-thirty in the morning. His daily routine started with shaving in front of a small mirror placed on the dining table, with a bowl of hot water and shaving soap nearby. I liked to watch Uncle Kaca Mata shave. He looked so different without his heavy glasses and with a white face covered with shaving cream.

Ahir, our houseboy, was always nearby in case Uncle Kaca Mata needed him to sharpen the razor or to get more hot water. Ahir was often scolded for not sharpening the razor enough, or for the water being too hot, or not hot at all. It was always this or that that didn't satisfy Uncle Kaca Mata. After shaving he went straight to the bathroom, which was in the backyard. He first changed from his leather sandals to wooden clogs, which were placed on the back veranda. His bath took at least half an hour.

Since my school started at seven o'clock, I had to wake up at six to be first in the bathroom. If I was late, I took my bath at the well, with Uncle Rir pouring water on me.

After his bath, Uncle Kaca Mata, still in his blue-striped pajamas, would return to the dining table to sip his strong black coffee (*kopi tubruk*). Then he would change into his neat clothes and wait for Uncle Rir to have breakfast together, always at eight o'clock. Uncle Rir always appeared in his pajamas for breakfast, while Uncle Kaca Mata was already neatly dressed.

After breakfast, Uncle Kaca Mata would go straight to his study to write or to read. For a few days before the sailing date of the Makassar- and Java-bound KPM ships, Uncle Hatta would be busy writing articles and letters to his friends and relatives in Java, Sumatra, Holland, and other places. On such days I only saw him at lunch time, then he disappeared into his study, and I could hear his typewriter rattling "ter-tik-ter" until after midday. On such days Uncle Rir took over Uncle Kaca Mata's class, and the bigger boys were given English and German lessons. During Uncle Kaca Mata's "ter-tik-ter" days, we school children made sure not to play too near his study.

After lunch Uncle Kaca Mata usually took a nap. He would wake up around three o'clock to give lessons to the afternoon classes. At five he would change into his walking shoes and ramble through the nutmeg forest for an hour or so, which was his only exercise in Neira. During his exile in Digul he had played soccer on the exiles' team, which played against the team of the policemen who were guarding them. When he got home from his walk, Uncle Kaca Mata sipped another cup of black coffee, took another bath, had his dinner, and then returned to his study. Ahir again served him black coffee around nine in the evening, and about midnight Uncle Kaca Mata would retire.

Uncle Kaca Mata reserved Saturday nights and the whole of Sunday for his friends, to visit them or for them to visit him. He had not as many friends as Uncle Rir. Bandanese said that Uncle Kaca Mata was too serious, too clever, and too busy.

Uncle Rir had no fixed routine, and in his Banda days lived more like an artist. Usually he woke up much later than Uncle Kaca Mata, but on many occasions he got up about five in the morning to take a stroll on the *Tita*, the beach of Kampong Ratu. During his morning walk he occasionally stopped to chat with the returning fishermen, who were bringing their catch to the fish market.

Often on school days Uncle Rir woke up early to cook my oatmeal porridge. Hatta and Sjahrir had their own cook and a boy servant, but the cook and servant lived outside and only came to work at eight in the morning, while my school started at seven. I wasn't used to having such a big breakfast, and longed for Halik's fried bananas.

After his breakfast with Uncle Kaca Mata, Uncle Rir would take a cup of tea to his room, and start reading or doing some typing. He took his bath at any time before noon, and would only change from his pajamas into his shorts and short-sleeved shirt when Uncle Kaca Mata shouted, "Rir, lunch is served."

Often Uncle Rir read and worked in his boxer shorts. He seldom took a siesta because we kids were mixed in with him, and he often played marbles or tops with us. He usually played for the girl pupils to prevent the boys from cheating the small girls out of their shiny marbles. Uncle Rir was very good at tops and showed us how to let a rotation top walk from his palm to his arm.

Does and Des Alwi in front of the house where Hatta and Sjahrir lived, 1937

Uncle Rir's afternoons were spent swimming or playing tennis or soccer. He played soccer on the Ratu team, which we Kampong China boys didn't like very much, but he wasn't such a good player, so we didn't really mind his playing for a rival. Uncle Rir declined to join the Ratu team when they played for the yearly "Wilhelmina Cup," which celebrated the Dutch queen's birthday. As a political exile of the Dutch, he asked why he should play to celebrate their queen's birthday.

Uncle Rir spent his evenings with the Baadillas and the Kampong China people, attending birthday parties, attending dance parties at Christian Bandanese houses or at the Baadillas (at that time the Baadillas were the only Muslims in Banda who danced), attending wedding parties of the Muslim Bandanese, rowing in the *orambai*[5]

---

[5] A boat propelled by paddles, with a capacity of up to fifty people. A helmsman beats out the rhythm for the crew, and when auxilliary sails are used, sits at the stern using a paddle as a rudder. In the past, the *orambai* was commonly used in inter-island trade in the Moluccas. See Willard A. Hanna and Nigel Simmonds, *Banda: A Journey Through Indonesia's Fabled Isles of*

on moonlit nights, and so forth. Uncle Rir only worked in the evenings if he had to write letters to his girlfriend in Holland or to some of his friends in Europe. (My job in the Hatta–Sjahrir household was to take their letters to the post office and to collect items from their post-office box.)

MEALS WITH THE UNCLES

The two uncles always took their breakfast and lunch together. Their breakfast consisted of bread, butter, and jam; or plain fried rice with leftovers from the previous night. I wasn't allowed to eat lunch alone but ate with the two uncles to learn table manners. On many occasions I didn't enjoy my lunch because I was afraid of Uncle Kaca Mata sitting next to me. For lunch we had a large *rijsttafel* [meal of many dishes, always including rice]. Soon I learned how to cook rice, and became such an expert that the two uncles let me cook *all* the rice.

Evening meals were open-ended. The uncles either went out for dinner, together or separately, at friends' houses, or had separate meals at our house. If at home, we ate the lunch's leftovers. Uncle Kaca Mata would eat alone, and Uncle Rir would eat with a bunch of kids. When friends came for supper the uncles opened canned corned beef or sardines.

Usually at about ten in the morning Uncle Kaca Mata would receive Halima, the cook, to arrange the daily menu and to give her some money for the market. The meals were simple, consisting of vegetables, fish, *sambal* [chili sauce], and two dishes cooked with coconut milk. Fried chicken was served on Wednesdays and Saturdays. On Friday goat meat was served; goats were usually slaughtered on Fridays by Bandanese Muslims.

Beef was only obtainable once a month, because a cow was only slaughtered when the so-called butcher had enough customers for the whole cow. The butcher usually came around when he had a proposed date for slaughtering a cow; he made a written list of the orders, noting how many pounds of which part of the cow each buyer wanted. A cow was only slaughtered when the list of parts was fully booked. I used to be one of the boys taking round the list from the butcher, visiting houses to take orders. The butcher gave us a two-cent commission on a one-guilder order. Only the well-to-do people ordered beef; most Bandanese stuck to fish, which was twenty times cheaper.

Occasionally some neighbors sent fresh fish to us, the two bachelors and a boy. It always arrived after our cook had returned home and thus had to be prepared right away. There was no electricity in Banda Neira, and the exiles were too poor to have a kerosene refrigerator. If it was a small grouper I could handle it myself, but if it was a big tuna fish an SOS was sent to our neighbor, Grandma Toos. When she got to the house with her knives she always said, "Why don't you handsome and wise gentlemen get married to lovely Bandanese girls, and have some one to cook for you?"

Hatta didn't think it was funny, but Uncle Rir would laugh loudly. Grandma Toos would first pluck a few limes from the tree in the yard and then go straight to the kitchen to operate on the tuna. After cleaning the fish with limes she usually stayed to cook it. Many times the tuna fish was given to Grandma Toos, and in

Fire and Spice (Kuala Lampur and Denpasar, Bali: Yayasan Warisan dan Budaya Banda, 1997), p. 165.

return she would send a plate of hot fried tuna steaks to us. On some other occasions Grandma Toos just dispatched her maidservant to tackle the fish.

During the tuna season, when the Banda Sea is as still as a mirror, most people forgot to eat other kinds of fish, because four to five pounds of tuna cost only a few cents. Salted tuna fish was a bit risky to produce because the colonial government monopolized salt production, and salt was more expensive than the fish itself. Also, salted tuna fish doesn't last long.

PARTIES AND BIRTHDAYS

The feast-loving Bandanese always looked for a reason to organize a party. The Baadilla family birthdays were celebrated with dance parties or with picnics at one of Banda's lovely beaches. Uncle Rir, being a good dancer from his student days in Amsterdam and Leiden, according to the Bandanese girls, taught us to dance the foxtrot, waltz, and even the tango. Uncle Kaca Mata never danced; he only watched while others danced, and when he was tired of watching, he either played bridge or went home. If the party was at his residence, he was always a good host, seeing that his guests had enough to eat and drink, and acting as if it were his own birthday party.

Uncle Rir's birthday was always celebrated in a big way. Every March 5 the Baadillas, neighbors, and friends would come to the *rumah besar*, some with food and some with guitars, to make a feast. They didn't bring *tuak* [sap of coconut flowers] or the locally made coconut or palm wine called *tjap tikus* ("Mouse Brand") because Uncle Kaca Mata was anti-alcohol, as were the older Baadillas.

Some older people asked me to find out the exact date of Uncle Kaca Mata's August birthday, but I didn't have any success in finding out. Even Uncle Rir didn't know. One day some guests at the residence happened to ask Uncle Kaca Mata when his birthday was. He replied, "Today." In fact, it was that day, but since he was known never to disclose the date of his birthday, nobody believed him. If they only knew that Uncle Kaca Mata never told a lie, then the whole mystery would have been solved.

Since we were only sure of the month of Uncle Kaca Mata's birthday, the Bandanese would organize a party for him one Saturday evening in the month of August. If he happened to be busy at the beginning of the month, then the party was postponed to the next Saturday evening.

There wouldn't be any dancing or gambling at the parties organized for Uncle Hatta. The Bandanese knew that Uncle Kaca Mata was a strict man, and the Bandanese respected him very much. Guitar-playing and joke-telling were allowed, because Uncle Kaca Mata loved Moluccan melodies, and some Moluccan jokes, as long as they were not too malicious. We kids used to perform some native dances on such occasions, and I was always chosen to be the clown, or to act like one.

The fun-loving aunties of mine would ask me to impersonate Uncle Kaca Mata's way of walking and talking. The incidents in the afternoon classes when Uncle Kaca Mata was angry at one of the pupils were my favorite subjects. I would start by calling *monyet!* to one of the children. I would point to one boy and tell him: "You monkey! You can't eat and sleep and do your arithmetic lessons at the same time."

I would also imitate Uncle Kaca Mata's way of walking for his daily afternoon exercise, by walking very fast and swinging my arms up and down. At the end of the show I would appear in a "knee to neck" swimming suit, wearing a pair of white tennis shoes. Everybody would burst out laughing, especially Uncle Rir, who could laugh very loudly. Uncle Kaca Mata would also laugh; after all, it was only a show to celebrate his birthday. Uncle Rir would point at me, and tell the crowd, "Look, he's wearing Hatta's swimming suit and his tennis shoes, including his socks. But I have never seen Hatta wearing socks when he was swimming." The crowd would again burst out laughing.

Such parties always ended late at night after plenty of Moluccan sing-songs where everybody joined in singing traditional rhyming four-line *pantuns*. Each person in turn sings his or her own *pantun* verse, often composed on the spot. Everybody joins in singing the choruses. The Moluccan *pantuns* usually originated in Ambon Island and spread to the other islands of Indonesia through Moluccan soldiers in the KNIL. Most of these *pantuns* were in the local Indonesian dialect of the Moluccas, but in Java or Sumatra these melodies were sung in real Indonesian phrases.

Some of the older Bandanese liked "double-meaning" *pantuns*, especially when Uncle Kaca Mata had gone home. Funny, but I never heard him sing. Uncle Rir was quite the contrary; he sometimes sang too much and snatched other people's turns.

During their time in Banda, Uncle Rir started to speak the Bandanese Malay slang, and continued to use it in later years when he talked with us at home, or with Bandanese guests. Uncle Kaca Mata always spoke Indonesian, with a Minangkabau accent. During his time in Banda he didn't want to learn the Bandanese dialect. He said it would ruin the Indonesian language if one spoke the Bandanese slang. We agreed with him, especially when we wanted to speak the "high Malay," as we used to call the Indonesian language.

HIDE-AND-SEEK

Saturday nights were always fun. At least a dozen friends and cousins would come to sleep in the uncles' eight-room house. We would cook our rice and prepare the fish ourselves. Uncle Kaca Mata was always missing on such occasions. We were too noisy for him, so he sought refuge at Dr. Tjipto's or the Sumantri's house. After the meal we usually played hide-and-seek in the dark backyard and the empty rooms, turning the furniture upside down. Uncle Rir would join the game and play with us like a real boy. One night Uncle Kaca Mata returned home early and was very mad to find his room in a mess. Some of the visiting boys had forgotten Uncle Rir's warning not to hide in that special extra-territorial room. We could hear Uncle Kaca Mata's favorite words when he was angry: "*Monyet, monyet, binatang, binatang kecil*" (monkeys and small beasts).

We of course hid under our beds or in the rooms' dark corners. Hatta called, "Sjahrir, Rir, Rir, are you there?"

We didn't hear any answer from our playmate uncle. Uncle Kaca Mata then lit his kerosene wall lamp (*lampu tembok*), but it did not provide enough light for him to fix his room and rearrange his disordered *kelambu* (mosquito net). Then we heard him walking toward Uncle Rir's room. He again called, "Rir, Rir, are you there?"

Still no answer from Uncle Rir. We were as quiet as mice. I held my breath when I heard Uncle Hatta pumping the tank of the Storm King kerosene lamp that could light up his room, the sitting room, the back veranda, and Uncle Rir's room. Now he would discover us; there would be no chance to play unofficial hide-and-seek with Uncle Kaca Mata. Our only chance was to sneak out through Uncle Rir's room before

Uncle Kaca Mata lit the powerful kerosene lamp. I wondered whether our playmate, the exiled famous young nationalist leader, Uncle Sjahrir, was also trapped inside his room. I knew he was not afraid of Hatta, because on several occasions they had heavy political debates with each other, but the illegal entry into Uncle Kaca Mata's room by some of my playmates was most embarrassing to Uncle Rir.

When Uncle Kaca Mata lit the kerosene lamp on the back veranda, and went to his room to light the lamp there, we crawled quietly to Uncle Rir's room to go out the door to the front veranda and street. To my surprise the door was already open. Whether Uncle Rir had sneaked out when Hatta arrived, or before, nobody knew. I rushed with some of the boys to their house, where we found Uncle Rir chatting with Grandma Toos and some other ladies, drinking hot ginger tea with pineapple rolls. Seeing us coming at midnight Grandma Toos made a hell of a noise, telling her grandsons to go to their rooms.

I told Uncle Rir that Uncle Kaca Mata was mad when he found that his room was upside down. Uncle Rir asked whether I had played in there. I said that I knew better than to hide in Uncle Kaca Mata's bedroom.

We left Grandma Toos's place and went back to the house. When we arrived, Hatta was reading in his study. Uncle Rir went to talk with him. I heard Uncle Kaca Mata saying to him, "These boys have been playing in my room, stepped on my bed sheet with their dirty feet, ruined my *kelambu*, knocked down my chairs, etc., etc."

Uncle Rir replied, "I am sorry, Ta (for Hatta). I had told them not to play in your room, but some of Des's friends haven't been here before. They were playing hide-and-seek, and probably some entered your room without knowing it was yours." (He didn't say that he was in the game also.)

Then he asked Uncle Kaca Mata what his program was for the next day, a Sunday. When he said that he had nothing in mind, the angry Uncle Kaca Mata was invited to join in our sailing venture around Banda Neira Island. He accepted, a sign that he had calmed down. Uncle Kaca Mata was worried in a fatherly way about breakfast for the ten naughty boy guests. But Uncle Rir told him there was nothing to worry about, "We'll just give them fried bananas and rice cakes from the peddlers."

Hatta replied, "I don't think these cakes are very clean for the boys to eat."

Uncle Rir then said, "I think it's all right, these kids have been eating them all the time. Well, Ta, I'll see you tomorrow at six. *Wel te rusten, Ta*" ("sleep well," in Dutch).

Uncle Rir thus concluded his conversation and went to bed. When everything was calm, the boys who were hiding in the back garden returned to their nests of extra mattresses and wild *pandan* leaf mats. My friends Perus and Jot (as we Bandanese pronounced George) also sneaked back from their grandma's house, intending to come along on the next morning's sailing trip.

SAILING TRIP AROUND BANDA NEIRA

We woke up early in the morning to prepare for the trip and to boil some water for our tea and Uncle Kaca Mata's extra-strong coffee. Some boys went to Halik's house in Kampong China, about half a mile from the house of Hatta and Sjahrir in Kampong Ratu, to fetch him and his fried bananas. Half an hour later the boys arrived back with Halik and his twin brothers, Hitam and Putih, carrying baskets with their fried snacks. We told Halik that if he let us *borong* (wholesale) his sixty cakes for fifty cents, he could join us in the sailing trip around Neira Island. Uncle Rir came to listen to our bargaining, and laughed when one boy said, "For forty cents you can take Hitam and Putih along." Uncle Rir paid Halik sixty cents, and he said that all three brothers could come with us.

Uncle Kaca Mata was now awake, and looked very sourly at me as he joined the breakfast table. He was interested in the small twins, asking where they came from. I replied that they were fried-banana sellers. "They look the same, don't they?" he said.

"Yes, because they are twins," I replied.

Hatta asked the twins what their names were. The boys answered simultaneously, "Hitam and Putih."

Hatta then said, "We better call them Bawang Putih and Bawang Merah." We all laughed. Bawang Putih and Bawang Merah is a well-known Indonesian children's story about twin brothers who were adopted by two different people, or sold to two different people by their stepfather. One of them became a king and the other a slave. (*Bawang merah* means red onion and *bawang putih* means garlic.)

At seven o'clock we departed from the house. First we walked to Negreh to borrow an *orambai* from Uncle Philippus for the sailing expedition. We had to wait until a little after eight o'clock for Uncle Philippus to return from church. Uncle Rir asked whether we could borrow his *orambai* for the sailing trip. But Auntie Philippus, the most respected lady of Negreh, did not want to lend us the *orambai* because, she said, the *orambai* was too small to accommodate thirteen boys and two adults. Uncle Philippus suggested that we could take his *ru-re-hee*, a bigger prau that is used for tuna fishing. However, he said that if we took the *ru-re-hee* we should take along a few professional rowers. He did not believe that we were strong enough to row around Neira. Uncle Philippus laughed when Uncle Rir told him that we intended to sail as well as row. He said, "It is very hard to maneuver a *ru-re-hee* when a sail is used."

Uncle Rir didn't like the idea of having some rowers with us; he wanted to sail, not to row, around Neira. I knew that Uncle Rir wanted to be the captain of the *orambai* and to hold the tiller and let the wind and the boys do the rest of the work. Halik found a solution by inviting two of his strong cousins to become our extra rowers. They were tuna fishermen and knew how to handle the *ru-re-hee* in time of emergency. Halik suggested that they act as rowers and advisers to the self-appointed *ru-re-hee* captain.

It was already nine o'clock when we got started. Uncle Philippus, at Captain Rir's insistence, produced the sail from one of his old outriggers to put on the *ru-re-hee*. The sail was so small that it looked more like a football club's banner than a sail. Bandanese living near the harbor area laughed at us when they saw our "banner-sail."

It was getting hot when we rowed past Neira harbor into Banda Bay. Uncle Kaca Mata, who was sitting in the middle of the *ru-re-hee* to avoid getting wet, put on his sun helmet, afraid of getting sunburned. With his white sun helmet he looked like Hayashi-san, the first mate of *Dai Ichi Tora Maru*, the Japanese merchant ship that used to call at Banda Neira. Only the gold teeth were missing. He could even have been Hatta-san. After all, *hata* is the Japanese word for flag. Hatta-san, or Mister Flag, and the banner-size sail were the two items needed to keep the *ru-re-hee* moving—one for the ballast and the other to catch the wind.

As we entered Banda Bay, a little breeze blew us toward the government pier. I suggested to the honorable captain that we go a bit farther out to sea, but the captain didn't agree. He wanted to go by Kampong Baru first, and from there sail toward

Pulau Pisang, and then turn toward Lautaka plantation at the other end of Neira. I knew what was coming when we sailed too close to the beaches of Kampong Baru. As I had foreseen, these beaches were crowded with Sunday picnickers. When we rowed past them with our sail up, the girls on the beach started shouting at us, "Hey, you! Are you going with your *pandan* mat sail to sleep on the ocean?"

Some girls who knew Sjahrir and Hatta shouted at them, "Hey, *abang* (brothers)! If you go back to Sumatra with that funny sail of yours, take us along."

The uncles laughed. At that time I was too young to realize why Uncle Rir wanted to sail the *ru-re-hee* near the Kampong Baru beach instead of going a little farther out to sea. He, of course, wanted to see the girls on the beach and to show-off being the *ru-re-hee*'s captain. He was only twenty-eight at that time, and a bachelor.

Soon we passed Kampong Baru, and couldn't hear what people were yelling. The small sail caught some wind, and the *ru-re-hee* moved ahead slowly toward Pulau Pisang.

It was already three o'clock in the afternoon when we reached Lautaka, and we were really hungry. We stopped at a clean beach for a swim and to gather some *kanari* nuts to fill our empty stomachs. Uncle Kaca Mata started swimming with his tennis shoes on. He always swam that way; he didn't want his feet to get hurt on the sharp stones. Jot and Halik came back with some young beach mangoes, but Uncle Kaca Mata would not eat them, they were too sour for him.

Halik tried to please him by giving him a handful of shelled *kanari* nuts. I didn't know what Halik was after by pleasing Uncle Kaca Mata. No boys dared to talk to Uncle Kaca Mata unless spoken to, and then we had to reply. But not Halik. He asked Uncle Kaca Mata all sorts of questions: where he came from, whether he could read the Koran, whether his mother was still alive, why the Dutch banished him to Banda Neira. Uncle Kaca Mata answered all Halik's questions, except the last one. Halik didn't give in, and said, "I know: You are more clever than a Dutch doctor, that is why they sent you away from Sumatra and Java."

We all laughed. Uncle Rir was so amused that he couldn't stop laughing. We liked Uncle Rir—he always smiled, and when something was funny he laughed out loud.

We spent about two hours in Lautaka Oceanside, and left for Sun Gate, a narrow strait that separates Gunung Api from Neira. The current was very strong when we entered the narrow passage, and it kept pushing us toward the open sea. The self-appointed captain didn't maneuver the *ru-re-hee* properly, so he was replaced by one of Halik's strong cousins. The new captain maneuvered the boat well, and cleared the narrow passage. By now we could see the lights of Negreh and Kampong China. When we arrived at the Philippus pier about nine o'clock, some mothers were waiting there. They seemed a little worried that we didn't get back to the pier before sunset. The two uncles apologized to the boys' mothers for causing some anxious moments. But Auntie Philippus said to Uncle Sjahrir, "You educated young man. Didn't my husband tell you to take some rowers along? Not bad, seven miles in twelve hours!"

We returned the oars and the banner-like sail to Uncle Philippus and rushed home to eat the *rijsttafel* that had been prepared earlier that day and had been meant for lunch. Before we left home that morning I had heard Uncle Kaca Mata ask Uncle Rir whether we'd be back before lunchtime. Uncle Rir had replied, "Yes, of course."

CHAPTER FOUR

BOATS FOR THE UNCLES

The two exiles liked boating and sailing so much that Uncle Kaca Mata decided to buy an *orambai* for our use, so I went with some friends to find one. We found a suitable one at the boat yard near the harbor, where a Saruan man called Uncle Sepos was a well-known *orambai* builder. However, Uncle Sepos asked twenty guilders for a prau that could carry about twelve persons. He didn't want to lower his price, but Uncle Kaca Mata had only reserved ten to twelve and a half guilders for an *orambai* fund.

We went to Uncle Philippus for advice; his advice on anything that concerned praus and the sea was taken seriously by the Negreh people. He told us not to buy a new *orambai* because one never knew whether a newly built prau would leak until it had been used for some time. Uncle Philippus suggested that we go with him to Lonthor village on Banda Besar to look for a suitable *orambai*. So that same afternoon I went with three friends and Uncle Philippus to Lonthor in one of Uncle Philippus's outriggers.

Lonthor lies about three nautical miles from the Philippus pier. We got there within an hour and went straight to Abang Johar's house. Abang Johar was a fisherman with eight grown-up sons. The Kampong China and Negreh kids respected the Lonthor kids—they are a tough lot and good fighters. We stayed close to the two older men and remained quiet, afraid to say something that might create trouble with the Lonthor boys. The four of us waited on the beach when Uncle Philippus entered Abang Johar's house for an *orambai* talk. Soon we realized that about a dozen Lonthor boys had surrounded us and were watching us. One of them asked why we were there, and one of Abang Johar's sons said that we had come to Lonthor to buy a prau.

One of the Lonthor boys said, "These Neira people can't build their own *orambai*. That's why they come here to buy one."

The Lonthor boys made fun of us and bullied us until we couldn't stand it any longer. Suddenly Nolsy Philippus, Uncle Philippus's eleven-year-old son (later a boxing champion), stood up and said, "Don't you Lonthor boys try to bully us just because you are in your own kampong and in the majority!"

The Lonthor boys responded to Nolsy's challenge, and soon we found ourselves fighting against nine or ten of them. The Johar sons didn't join in, but watched the fighting with pleasure. Before we realized it, the two men had come out of the house to stop the fighting. Abang Johar chased away the unfriendly Lonthor boys with an oar and scolded his sons for remaining quiet instead of warning him.

Uncle Philippus was very angry. He told Abang Johar to come to Neira if he wanted to sell an *orambai*. Then we went back to Neira, Nolsy with a bleeding nose, me with a torn shirt, and the two other friends looking shabby.

The next day Abang Johar arrived in Neira with his eight sons and two small *orambai*s. We fetched Uncle Rir and Uncle Kaca Mata to see the *orambai*s. They came to have a look, but let Uncle Philippus do the bargaining and choosing. He picked the six-rower *orambai*, and paid Abang Johar ten guilders. It was a very easy transaction: no receipt, just an exchange of ten guilders for one *orambai*, the usual Bandanese way of selling things.

Uncle Philippus was happy that the two exiles and their friends had their own *orambai*, so they wouldn't bother him again to borrow one of his praus. Soon, all the Kampong China and Negreh people knew that Uncle Kaca Mata had his own *orambai*, and his status changed to that of an *orambai* lender. Almost every week people came to the house to borrow the *orambai* for a picnic, or to fetch coconuts, sweet potatoes, tapioca roots, fruits, and vegetables from their *kebuns* [gardens] on the other islands. Usually, after the borrowers returned the *orambai*, they gave Uncle Kaca Mata some of the items they had brought from their gardens. Fruit was the gift that Uncle Kaca Mata liked most. He didn't like sweet potatoes or tapioca, finding them too heavy; he preferred bread or fried rice for breakfast. Uncle Rir, on the other hand, would eat anything.

Left to right: Sjahrir, as captain of the Bandanese *orambai* that belonged to Hatta; Bachtul and Munir (Hatta's Sumatran students); three of the children "adopted" by Sjahrir—Mimi (Des's cousin), Lily (Des's sister), and Does (Des's cousin)

Uncle Kaca Mata's *orambai* was kept on a small beach near Uncle Philippus's pier. Uncle Kaca Mata seldom used the prau—unless we invited him to join us on a rowing trip in his own *orambai*. We children looked after the *orambai*. Uncle Philippus acted as its guardian, in case the boys might use it for such purposes as taking foreign tourists to see the coral gardens, ferrying the passengers of the KPM steamers to Neira, or using the *orambai* to steal fruit off Gunung Api Island. Such things had happened, and Uncle Kaca Mata was very embarrassed. Imagine—a known nationalist leader and political exile renting his prau to tourists, or using it to carry passengers to and from a KPM steamer in competition with the Bandanese *orambai* owners, or, worst of all, using the prau to steal fruit.

All of this was reported to Uncle Kaca Mata by the most respected lady of Negreh, Auntie Philippus, when she met him at Taukeh Tan's shop. She told him about his *orambai* being used to ferry KPM passengers by the naughty boys who played with the fried banana peddler, which wasn't so bad, because the Philippus boys did the same thing with their praus. The worst of it was the boys used the prau to steal young coconuts and *jamblang* (plums) from Madame de Branz's plantation at Uluwero, on Gunung Api. Madame de Branz, the richest widow of Neira and the proprietor of Banda's only hotel, the Hotel de Branz, was a church friend of Auntie Philippus. In fact, she had reported to Uncle Rir before, but the children's friend, Uncle Rir, didn't take any notice, but only said to Aunt Philippus, "Oh, these naughty children."

Uncle Kaca Mata was, of course, mad at me—even when the records showed that on such-and-such days, as reported by Auntie Philippus, I was at school or in class at the house. I did admit to Uncle Rir, during a "man to man" talk, having been with the Sunday morning *jamblang*-stealing gang. "But," I told him, "it wasn't stealing, we just plucked the fruits from the tree branches that were hanging low over the water."

Uncle Rir asked me whether Halik had used the prau to ferry passengers from the ship to the *los*. I told him that Halik was really only interested in selling his cakes on the ship. Since the steamer is at anchor far from the *los*, he must use some prau to get there. On his trip back he might take some passengers to the wharf.

Uncle Rir asked me why Halik didn't use his *kolee-kolee* (dugout canoe) to go to the ship. Laughing, I replied, "What? Use the *kolee-kolee* to carry cakes to the ship? It's too small. He'd get wet, and his fried bananas would be soaked in sea water. And if a powerful motorboat from the ship passed too close, its waves would probably capsize the *kolee-kolee*. Poor Halik would lose all his cakes and the earnings he put underneath the banana leaves inside his basket. When he got home, his mother would smack him with a rattan cane or even with one of the oars that Halik kept in the house."

SJAHRIR BUYS A *KOLEE-KOLEE*

Uncle Rir became interested in a *kolee-kolee*. After many pleas from me, he bought one, for only one guilder, from one of the Saruans who often came to Neira to sell these dugout canoes. The one he bought was small, but it could carry two people.

We boys drilled and trained Uncle Rir to ride in it. The first lesson was how to step into the *kolee-kolee*, not from the water, but from the dry steps of the Philippus pier. Every time Uncle Rir put one foot on the *kolee-kolee* the canoe swayed and moved, leaving him on the steps or in the water. So we suggested that he get rid of his heavy clothes and wear only his boxer shorts. He followed our instructions. Auntie Philippus, who was watching the lessons from the pier, disappeared into the house.

Uncle Rir shouted at her, "Hey, Auntie, what's the difference between boxer shorts and swimming trunks? You didn't run away when you saw me with swimming trunks on last time."

Auntie Philippus shouted back from inside the house, "Look, educated young man, I am not shy at all. You are much younger than some of my sons who are now in the marines or in the army. Why should I be afraid of your boxer shorts?"

Everyone laughed. She continued, "I went inside because I want to prepare some *kolak* (coconut milk porridge with brown sugar and bananas or sweet potatoes) for you and your young friends. If you all get tired from the *kolee-kolee* lessons, come inside the house for some *kolak*."

Uncle Rir was prepared to get wet, and with his boxer shorts as his swimming costume, the lessons went well. Soon he disappeared with the *kolee-kolee* behind the *los*. I hoped he wouldn't go to Kampong Baru to show off for rowing a *kolee-kolee*—in his boxer shorts. He soon returned to the Philippus pier with the *kolee-kolee*, but he couldn't climb out of it, and we had to hold it so he could step out.

Soon Uncle Rir learned how to balance his body, and you could see him in his *kolee-kolee* almost every afternoon. To be able to have regular sessions in the *kolee-kolee* he cut short our afternoon classes. Although I quite liked this, I was not so happy that he had acquired the *kolee-kolee* sickness—he wanted to use it for himself most afternoons. Sometimes I could also come along, but only as a crew member. He wanted to be at the helm all the time, while I had to sit in front and paddle on the right side. Uncle Rir would only paddle on the left side because he was right handed—like most people are, including me. He hadn't much experience with the *kolee-kolee*, but acted as if he were already qualified and didn't want to listen to his small instructor any longer. He completely forgot that we boys were his *kolee-kolee* teachers. He probably wanted to obtain some *kolee-kolee* experience the hard way, but when his *kolee-kolee* overturned in the middle of the lagoon, Uncle Philippus always rushed out in his outrigger to rescue him. If we boys capsized far away from the pier or the *los* we would just empty out the water, climb back in, and off we would go again.

Although Uncle Rir knew how to empty the water from inside the *kolee-kolee*, he had a hard time learning how to climb back in, and depended on Uncle Philippus to rescue him. We boys, watching from one of the piers near the *los*, would boo them, and tell Uncle Rir, "You see what happens when you don't listen to our instructions!"

He would reply, "OK, boys, teach me how to climb into the *kolee-kolee* from the water."

So we taught him, and soon he was qualified, and even beat us in the *kolee-kolee* races. "Obviously you win against them," said Auntie Philippus, "You are much stronger than the whole lot of your young friends."

To Lonthor for a Sailboat

After graduating from the *kolee-kolee* class, Uncle Rir wanted a bigger prau that he could sail in Banda Bay and Neira harbor. Uncle Kaca Mata's *orambai* was not good enough for him because it had no proper sail and no rudder. He also realized that we boys were not strong enough to row the *orambai*. I was very happy when Uncle Rir told me that he intended to go to Lonthor to purchase a small sailing boat, because I thought if he had his own prau, the *kolee-kolee* would be in my solid control.

So one Sunday we boys went to Lonthor with Uncle Rir in Uncle Kaca Mata's *orambai*. Uncle Kaca Mata didn't want to come along; he was too busy at home writing articles and letters to his friends and relatives.

We arrived at Lonthor and went straight to Abang Johar's house. He was very friendly to us, as were his sons, especially when they saw us coming with a bunch of twelve boys, including Halik. Halik was recognized among us boys as a good fighter, so Nolsy asked Halik to go to Lonthor with us, just in case the Lonthor boys wanted to create trouble. Halik agreed to come along because he was of the opinion that those Lonthor boys would never attack us when he was around.

The Lonthor crowd who had fought us before came with more boys, but they stood a distance away. As long as we were with an adult they didn't try to touch us. We were also like that. Somehow our child's world recognized adults as a kind of authority; we respected them, probably because they were bigger and stronger than us.

Abang Johar showed us his praus. Some were new and unpainted. They smelled nice; by smelling their planks we could tell what kind of wood they were made of. Uncle Rir did not want to use an *orambai* as a sailing boat. He said, "They are not comfortable, and are rather clumsy looking, with both ends looking the same and having no helm."

Even when Abang Johar promised to convert it into a sailing boat by installing a permanent mast and rebuilding the stern for the helm, Uncle Rir was not satisfied. He didn't like the idea of turning an *orambai* into a "professional" sailing boat because the body would still be the same—broad and clumsy.

Than Uncle Rir saw a large *kolee-kolee*, made from a giant *pitaor* tree trunk. It must have weighed half a ton and was so large that it could carry at least eight gunny sacks of nutmeg. We boys quite liked it because it could probably carry all of us, twelve boys and two adults, but we didn't like to turn it into a sailing boat. We thought it would be crazy to turn a dugout piece of a tree trunk into a streamlined sailing boat. But Uncle Rir was happy with it. He bought it for eight guilders, because it was eight times bigger than the one-guilder *kolee-kolee* of ours. Abang Johar was glad to get rid of his fantastic-size *kolee-kolee* at that price, because even for a lower price no Bandanese would buy such a big *kolee-kolee*. There was too big a risk when a large canoe capsizes. Abang Johar looked astonished when Uncle Rir told him that the *kolee-kolee* he had bought was going to lose its tail when converted into a sailing boat.

A DUGOUT BECOMES A SAILBOAT

When we arrived back at the Philippus pier, old man Philippus said, "*Astaga!* ('Goodness' in Bandanese–Malay slang.) I have never seen such a large and ugly looking *kolee-kolee* before."

We told him that the large and ugly looking *kolee-kolee* was going to turn into a shapely sail boat with a mast and real helm. Uncle Philippus shook his head, saying, "I should have come with you to Lonthor to pick a real prau to be used as a sailing boat."

Said Uncle Rir, "Well, you'll see what a nice boat it is going to be when Sepus makes the alterations."

Uncle Philippus recognized Sepus as a first-class boat builder, but turning a giant *kolee-kolee* into a shapely schooner or a sailing boat is something different. Thank goodness Auntie Philippus was not there when we arrived. Otherwise Uncle Rir certainly would have received plenty of commentary, such as: "You educated young man, being cheated by the Lonthor prau seller."

Uncle Rir's gigantic *kolee-kolee* was sent to Sepus, the boat builder, to be converted into a sailing boat. Uncle Mat, my favorite uncle, went to the Tjotjo Baadilla pier to give some advice to Sepus on how to change a dugout boat into a yacht. But when he saw the *kolee-kolee* he shook his head and said, "How is it possible to turn that into a yacht? This big canoe doesn't even have a keel."

Sepus told him that the "gentleman" had ordered him to saw a piece off from one end and close it with some planks, so that a helm could be placed at the stern with an extra plank seat for the helmsman. Uncle Rir also ordered Sepus to put a real mast made of wood, not bamboo, in the middle of the boat.

Uncle Mat asked Sepus, "How much do you charge the gentleman for this kind of alteration work?"

Sepus told him about seven guilders, excluding the khaki drill material for sails. Uncle Philippus commented that with that much money Sepus could build a silver-plated mast. Sepus didn't like that joke, but said that he had promised the gentleman to follow his instructions, and he would stick to it.

Every afternoon we children would go with Uncle Rir to the Tjotjo pier to see the progress on the future yacht. It seemed as if Sepus found it difficult to close the opening of the bow or stern of the *kolee-kolee*. The *kolee-kolee*'s edges are too thin for a wooden pin, but an iron nail would quickly rust, especially in sea water, and the prau's body would collapse, or "peel off," as we said in Banda.

To divert the little "inspectors'" attention, Sepus concentrated on building the mast and the two pieces of sail. When we returned some afternoons later, the stern was already covered with one piece of wood and the rear edges were caulked with tar-wax. Whether Sepus had hammered nails in it or used wooden pins, nobody knew because it was sealed off with the tar-wax. The helm consisted of ordinary planks, forming a sort of portable helm. The handle could be removed, so that without the owner's consent nobody could use the yacht. The owner could keep the helm's handle at home when he didn't want people to use his yacht. We boys didn't like the removable helm handle because that meant we had no freedom to use the yacht without the owner's consent.

The pseudo-yacht looked so nice, especially when Sepus touched up the yacht's bow to make it look like a real schooner, and added a shapely long bowsprit to tie the line of the front sail. However, Auntie Philippus still called the boat a *kolee-kolee*, even if it had been turned into a so-called yacht. Uncle Rir told her that it was no longer a *kolee-kolee*, but a prau *layar* (sailing boat). Auntie Philippus replied, "It is still a *kolee-kolee* to me. Once a *kolee-kolee* forever a *kolee-kolee*."

At first we intended to paint the yacht red and white, but Auntie Philippus didn't like it. She said the Dutch *controleur* would confiscate the boat because red and white were anti-Dutch colors. Halik was also against painting the yacht red and white. Quietly he told us the reason: if we painted the yacht red and white, then it would be a Dutch flag because the body of the boat would be red and white and the sea below it blue, the colors and design of the Dutch flag. We agreed, and finally chose blue—which in fact was the only color Koon could provide from his father's shop, free of charge, of course.

Then it came time to choose the yacht's name. Some boys suggested the name *Neira* for the yacht, but it was already used by one of the Kok's motorboats. "How about *Gunung Api*?" asked Halik. Someone said, "No, no. Some day Gunung Api will erupt. We don't want the yacht to erupt, do we?"

Some boys suggested that we use names of fish, but the names of good fish were already used for the boats of the fishermen. There were so many praus in Banda Neira that we ran out of names, especially of islands and of fish.

Somebody suggested naming the yacht "Sumatra," because Uncle Rir was born there. Uncle Rir didn't agree, but suggested naming the yacht "Indonesia." Koon didn't know what Indonesia meant and asked Uncle Rir if it was a bird. We all laughed. Halik made the explanation to Koon, because from mixing with the exiles Halik had begun to understand things. He even knew why these people from Java and Sumatra were banished to Banda Neira. He told Koon that Indonesia is the Malay name for the Netherlands Indies. Koon said he had never heard of it before. Uncle Rir explained to Koon that in the Dutch schools this name was never mentioned, because the Dutch teachers don't want their colony to be called "Indonesia." He then told Koon that the word Indonesia is like the word "Chung Hua" or "Tiongkok" for China. The Dutch called this country "Indie" or "Nederlands Indie," but we call it "Indonesia."

At last Koon understood the meaning of "Indonesia." He ran home to get some black paint and a collection of forms for the letters to be painted on the side of the boat. Koon did the painting himself; he was very good at it.

LAUNCHING THE YACHT *INDONESIA*

Some Negreh people told Uncle Rir to have a *selamatan* [ceremonial meal] and sacrifice a goat before the boat was launched. Uncle Rir said that the yacht was too small to sacrifice a poor goat, but *roti kismis* (raisin bread) would be served after the launching.

The next morning we were ready. A basket full of raisin bread, hot from Auntie Philippus's oven; Halik's fried bananas, a donation from him to honor the occasion; and Koon's *rozen* [rose] syrup were all ready to feed the guests. About thirty children were present: the afternoon class, my friends, and several gate-crashing Negreh children.

Before the yacht was launched Uncle Rir sent me to a Chinese shop to purchase a bottle of champagne to crash on the yacht's bow. The Chinese shopkeeper didn't know what champagne was, and neither did I. Together with the Chinese shopkeeper I inspected all the bottles inside his shop just to find a label that sounded something like "sampain." Then I discovered a bottle on whose label was written in Dutch something like: "This lemonade tastes like champagne." This must be the one, I thought, but how come the price was only ten cents? Uncle Rir had told me that I must be careful when I carried the bottle of champagne because it would be expensive, over one guilder. I took the bottle, hoping that the Chinese shopkeeper had sold the "sampain" below its cost.

When I got back to the Tjotjo Baadilla pier, everybody was waiting for me. "Quick," Uncle Rir said, "where is the bottle?" I gave it to him. He screamed, "This isn't champagne, this is lemonade!" I asked him to read the label. He smiled and said, "Never mind. This will do."

To myself I said, "Of course this bottle is all right; it cost only ten cents. Why waste over one guilder just to crash it on the yacht's bow?"

We children watched Uncle Rir tie the small lemonade bottle on one end of a piece of string and the other end on the yacht's bow. With the bottle in his hands he stood in front of the yacht and said loudly, "I name this ship *Indonesia*." (I wondered since when a *kolee-kolee* was a ship.) Then Uncle Rir let loose the bottle on the yacht's bow. The bottle didn't break.

"Break the bottle with a stone; that would be much easier," Halik said. Uncle Rir told him to be quiet. We kids thought it was crazy to try to break a bottle on something made of wood. We had never seen or heard of people breaking a bottle on a prau's bow.

Uncle Rir then held the bottle tightly in his right hand and knocked it with force on the bow of his beloved yacht. The bottle broke in two, making a deep cut in Uncle Rir's right palm. A mixture of lemonade and blood spilled in front of the yacht. Lots of blood came out of Uncle Rir's hand. Some small kids ran away; some thought that Uncle Rir had lost his hand when he wrapped it in his white shirt and the shirt soon turned red.

Nolsy ran home to call his ma. Auntie Philippus came running with some church ladies, bringing along cotton and bandages. Uncle Rir smiled while the ladies nursed his hand. He told us to carry on with the celebration, which was to tackle the raisin bread and fried bananas. The Negreh ladies told him that if he had sacrificed a goat for the launching, as was the Bandanese custom, this blood-spilling accident would not have happened. Since he didn't listen to them, he sacrificed his own hand. Uncle Rir smiled and told them that he didn't understand how the ladies could go to church and at the same time believe in the *foe-foe*.

"Well," said Auntie Philippus, "we go to church because we are Christians, but we are also Bandanese. Born on Banda's soil, we should follow the Bandanese customs inherited from the *tee-tee-moyang* (ancestors)."

Everybody was so busy nursing Uncle Rir and eating raisin bread that we completely forgot to launch the yacht. With the assistance of the church ladies and Sepus we children managed to push the yacht into the water. "Hooray!" we screamed when the yacht drifted on to the water. We were glad that it didn't capsize. Even the mast didn't seem to be too heavy for the ex-*kolee-kolee*. At last we saw old Sepus smile; he was happy when Uncle Rir paid him the balance due him, and presented him with a sarong. We children all climbed into the yacht. Uncle Rir wanted to join us, but Auntie Philippus told him that he better stay with the ladies if he wanted his hand to heal.

She said to Uncle Rir, "Look, you educated young man, you still have plenty of time in the future to play with your *kolee-kolee* toy."

Uncle Rir promised her that he would only sit as an ordinary passenger instead of being the helmsman. Sepus was then put in charge of the yacht. We raised the sails, but there wasn't any wind. We returned to the pier and left the yacht to be looked after by Sepus. Before we left the yacht, Uncle Rir, with his right hand bandaged, still managed to dismantle the helm-handle with his left hand. He took it with him to the house. That meant nobody could use his toy without his permission.

CHAPTER FIVE

LIFE WITH THE EXILES

The political exiles always got together once or twice a week to discuss the Indonesian political situation, Indonesia's future, and the general world situation, such as the civil war in Spain and the Sino–Japanese War. They usually stayed up until late at night at Uncle Tjipto Mangunkusumo's place. Uncle Tjip was already a sick man; he suffered from asthma and couldn't leave his house, especially in the evening.

THE OTHER EXILES IN BANDA

Sometimes I joined the uncles on Saturday evenings for dinner at the Tjipto's. While the gentlemen had their political discussions I would play with the two Tjipto boys, Donald and Louis. They were much older than I, and were already studying in Uncle Kaca Mata's class, taking math, English, French, and German lessons. Louis, the younger of the two, designed and built his own miniature boats, while Donald built and supplied them with small engines. They did not build miniature *kolee-kolee* or *orambai*, but real small schooners and even small KPM boats with real engines. Nearly every Sunday morning, they tried out their miniature boats at the beach near the fish market, which was not far from their residence. I was always invited to come along when they tested their boats—to act as a "lifeguard" and boat-rescuer in case the small boats wandered too far out to sea, or when they sank and disappeared in the depths. Donald and Louis could not swim because their mother did not allow them to swim. She was afraid the boys might catch cold and get asthma. Sometimes, sneakily, we persuaded Donald and Louis to try to swim. Donald tried, but was afraid of deep water. He refused to be taught and only swam in knee-deep water.

Uncle Tjip was always in pajamas, even when he had guests. He was very nice to me. Every time I visited the Tjiptos I had to greet Uncle Tjip by shaking his hand. He would then put me on his knees. I did not mind shaking his hand, but didn't like sitting on the knees of a pipe-smoking Uncle Tjip. On many occasions when I visited the house with Uncle Rir I tried to avoid Uncle Tjip by entering the house from the backdoor and going straight to Donald's and Louis's study. Uncle Tjip would ask Uncle Rir where I was, and Uncle Rir would point toward his sons' room. Then Uncle Tjip would call me, with his strong Javanese accent, "Duwes (Des), you forgot to greet me."

I would come out of the boys' room, go to him, and shake his hand. He would then ask, "Why didn't you come and say hello to me? You little so-and-so."

I was a straightforward boy, and would tell him that the reason was that he smelled of tobacco. Uncle Tjip was amused, as were the others sitting with him.

Uncle Rir liked and respected Uncle Tjip. Uncle Rir told us that when he was a senior high-school student in Bandung, a friend took him to a political meeting to hear Dr. Tjipto Mangunkusumo speak. That was the first time that he listened to an anti-colonial speech by a nationalist leader. He did not know much about politics in those days, but that night, hearing speeches by the pioneers of the Indonesian independence movement, his eyes were opened. In fact, that night changed his career, his future, and his life.

This postcard shows Kampong China from an overview. To the left of Fort Belgica is Hatta's house. Next door is the jail.

The Iwa Kusuma Sumantris lived opposite my school. Their backdoor was only a few yards from the uncles' house. Uncle Kaca Mata had a fixed program of dining with them every Saturday night. He would visit the Tjiptos first, and then would go to the Sumantris. Uncle Rir did not visit the Sumantris as much as he did initially, and later ceased visiting them altogether. He was very attached to the Tjiptos and had made many friends among the Bandanese. However, political differences with Mr. Iwa Kusuma Sumantri were the main reason why Uncle Rir stopped visiting the Sumantris. There were already some differences between Uncle Tjip and Mr. Sumantri before the two uncles came to Banda, and the two families did not see each other often. Iwa Kusuma Sumantri's pro-communist opinions were probably the reason why Uncle Rir, and even Uncle Tjip, parted with Iwa Kusuma Sumantri. They met, but not as often as before.

Uncle Kaca Mata seemed neutral in this matter. He was as anti-communist as Uncle Tjip and Uncle Rir, but was probably trying to convert or to soften Iwa's opinion. To Uncle Rir's surprise, Mr. Sumantri engaged a Bandanese Arab to teach him to read the Koran. Whether that was Uncle Kaca Mata's influence, or Iwa had just changed from a pro-communist to a pro-Muslim position, nobody understood. Later Uncle Kaca Mata explained that Iwa took those Koran-reading lessons just to know more about Islam for his own personal need and for his future political career, since the majority of the Indonesian population embraced the Islamic faith.

Uncle Tjip and Uncle Rir were also surprised that Mr. Sumantri had engaged a pro-Ibn Saud religious teacher. They were angry with Iwa Kusuma Sumantri because, under the Ibn Saud reign, before World War II, the Saudi Arabian government had been reporting on anti-Dutch Indonesians and even turning some of them over to the Dutch East Indies government, especially among the hajis on the pilgrimage. Some anti-Dutch Indonesian students had been deported by the Saudi Arabian government to Indonesia, where they were arrested on arrival. In addition, Mr. Sumantri's religious teacher was very close to the pro-van der Plas[1] Al Irshad Muslim movement.[2]

THE *GEZAGHEBBER*

It happened that the young *controleur* was replaced by an old, tough *gezaghebber* [administrator], Mr. Kloosterhuis. *Gezaghebber* was the same rank as *controleur*, except that a *controleur* had to be a university graduate, and could climb to the ranks of assistant *resident*, *resident*, governor, and even governor-general. A *gezaghebber* couldn't be promoted because he was not a university graduate; he had only passed a special two-year course after finishing a three-year secondary school or failing his studies at Leiden University. A *gezaghebber* was just a *gezaghebber*, and would remain a *gezaghebber* for the rest of his life.

Kloosterhuis was a tough, old colonial officer. Even before he came to Banda, he was already well-known in the Moluccas as a tough sort, who had served in Ternate, in the North Moluccas, and in Fak-Fak in New Guinea. He jailed people for not paying their taxes, and turned a Muslim cemetery into some government godowns in Ternate. His first act in Neira was to stop the fruit sellers from selling their fruit in front of the *los* when a ship arrived.

In Banda he didn't like the political exiles. Soon he ordered the sick Uncle Tjip to come in person to collect his government allowance at the district officer's office. Uncle Tjip didn't follow Mr. Kloosterhuis's order. Instead he sent the *gezaghebber* a nasty note, saying that if he had dared to oppose the Dutch governor-general in Batavia, he would dare a thousand times more to oppose a mere *gezaghebber*'s order.

"Who do you think you are?" Uncle Tjip wrote, "You can't expect me to follow your order just to collect 150 guilders, which is not even your own money. Your government pays me that amount, not because they like me or pity me, but because they don't allow me to earn my own living and banish me to this island."

Kloosterhuis didn't dare to act, and Auntie Tjip was allowed to collect her husband's allowance. But Kloosterhuis wasn't silent either. He sent a report to his superior, the *resident* of Ambon, requesting that the political exiles at Banda Neira be banned from going to the other Banda islands because they were supposed to be in exile only in Neira. Kloosterhuis probably had in mind Uncle Rir's sailing boat and

---

[1] Dr. Charles van der Plas was considered by many Indonesians to be better informed on their country than any other Dutch official, and is said to have been thought by many to have been the head of the colonial political intelligence service. Acts of the colonial government exhibiting "shrewd intelligence" were often attributed by Indonesians to van der Plas. See Kahin, *Nationalism and Revolution*, pp. 317, 379 n72.

[2] Described as a modernist and reformist "Arab organization" by Harry J. Benda, *The Crescent and the Rising Sun: Indonesian Islam under the Japanese Occupation, 1942–1945* (The Hague and Bandung: W. van Hoeve Ltd., 1958), pp. 235 n36, 237 n53.

Uncle Kaca Mata's *orambai*, that often cruised to Banda Besar, Gunung Api, and Pulau Pisang.

A few months later the exiles were called to appear at the *gezaghebber*'s office. Kloosterhuis gave them the news he had just received from the government: that from now on the exiles were not allowed to leave Banda Neira Island without his permission. Uncle Rir then asked him whether this meant that the exiles couldn't row or sail in the inner bays of Banda Neira. Kloosterhuis told him that they could do this, but they were not allowed to visit Banda Besar, Ai, Run, or other islands that lay over a mile from Banda Neira. Gunung Api, just a yelling distance from Neira, was not included in the ban.

When the two uncles returned from the meeting with Mr. Kloosterhuis, Uncle Rir commented that the government must be silly to think that the exiles might run away from Banda to some other country. He said, "The Dutch don't expect that my yacht could reach Australia or the Pacific, do they?"

At last Uncle Rir admitted that his yacht could not reach the open sea. Despite the ban, Uncle Rir still visited Lonthor, on Banda Besar, and Pulau Pisang. Uncle Kaca Mata was not so interested in going to the other islands even before the ban was imposed. In some of the villages on Banda Besar, Uncle Rir wasn't even recognized as "Sjahrir" by some Dutch *perkeniers*. He looked like some of our big cousins and friends, especially when he wore only shorts with no shirt.

The ban imposed on the exiles seemed not to satisfy Kloosterhuis. He wanted to take further actions to make their lives more miserable. He couldn't stand that the exiles enjoyed "happy" lives despite his ban. It seemed as if Mr. Kloosterhuis considered them his own personal enemies. It could have been Uncle Tjip's letter, or it could have been that he had nothing better to do in such a peaceful place as Banda.

The next action the *gezaghebber* took against the exiles involved the afternoon classes. Kloosterhuis first sent his police chief to tell Hatta and Sjahrir that they were not allowed to teach pupils over the age of sixteen. Next, Kloosterhuis sent the police chief to tell the two exiles that they were only allowed to teach the children of three families; any others must be registered and their names must be sent to the *gezaghebber*. Hatta told the police chief that, in fact, only children of three families were taking lessons in the afternoon classes: the Baadilla, Maskat, and Mangunkusumo families.

Our school was watched by plainclothes policemen. The *gezaghebber* wanted to make sure that only children of the three families were studying in the classes of the two exiles. The policeman also noted down the names of people visiting the uncles.

THE UNCLES MOVE HOUSES

When the European war started, Sjahrir decided to marry his Dutch girlfriend, Maria Duchateau, who lived in Amsterdam, because only by marrying her officially would she be allowed to leave the Netherlands and join him in Banda Neira.[3] He made preparations to marry her by proxy and to receive her and her two children by a previous marriage. We knew her as "Auntie Mies" because her picture was on his

---

[3] They had married in an Islamic ceremony in Medan in April 1932. But the Dutch authorities, who learned that she had not been formally divorced from her first husband, Sol Tas, had the marriage declared void and deported Maria back to the Netherlands. See Rudolf Mrázek, *Sjahrir: Politics and Exile in Indonesia* (Ithaca, NY: Cornell University Southeast Asia Program, 1994), pp. 111–12, 197.

desk, together with her children, a boy and a girl, by her first husband, a Dutch journalist. Auntie Mies had a sharp nose and was blond. I told Uncle Rir that when his stepson came to Neira I would dare to fight him and beat him up. Uncle Rir just laughed. In the meantime, the European war became hotter, and the Germans occupied the Netherlands. Finished were the hopes of getting Auntie Mies and her children to Banda Neira.

Sjahrir's political life and his future as a nationalist would have turned out differently if his Dutch wife had joined him in Neira. So, too, the futures of us adopted children would have been different. Auntie Mies was not an easy person, and if she had come to Banda, I am sure she would have sent us away from Uncle Rir.

Because of the noisy adopted children, and the preparations to receive Auntie Mies and her children, Uncle Rir moved to one of the Baadilla houses, leaving Uncle Kaca Mata alone in his eight-room *perkenier*'s residence. Uncle Kaca Mata, finding his house too large for him, moved to a smaller house, still in Kampong Ratu, only a hundred yards away from Uncle Rir.

Uncle Kaca Mata's new house was in the neighborhood of the Neira prison. It was one of those *perkenier* houses built in the beginning of the nineteenth century. It was quite large and rather high above the street. To reach its front veranda from the street, we had to climb one of the marble staircases situated at each end of the house. The railing on the front veranda was made of V-shaped iron bars, topped with a thick wooden plank. It looked almost like a ship's railing, except that seven feet below was not water but a hard black-soil street of Neira. Thick walls and large glass doors with wooden frames separated the front veranda from two large rooms and a sitting room. The back veranda looked almost like the front veranda except that it had no railing. A long, narrow backyard separated the house from a pavilion with five smaller rooms. Two of these rooms were used for our classes, one as a dining room, one to store provisions and old newspapers, and the last room was for Ahir, the houseboy and gardener. The back door, or rather the side entrance, came straight from the street and was always locked except in the afternoons when it was opened to let us come to class.

After Uncle Rir and Uncle Hatta lived separately, the schedule for the classes they taught was divided into morning classes for the non-school-going children at Uncle Kaca Mata's residence, and afternoon classes for the school-going children at Uncle Rir's residence. By this time, three Minangkabau students from West Sumatra—Bachtul Nazar, Munir, and Damanhuri (whom we called Daman)—had been sent by the Koperasi group of Bukittinggi to study economics and banking with Uncle Kaca Mata.[4] These students, who were about twenty years old, had finished secondary school in Sumatra and were sent by those who had supported Hatta when he studied at Rotterdam University. They were housed at my auntie's place (the widow of Uncle Ding, mother of Wachi).

The *gezaghebber*, Mr. Kloosterhuis, didn't react to the arrival of these new students. He may have been told by the colonial authorities to be more lenient toward the exiles because, after the outbreak of the war in Europe, the Dutch

---

[4] Anwar Sutan Saidi, director of the branch of the National Bank, sent three students (no names given) from Bukittingi to study with Hatta. Deliar Noer, *Mohammad Hatta: Biografi Politik* (Jakarta: Lembaga Penelitian, Pendidikan dan Penerangan Ekonomi dan Sosial, 1990), p. 141.

government hoped for the support of the nationalist leaders, who were considered anti-fascist.

Twice a week Uncle Rir gave the students from Sumatra and the Tjipto boys lessons in English and German in the morning, while Uncle Kaca Mata taught them economics and math the other four days. When these students started attending classes before noontime, it changed the quiet morning life of the two exiles completely.

After the two uncles lived in separate houses, both the school-going children (including me) and the non-school going children (including my cousin Mimi and my sister Lily) had afternoon lessons twice a week with Uncle Sjahrir. We went to Uncle Kaca Mata's house three days a week for the afternoon lessons, and for our Saturday lunch. We enjoyed eating at Uncle Kaca Mata's house because the food was better and had more variety than at Uncle Rir's house. Uncle Rir, in fact, didn't care much about food, although he was a fish lover and was particularly fond of *lokki* (a body like a crayfish, it only comes out of its hole in shallow water when the tide is low; the Latin name is *squilla lutaria*). *Lokki* fried in coconut oil with sweet soya bean sauce was Uncle Rir's most favorite food during his Banda Neira days.

Uncle Kaca Mata, who loved cats, kept a few male cats at his new house. He gave them names such as "Hitler," "Mussolini," and "Franco," names of dictators he hated.

Uncle Rir had a dog, called Jojy, who barked every time a policeman came near the house. One night a policeman shot Jojy when he wandered too far from the house. Jojy, badly wounded, still managed to crawl to the front veranda of the house, and died in front of Uncle Rir's room.

THE ADOPTED CHILDREN AND LITTLE ALI

Uncle Rir tried to raise his adopted children in a disciplined way. We had to cook our own evening meals. We had only one pair of shoes, three shirts, and three pairs of shorts each. The shirts he tailored himself. The pockets were either too small or too big, or not straight enough. He even made dresses for Lily and Mimi, my sister and cousin, and the small girls wore those dresses with pride.

When we had just moved from Uncle Kaca Mata's house and were staying at the house belonging to my uncle, my father's brother who was married to one of my mother's sisters, Uncle Rir adopted my uncle's grandson Ali, who was just one month old. Ali had been born in Dobo, and was brought to Banda Neira by his mother, who was so sick with malaria that she was not able to attend to the small baby. Uncle Rir volunteered to look after little Ali; he fed him with canned milk and other baby food. The baby grew to be a healthy boy, and Uncle Rir refused to return him to his mother when she recovered from her illness and was about to return to her husband, a pearl fisher, living in Dobo. After much discussion and pleading, she at last allowed Uncle Rir to keep baby Ali until further notice. She then left for Dobo to join her husband. Uncle Rir attended to little Ali like a real mother: bathed him, fed him, and even took the small baby boy on several of his sailing junkets in the lagoon.

Sjahrir and the Bandanese children. Standing, from left: Aunt Silva,
Mimi (Des's cousin), Aunt Irma, Lily (Des's sister).
Sitting: Ali (Sjahrir's adopted son), with Sjahrir.

SJAHRIR MOVES TO THE *RUMAH BESAR*

When Grandma died at the age of seventy-six, we children asked Uncle Rir to
stay in the *rumah besar* and look after its priceless collections. Our mothers and
fathers supported us because they were afraid that if the house were unoccupied, the
Baadillas from outside Banda Neira might come and claim items in the collections of
Grandfather and Grandmother as their inheritance. A couple of days before Uncle
Rir moved to the *rumah besar*, the medals that Grandpa Tjong received from the
Dutch queen disappeared from the large glass case in which they were kept, and

couldn't be traced. Who pinched the medals nobody knew, but rumors said it must have been the eldest son, Abdullah, who didn't like the idea of Uncle Rir staying at the *rumah besar* because he would not be able to lay his hands on the remaining items in Grandfather Tjong's collection of rare Bandanese and Moluccan species.

After Uncle Rir moved from Kampong Ratu to stay together with the kids at our grandparents' house, he automatically became a member of the Baadilla clan. When Grandma was still alive she told Uncle Rir, "I wish you were one of my sons, my fifteenth child." Uncle Rir was so involved with the Baadillas in their affairs that he became not only a son, as Grandma had wished, but also the judge, adviser, and consultant of the clan.

The *rumah besar*, where we now stayed with Uncle Rir, was one of the most luxurious and beautiful houses of Neira. It was built by our great-grandfather in the first half of the nineteenth century, the era when Banda was the richest island group of the Indies. The house had colorful tile floors, the verandas had bluish-white marble floors. The floors of the sitting and dining rooms had beautiful designs, and their crystal chandeliers tinkled when a little breeze blew through the house. The sitting room contained antique furniture and old porcelain plates, and the two largest sleeping rooms were furnished with large mahogany beds. The front veranda was decorated with large porcelain flower pots. When we moved in after Grandma's death, we transferred all those antiques to the "museum" in the pavilion on the right wing of the house, and replaced them with Uncle Rir's own modern furniture that he bought at the auction of an outgoing Dutch schoolteacher.

Our lunches were prepared by my mother in her house and brought by *rantang* [set of stacked containers for transporting food] to the *rumah besar*. The dinners were prepared by us, the foster children. Uncle Rir only cooked when he received some *lokki* from his fishermen friends, or when I brought home some crayfish after a day's outing and *lokki*-hunting along the beach during low tide.

I was happy to have Uncle Rir stay in Kampong China, near the *los* and the backyard between the *rumah besar* and the Kok's godown with my deer and birds. Only the fruit trees of the backyard were no longer fully under my control because Uncle Rir liked the rose apples and sweet mandarins that grew there. I didn't mind his climbing the trees and picking the fruit, but every time he wanted some fruit, the whole class joined him and picked more fruit than they could eat. The kids were so wild in climbing that they broke many branches, ruining the young fruit. I had a couple of fights with some boys of the afternoon classes and became the most unpopular boy of the Uncle Rir crowd.

During this time my mother made me join the Boy Scouts. I hated it because twice a week I had to wear the silly Boy Scout uniform. The leather boots would become too small within a couple of months because I was growing very fast. To buy new shoes every two or three months was not possible, so I started wearing Uncle Rir's shoes, especially his white leather shoes, which were one size larger. Uncle Rir didn't say anything as long as I cleaned his shoes after wearing them.

One day our Boy Scout club had to parade in front of the visiting Dutch *resident* from Ambon, the capital of the Moluccas. I had no comfortable shoes for the march, and white shoes were not allowed for the parade. I found a solution by painting Uncle Rir's white shoes with black Chinese ink, and wore them in the parade. Uncle Rir was mad when he discovered that I had turned his white leather shoes an ugly black color. For a week he didn't speak to me, and prohibited me from joining his sailing junkets. Those kinds of punishment didn't hurt me at all. On such occasions I didn't go to the afternoon classes and would disappear from the house for a couple of days to stay with an old great-auntie or sleep at my mother's house. My afternoons then were mostly spent swimming or diving for coins whenever a KPM or tourist ship was in the harbor.

As for sailing, there were enough *kolee-kolee* and praus to borrow from friends in Negreh. Many times I quietly used Uncle Rir's private yacht or Uncle Kaca Mata's *orambai* to take white tourists to see the coral sea-gardens of Banda, or ferried some passengers and sailors from the ship's anchorage to the *los* or government pier. I became a rascal, as some people said. I preferred to swim or climb fruit trees than to learn how to play tennis with other "decent" children.

READING TO AUNTIE MALI

We children loved to come along with Uncle Rir on his twice-a-week afternoon visits to Auntie Mali,[5] a Eurasian lady from Medan. Uncle Rir, who was brought up in Medan, had known her during his childhood years. Auntie Mali, now quite elderly, had known Uncle Rir when he was only a boy of ten. For nearly twenty years she hadn't seen him because she was transferred to several parts of the Moluccas and later to Banda Neira. She had worked in the *controleur*'s office at Neira as chief clerk, but had had a stroke a decade ago and half of her body was paralyzed up to her neck. Fate brought the two of them to Banda where they met again after twenty years, he as a political exile and she as a paralyzed old lady with a small pension.

Auntie Mali loved Banda Neira so much that she refused to go back to Medan. She couldn't walk properly and had to be supported when she went from one part of the house to another. She stayed in Kampong Baru, in a cozy little house, with a large garden full of roses and other lovely flowers. Every time we visited her, we children helped Uncle Rir carry her in her rattan armchair to the front veranda. Uncle Rir would play her old collection of waltzes and tangos on her Gramophone, and we kids had to dance so that Auntie Mali could enjoy watching us. Because of her condition, Auntie Mali could only speak softly. She would whisper, "Bravo, bravo, young children."

Usually we stayed to dine with Auntie Mali. Her old servant just loved to cook for the little guests with their adopted daddy. After the evening meal, Uncle Rir would read to Auntie Mali, and we children would relax on the sofa waiting for Uncle Rir to finish reading. Out of respect for Auntie Mali, we children remained as quiet as mice when she listened to Uncle Rir, who read Dutch like an educated Dutchman.

Often we children were already asleep when Uncle Rir finished reading to Auntie Mali. He would wake us up, and little Ali would always break the peace by crying loudly when he was awakened. We would then go home, walking through the quiet, dark streets of Kampong Baru, Kampong Ratu, and then Kampong China, with Uncle Rir carrying Ali on his shoulders, and the other half-asleep children trailing behind.

---

[5] Miss Malia Mulder, whose grandfather was a colonial official in Banda in the mid-nineteenth century. In Sjahrir's *Out of Exile*, he gives her the pseudonym "Nellie Cresa," and mentions reading to her.

THE KIDNAPPING OF ALI

Ali's grandmother from his mother's side (not a Baadilla) lived in Kampong Baru and occasionally came to the *rumah besar* to see her grandchild. But she was not allowed by Uncle Rir or the other adopted children to take Ali to Kampong Baru. One day when Ali was about two years old, he disappeared. Some kids told us that his grandmother, with the help of some of Kampong Baru's bigger boys, had kidnapped Ali and taken him to Kampong Baru. The whole *rumah besar* and the Kampong China relations were in an uproar. Uncle Rir couldn't claim Ali back because he refused to quarrel with the relatives of Ali's mother. Ali's grandfather from his father's side (my uncle, my father's brother), and Ali's grandmother (my auntie, my mother's sister), were fetched. They told Uncle Rir that the other grandmother probably only wanted to keep Ali for a day or two and would soon return him. They couldn't do much because they also wanted to avoid quarreling with the relatives of their daughter-in-law.

In many things the other kampongs in Neira considered Kampong Baru as a rival. It had a good and strong soccer team, and won the race against other *belang* of the Banda group. It was also the kampong with the largest Muslim majority, not like Kampong China with its mixed population of Muslims, Christians, Eurasians, and Butonese.

We knew that an official delegation from Kampong China to claim Ali back would be turned down, so we decided to take a "wait-and-see" attitude. But after two days Ali had not been returned. Uncle Rir was very upset, as were the other adopted children and the afternoon classmates, some of whom came from Kampong Baru. We were all so used to the small Ali that we felt lonely without him. We then decided to kidnap Ali from Kampong Baru, although it would be very hard to do, especially when everyone was related to each other.

Husein Maskat, one of the boys in the advanced class of Uncle Rir, who came from Kampong Baru, decided to become our "spy" because of his loyalty to Uncle Rir and his liking for Ali. One day Husein told us that on his way to the afternoon class he saw Ali playing in the street with some small kids. He also told us that between two and five o'clock in the afternoon almost every big boy in Kampong Baru was in Koran-reading class. We decided to kidnap Ali that same afternoon, and three of the boys proceeded to Kampong Baru. It was an easy job. When Ali saw us coming, he ran to us. One of my bigger cousins carried him on his bike, and we sped away to Kampong China. The reunion with Ali was a happy one. Even the Chinese shopkeeper, Chong Eng, whose shop was in front of the house, was happy to see Ali back with Uncle Rir, and sent a few pounds of peanuts and sweets to celebrate the occasion. Uncle Rir gave Ali a bath because everybody who embraced him said that he smelled of tuna fish. Most Kampong Baru people were tuna fishermen and consumed a lot of tuna. After this incident we guarded Ali and would lock him inside his room when the afternoon classes began.

Ali was a strong and healthy boy of two when his mother returned from Dobo with two more sons, who were born there after Ali. The mother didn't try to claim Ali back from Uncle Rir.

HISTORY AND GEOGRAPHY LESSONS

The two uncles always gave books as birthday presents to the adopted children. The uncles, in fact, coached us to read books suitable for our ages, but, being a curious boy, I was always interested in reading other books from Uncle Rir's bookshelves. Among his books that most interested me were those about revolutions and wars. Uncle Kaca Mata presented me with several books on my twelfth birthday: *Uncle Tom's Cabin, Baron von Munchhausen,* and *Don Quixote.* I liked those books, but considered Munchhausen[6] and Don Quixote funny and stupid. The uncles also gave us Indonesian books to read, and books about Sumatra and Java to acquaint us with the situation and folklore of our brothers on the other, bigger islands of Indonesia.

By the age of twelve, when I was a fifth grader, I was already aware of the Dutch East Indies government. Reading books and learning Indonesian history and nationalism from our uncles, I began to realize that the Dutch East Indies government was in fact not the government of our people, but merely the colonizer and oppressor of Indonesia.

And I just did not understand why they kept those political exiles away from their families and homes.

At thirteen I began to face some troubles at the Dutch school for not seriously learning Indonesian history from the Dutch textbooks. Our Indonesian history lessons in the afternoon classes differed completely from the lessons and textbooks we had in the Dutch school. In the Indonesian history we were taught at home, we learned that Teuku Umar of Aceh and Diponegoro of Central Java, who had organized uprisings against the colonial government, were heroes. In the Dutch school we were taught that these men were bandits. I considered it pure nonsense that Diponegoro was referred to in the Dutch textbooks as a jealous prince who rebelled against the Dutch authority. Teuku Umar, the Acehnese leader who fought the Dutch during the Dutch–Acehnese War (1873–1904), was called an "opium addict."

A great deal of time at school was devoted to the study of the history of the "fatherland," as the Netherlands was called. School songs never mentioned a word about Indonesia, but were always based on the "beautiful fatherland" of Holland, the Dutch royal family, and the tri-color Dutch flag.

An incident occurred during one of the geography lessons at school. As I was the biggest boy, I was called upon to fetch the map of the Netherlands and to place it in front of the class. But the map was too heavy for me and it fell to the ground, making the other children laugh. It happened that the headmaster, Mr. van Toledo, was passing the classroom. He came into the class, slapped me, and ordered me to go to his office, where I was questioned as to why I had dropped the map. Mr. van Toledo wanted to know whether I dropped the map on purpose or at the instigation of Sjahrir and Hatta. Before sending me home, he asked me why I lived with the "communists," since my grandfather had been a most respectable man and loyal to the Dutch government. I replied that I did not know who the communists were and that the gentlemen with whom I lived were nationalists. Mr. van Toledo than grabbed me by my shirt, pulled me close to him, and while shaking me told me that they were communists, which was the reason they were sent into exile. He then warned me that if I did not learn my geography and history lessons about the Netherlands he would see that I was not promoted to a higher class.

---

[6] Munchhausen was a German soldier, adventurer, and teller of tales (1720–1797).

I rushed home and told Sjahrir about the incident. He gave me fatherly advice, telling me to behave well at school and to learn my lessons irrespective of the ill feelings I might have toward the Dutch. However, later that evening I overheard Sjahrir and Hatta talking about the incident, and Hatta remarked that Mr. van Toledo was probably a fascist. Hatta was right. We later learned that Mr. van Toledo belonged to the National Socialist Bond (NSB, the Dutch fascist party).

Often I was insulted in front of my classmates and the schoolteachers, by being called a *buaya* (crocodile), or a communist, for mixing with Hatta and Sjahrir, the enemies of the authorities. I became fed up with the school after being called a crocodile, but I didn't mind at all being called a communist, since I didn't know what it actually meant, but thought that those who fought the Dutch authorities, or the Dutch school authorities, were called communists. I was also fed up with the Dutch school because my extra lessons in the afternoon classes and the books I read at home had put me ahead of most of my classmates.

Two things probably kept me from being booted out of the European school: I was not dumb, and I was the grandson of Tjong Baadilla. Although I was ahead of most of my classmates, I had to sit for one more year at school, for "not knowing" the history of Indonesia, as they put it, and because my mark for the Dutch language was below average. The bad mark for Dutch was, I thought, a made-up reason, to prevent me from going to a high school. Since Dutch was the only medium of instruction in secondary schools and academies in the Indies, if a student failed Dutch in his final examination, which was the entrance examination for secondary school, he had had it, especially if he had reached the maximum age, sixteen, for the European Elementary School.

Uncle Kaca Mata was always angry when I showed him my report card with red marks for history and Dutch. He scolded me for not learning my lessons well. Although Uncle Rir understood my problems at school, even he suggested that I should study harder and said that I would understand these problems more clearly when I grew up.

The situation at school became a little better for me after the mean class teacher, Mr. van Delden, had a stroke and collapsed in front of the class. A week later he died of a heart attack on board the KPM ship on his way to a hospital in Makassar. A few months later Hitler attacked the Netherlands and occupied it within a week. Mr. van Toledo, the headmaster, was arrested for being a member of the National Socialist Bond. A special team of Dutch police inspectors came especially from Ambon to search van Toledo's house and to interview school children about what he had told them about Hitler and the Germans. Many of us at school told the police investigators that the headmaster had shown us Hitler's book, *Mein Kampf*, played Nazi songs on the Gramophone in the class, and told us that German airplanes were much better than the British.

At van Toledo's house the police team found much evidence that he was a member of the NSB. He was shipped to Ambon in the corvette *Aru*, a Dutch warship that sailed among the islands of the Moluccas.

Mr. Antrag, my new classroom teacher, was a little better than Mr. van Delden, but the new headmaster, Mr. Zwerus, was no better than van Toledo. He didn't make us listen to Nazi songs as the old schoolmaster used to, but instead taught us to sing the new Dutch song called "Nederland zal Herrijzen" (Netherlands Shall Rise Again). With the new teacher, new headmaster, and their fatherland occupied by the Germans, I had no chance to pass to a higher grade. My poor marks in Dutch and history would have kept me from going to a high school in any case (hell, we didn't even have a high school in Banda). Weakness in the Dutch language was the main reason why so many Bandanese failed at school and became fishermen. Unlike the Ambonese, we Bandanese didn't like to speak Dutch. Even the majority of the Bandanese *burgers* preferred to speak Bandanese–Malay, rather than the language of their forefathers.

CHAPTER SIX

APPROACH OF WAR

When the war started in Europe, some *perkeniers* and several Chinese bought radio sets. Banda suddenly became closer to the rest of the world. Koon's father, Ho Kok Chai, placed his radio in the left wing of his house so that Uncle Rir, his neighbor, could listen to it. Soon Uncle Rir was at Ho's house practically every night to listen to the broadcast of world news from Radio Batavia and from foreign stations. Bandanese gathered every night in front of our house to listen to Uncle Rir's commentaries about the news. Even Uncle Kaca Mata often came to the house in the evening to chat with Uncle Rir and the visitors about the world situation. We served them ginger tea and peanuts.

Radio news was important to the Bandanese. Chong Eng, a pro-Japanese Chinese, became jealous of Ho Kok Chai, a pro-Chiang Kai Shek man, because of Uncle Rir's regular visits to Ho's place to listen to the radio. Chong Eng then bought his own battery-operated radio, and invited Uncle Rir to come to his house to listen to his new radio. Uncle Rir was in a quandry—he didn't know what to do, since both Ho and Chong Eng were neighbors. He decided to stick with Ho for the evening news, and in the morning he crossed the road to listen to Chong Eng's radio. However, that wasn't enough to satisfy Chong Eng because in the evening Ho got a bigger crowd in front of his house to listen to Uncle Rir's commentaries than Chong Eng got at his shop in the morning. Chong Eng changed his tactics and gave Uncle Rir his radio. He wasn't afraid to do this, although he knew that he might come under suspicion from Kloosterhuis. "Hell," he said, "he is my best customer. I deliver better goods and foodstuff than any other Chinese."

Ho, angry about the whole situation, took his radio set and his young wife for a rest at Bemo, Seram, waiting for Chiang Kai Shek to win the war. Ho rather liked Uncle Rir's anti-fascist attitude, but Chong Eng's intrigues were too much for him. Also, Ho was losing followers among Banda's Chinese, who were changing their attitudes from anti-Japanese to neutral and then to pro-Wang Ching Wei, one of the older Kuomintang leaders [who defected to the Japanese and headed their puppet government in China].

The *perkeniers* and other Dutch residents of Banda Neira were not so interested in the news or world affairs in general. They mostly tuned their radios to Nirom Broadcasting Company in Batavia for its music.

Kloosterhuis wasn't happy about the Bandanese who gathered every night at the house to listen to Uncle Rir. He dispatched plainclothes native policemen as informers to listen to the commentaries, but we knew who these police informers were. Everybody knew who they were, after all, Banda had only about a dozen policemen. In any case, Kloosterhuis had to do his duty to watch the exiles. Even when his own country was already occupied by the Germans he remained as colonial as ever. Anti-Dutch feeling began to spread, not only in Banda, but in the other Molucca Islands as well.

Chinese Kapitein Ho Kok Chai and one of his daughters

Just before Hitler attacked the Netherlands, the Bandanese formed a club called "Persatuan Banda Muda" [Young Banda Association], and made my real father the club's secretary. It was more of a reading club than a political movement, and was supplied by the exiles with books and newspapers. Soon after the Netherlands was occupied by the Germans, Kloosterhuis banned this club, and all non-Dutch clubs and social gatherings. Several Bandanese were arrested and sent to Ambon, charged with being pro-German. Actually, those arrested were ordinary people who had not the slightest idea of what fascism was, but were just glad that the Germans had occupied the Netherlands. This was particularly true of some Muslim Bandanese who hated the unchanged colonial policy of the Dutch so much that any country attacking the Netherlands would automatically be their friend. Not knowing the danger of fascism, they somehow hoped that the Japanese would soon come to chase the Dutch from the Indies. They expected the Japanese to bring changes, or at least a policy better than that of the Dutch.

In 1939 the Tjipto and Iwa Kusuma Sumantri families were moved to Makassar, where Dr. Tjipto made a statement opposing fascism. It seemed that with the outbreak of war in Europe, the Dutch authorities were more concerned about fascism, and realized that the nationalists were more inclined to support Western democracy than fascism. However, Tjipto and Iwa still had the status of political exiles.

CONSCRIPTION OF DUTCH NATIONALS

During the approach of the Second World War some of the *burgers*, being considered Dutch nationals, were conscripted, but some were not. There was a big outcry among the *burgers*. Some of those conscripted protested: some asking why only they had to face death and not the other *burgers*; some complained about being sent to Ambon for military training instead of staying behind to defend Banda when the Japanese attacked. Those not conscripted complained of not being considered "European."

Uncle Barentz, a KNIL pensioner, was one of the Bandanese *burgers* who complained about not being conscripted to fight the Japanese. After all, everybody in Banda knew that he was once a sergeant-major in the constabulary, and had plenty of fighting experience in Aceh during the uprising against the Dutch around the end of the last century. He claimed that, although he was fifty-eight years old, he could at least serve another seven years until he was sixty-five. He complained to all who passed by his house that he was not being enlisted into the army.

In one case, the KNIL conscripted only two of the six Schelling brothers. The two conscripted were about the age of forty, and the four others, who were younger and healthier, went unnoticed. Uncle Wim, one of the four not conscripted, said of one of the two conscripted, "John is much darker than myself, is illiterate, cannot speak Dutch—and still he is conscripted."

Later Mr. Kloosterhuis explained that he was not at fault because he could not help it if the fathers of those not conscripted had not registered them when they were born. In the case of the Schelling brothers, it seemed that their long-dead father, to avoid paying the one guilder and fifty cents registration fee for each European birth certificate, did not register all his children, especially as he had about ten of them. So the lucky, or unlucky, ones became European, and the rest plain Bandanese.

ATTITUDES TOWARD THE DUTCH AND JAPANESE

The Dutch residents of Neira continued to live as if nothing had happened, except that they held more parties at the *Societeit* to get funds for the "Netherlands Shall Rise Again" campaign. We schoolboys had to go around Neira to sell paper *oranje* [orange, the color associated with the Dutch royal family] flowers for the fund so that the Dutch government in exile in London could use the money to buy planes and other war materials. In one of those fund-raising strolls, Jot and I were only able to sell a few *oranje* flowers, earning only fourteen cents. Back at school the headmaster called us lazy, since other groups brought back over ten guilders from their *oranje* flower outings.

When I told Uncle Rir, he laughed loudly, especially when I told him that Jot and I were chased by a lady with a bamboo broom at Kampong Baru because she thought we had entered her house to steal her mangoes. I asked Uncle Rir whether he would have bought some *oranje* flowers if we had come to the house. He said that he would rather give Jot and me some money as a gift than give it to the Dutch, because, he said, the Dutch still had plenty of money in Indonesia and in London.

Why, he asked, should they bother the kampong people with the so-called fund to kick the Germans out of Holland?

Later we learned that the total amount collected in Banda Neira for the "Netherlands Shall Rise Again" fund was not more than two hundred guilders, including donations from the rich *perkeniers* and the big business people of Banda. For the average Bandanese, the war in Europe was just considered a struggle in which the Dutch colonial rulers would be punished by Providence for the evil oppression they had brought to the Bandanese and other Indonesians.

That was why the Japanese were initially liked in Banda. Whenever the Japanese ship the *Dai Ichi Tora Maru* arrived at Neira on its twice-monthly visits, once from Makassar and once from Babo, people gathered at the *los* to see the ship and chat with the crew. The Japanese sailors were so friendly and so generous, giving out free medicine and biscuits, that most Bandanese expected radical changes and hoped that the Japanese would soon come to take over Indonesia from the Dutch. The Joyoboyo prophecy, in combination with the *foe-foe*, were whispered and spread everywhere. According to the Joyoboyo prophecy, a yellow race would replace the white race, but would only reign over Indonesia temporarily (*seumur jagung*, the life of a corn plant). The Bandanese *orang tua-tua* and the *orang halus* would help the yellow race kick out the Dutch.

Anti-Dutch feeling grew stronger and stronger. Even the Chinese in Banda, who had disliked the Japanese because of the Sino–Japanese War, slowly began to change their attitude. But the Dutch colonials seemed not to realize this change. Instead of taking a more liberal attitude toward the population they remained arrogant. Kloosterhuis even jailed several Bandanese who openly said that the German and Japanese planes were faster than the Dutch planes.

Suddenly one morning Uncle Tjip arrived in Neira in a Dutch government steamer on his way from Makassar to Sukabumi, West Java, where he was being sent by the NEI government. The steamer only stopped for a day at Neira. The three exiles—Uncle Rir, Uncle Kaca Mata, and Uncle Tjip—locked themselves in Uncle Kaca Mata's study to discuss important matters, such as attitudes toward the Allies and toward the Japanese. Uncle Kaca Mata told us kids that we must not disturb them. Even at lunch we were not allowed to sit with them, but had to eat in the kitchen. Just before Uncle Tjip's departure we had a chance to ask him why he hadn't brought Donald, Louis, and Auntie Tjip along to Banda. He told us that Donald was already in Jakarta to study at a technical college and that Louis and Auntie Tjip had left directly for Sukabumi on a different boat.

We saw Uncle Tjip off at the government pier, while Mr. Kloosterhuis watched from a distance. He was wearing his official uniform, with a white cap and gold trim. He didn't even shake Uncle Tjip's hand when Uncle Tjip left to be ferried to the waiting steamer. Kloosterhuis looked as arrogant as ever, as if nothing had happened to Holland. The Bandanese gathered in groups near the pier and on the beach to get a last glimpse of Uncle Tjip. When Uncle Tjip arrived in Java he tried hard to secure the release of the two uncles from their internment, but for a long time nothing happened.

WAR COMES TO THE INDIES

Early in the morning of December 8, 1941, Uncle Rir got the first news of the Japanese attack on Pearl Harbor from Radio Manila. Later in the day everybody had heard the news, but my Dutch schoolmaster didn't believe me when I told him about the Japanese attack and the declaration of war by the Allies. He laconically told me that he only believed the news from his own government. A few minutes later the headmaster entered the class and in a loud voice read the news from a cable received from the *resident* in Ambon. The cable also said that all Europeans in Banda Neira should report at once in their militia uniforms to Kloosterhuis's office. All hell broke loose at school. The schoolchildren were sent home to wait for further news of the school schedule because all of the teachers, being Dutch nationals, were Netherlands East Indies conscripts, and had already had some military training in Ambon.

On December 9, the next day, the corvette *Aru* arrived at Banda to pick up the teachers and other Bandanese European militia members. Forty Europeans assembled at the *los*, with our schoolmaster as sergeant in his too-small uniform, to wait for Kloosterhuis's arrival and to be shipped away. Soon they left Neira harbor, and the speedy corvette quickly disappeared behind Gunung Api in the direction of Ambon. That was the last time we saw most of them. Some were killed at Ambon during the Japanese landing, some died in Japanese prisoner-of-war camps. Only one of the ELS teachers returned to Banda Neira. He had managed to escape to Seram Island with some of the Bandanese *burger* conscripts, where they managed to hire a sailing boat. They returned to Banda two weeks after Ambon had fallen into Japanese hands.

The Netherlands East Indies was now at war. Civil watches to report enemy landings at Banda Neira were organized, as if the dozen rifle-armed policemen were able to fight the Japanese. An air-raid alarm system using gongs and *tifas* was formed, and first-aid and food distribution systems and other war precautions were organized. Uncle Kaca Mata was appointed head of food distribution; he ordered all fields, parks, and empty ground at Neira to be turned into tapioca and corn fields. Uncle Rir was, of course, appointed as head of the listening post. When the Dutch authorities in Ambon heard of the "high appointments" given to the two exiles by the colonial-minded-turned-progressive Kloosterhuis, they ordered them cancelled. Kloosterhuis was so embarrassed by the order of cancellation from his superior in Ambon that he sent his aide, the former sergeant major Pieters (veteran of the Aceh war), to the two uncles to apologize for the mistake and to ask them to stay on as "advisers."

By the time the two uncles received the news about the cancellation of their appointments, the empty fields had already been planted with corn and tapioca. In fact, that probably saved Neira from starvation during the Japanese Occupation. Uncle Rir kept listening to the radio. The *rumah besar* was practically turned into a center of radio reports and the nerve center of Banda Neira. The only person who didn't visit the house was probably Kloosterhuis, but he still sent his aide and adviser, sergeant major Pieters, not to spy but to get advice on how Banda Neira should be run in war time. The people needed advice and leadership, not from Kloosterhuis, but from the Indonesian nationalist leaders who had been in exile in Neira for nearly six years.

The Japanese in the meantime had taken Minahasa, North Sulawesi, and already occupied some parts of South and Southeast Sulawesi, including the important military airfield of Kendari. Ambon was heavily bombed by the Japanese several times, as were the oil towns of Babo and Sorong, in New Guinea. Bandanese from these areas fled back to Banda. Hearing about the horror of Japanese bombing from the refugees, the Bandanese at last started building air-raid shelters. The Kok's godown backyard was turned into a large air-raid shelter. It cost me a few fruit trees when the shelter was built, but my large rose apple tree was not cut down because it was filled with young fruit, and food was what the Bandanese needed most in time of war. Anyhow, who said that the Japanese were going to bomb Neira? After all, the *Dai Ichi Tora Maru* crew knew that we had no military installation at Banda Neira, but only nutmeg trees.

About two weeks after the outbreak of the Pacific War, the Banda Neira hospital was moved to a large house belonging to the Koks at Kampong China. Uncle Rir asked Pieters why the old hospital had been emptied. Pieters said that he couldn't explain since it was "top secret." Then early in the morning just before Christmas, a large ship arrived at Neira harbor. The whole harbor area was cordoned off, and the population was warned to stay indoors until further notice; anyone who disobeyed that order would be shot on the spot. As our house was near the harbor we could see what was going on. First about fifty military policemen disembarked at the *los* and took positions around the harbor area. Then another fifty were spread along the road between the harbor and the old hospital.

Suddenly we saw short people wearing kimonos, and carrying *rantang*s, pillows, small bags, and other personal belongings, coming out from the harbor entrance. The group consisted of about forty Japanese, including children, who were marched to the old hospital. They were escorted by about another fifty military policemen, some of whom were carrying machine guns. As they passed our house, my mother cried, "Look, there is the Kinoko family, of the ice cream and cake shop in Ambon."

Most of the Japanese prisoners were civilians from Ambon, Ternate, and Manado. They had been living there for years, and hadn't bothered to return to Japan before the outbreak of the Pacific War. Uncle Rir laughed at the procession, saying, "It is silly to use about 150 soldiers just to escort forty old Japanese with their wives and children. One soldier with a rifle would be enough."

Some Bandanese pitied the Japanese prisoners. Some ladies who knew the kind Kinoko family of Ambon discussed sending them some cakes, but their husbands warned that they would be shot if they went near the old hospital. An old auntie of mine who had been pro-Dutch suddenly changed sides and became pro-Japanese after she saw the heavily armed soldiers under their Dutch commander escorting the Japanese prisoners.

Neira was suddenly full of soldiers wearing "MP" insignia on their shirtsleeves. Most were Ambonese. They did not spend much money, unlike the passengers of the KPM ships who used to visit Banda. In any case, except for the local fruit, there was nothing much to be sold. Rice and sugar were already rationed, and the provisions on hand in December were only enough to last until February. Sago biscuits still arrived from Seram Island by prau, but not as often as before. The harvest of tapioca and corn in March would help ease the shortage of food.

The 150 KNIL soldiers stationed at Neira to look after the forty Japanese civilian prisoners were a menace to the proud, poor, and peace-living Bandanese. They drilled the adult male population to march with hunting rifles, taught them how to extinguish fires in case of Japanese bombing and to black out kerosene lamps at night, and, last but not least, disturbed the beautiful Bandanese girls.

Suddenly one morning a large liner-turned-troop-transport arrived at Neira and took the KNIL troops and their Japanese prisoners to Timor Island. It was a relief; Banda was again quiet. Kloosterhuis again became friendlier and sent Pieters to Uncle Rir and Uncle Kaca Mata to ask for their advice on food distribution. The last part of January 1942 was an exciting time: all sea communication between the Banda Islands and the rest of the world was broken. The KPM ships had ceased operating throughout the archipelago. Even the praus from Seram didn't come bringing sago. The price of tapioca went up, and people began to consume more fish than any other staple. Practically every Bandanese caught his own fish.

Most Bandanese in the civilian watch carried hunting rifles and small gongs to warn of any Japanese landing; they also took along their fishing gear so that they could guard and fish at the same time. My Old Man was appointed chief of the civil watch, or as we called it, the "unarmed home guard" of the Kampong China and Negreh district. Those on night patrol, usually armed with a double-barreled shotgun borrowed from an old *perkenier*, and carrying sleeping mats, blankets, a coffee pot, and fishing lines, always ended up at the *los* to fish and to sleep. Every time the easy-going patrol passed a group of Bandanese sitting on the porch in the evening, they were greeted by shouts such as, "Did you see some Japanese?" or "Did you catch a Japanese submarine on your line?"

Nearly every night, and especially on moonlit nights, almost every Bandanese was on the street, on the beaches, on the piers, and, naturally, at the *los*, because of the blackout order, and the involuntary blackout because Banda had no more kerosene for lamps. On dark nights, some people just sat in front of their houses waiting for the war to finish or for the arrival of the Japanese, whom they thought were going to bring cheap food, clothes, and kerosene.

THE UNCLES LEAVE BANDA

After Pearl Harbor was attacked by the Japanese in December 1941, and the Dutch East Indies government declared war on the Japanese, the Dutch governor general in Jakarta ordered that Hatta and Sjahrir be brought back to Java. Before the exiles decided to go they made a proposal to the governor general to allow them to take the children they had adopted in Banda with them. The governor general agreed.[1]

The families of the adopted children conferred for two days with the uncles, with Uncle Hatta as chairman, as to who should go with the two uncles and who should stay. Little Ali was top priority. It took almost a day for everybody to agree that Ali should go with Uncle Rir; Ali's real mother fainted twice during those family sessions. The decision on whether I should go along was a quick one. All the families wanted to get rid of the scoundrel Des as soon as possible. Lily was also easy: she was the eldest, and could act as half-sister and half-mother to the younger kids when we were far away from Banda. Mimi must go along because she was considered the cleverest of the lot, but her mother kept crying during the whole session. Ali's grandfather objected when it was suggested that Ali's older brother, Moh, could also go. He told Uncle Rir, `"You can't take two of my grandsons. No, Sir, one is enough."

The departure time was far from definite because sea communication had ceased with the exception of military ships that only carried troops and important Dutch

---

[1] For Sjahrir's account, see Sjahrir, *Out of Exile*, pp. 225–26.

officials. Makassar was about to be attacked, and the Japanese were in control of nearly all the airfields in Sulawesi. Thus, sea and air links between the upper part of the Moluccan Archipelago and Java were practically cut off.

In the early morning of January 31, 1942, the air-raid alarm sounded again when a plane was heard circling above Neira. A Catalina amphibious plane soon landed in front of the *los*. People thought it must be a Dutch plane because the two crew members who were paddling to the *los* in a rubber dingy were *orang putih* (white men). They were two tall American flyers of the United States Navy.[2] They walked past our house on their way to see the local Dutch official, Kloosterhuis. Seeing them pass the house Uncle Rir shouted, "This is it, this is it. Get ready everyone, we are leaving."

I felt stiff when he said that; I wasn't prepared at all to leave beautiful Banda. I wanted to cry, but couldn't. A few minutes later Kloosterhuis sent a policeman to the house to tell Uncle Rir that we should be ready for take off in fifteen minutes. Our families and a crowd of Bandanese rushed to the house, some crying, some shouting to beg Uncle Rir to stay. I rushed to Uncle Hatta's house to see what was going on there. Hundreds of people were in front of his house, also pleading that he not leave. As Uncle Rir later described the scene:

> We had to leave before daylight, because otherwise it would not be possible. The Japanese were on Ambon and their planes were expected to follow the Catalina at any moment. All of Banda was on the dock—half awake, half dressed, unwashed, and frightened—to see us off. The people had acquired such confidence in us that I felt as if I were committing desertion.[3]

I rushed back to the house and my mother embraced me and cried; my younger sisters followed me and cried; the old servant Nina embraced my legs and asked me not to go. Jot, Halik, Koon, and many other friends looked at me with sad eyes.

An old lady who used to come to the house to chat with Uncle Rir screamed loudly and begged him to stay. Uncle Hatta arrived from Kampong Ratu with a small bag, followed by a crowd of silent and sad-looking Bandanese. We left the house to proceed to the *los* followed by a crying and sad-looking crowd. At the *los* more people were waiting—almost every Bandanese of Neira was there. *Kolee-kolee* and praus arrived from Gunung Api with more people. Their village head said loudly, "Please *tuan-tuan* [gentlemen], don't leave us!"

Auntie Philippus also shouted and begged the two exiles to stay and lead the Bandanese. Kloosterhuis arrived on his bicycle; he shook hands with the two uncles, which was his first handshake with them.

The American Navy Captain of the Catalina said that all who were planning to go on the flight had to be weighed, together with their baggage. Because Makassar was under attack by the Japanese and Kendari was already in Japanese hands, the plane would have to fly straight to Surabaya without refueling, a twelve-hour flight.

---

[2] The pilots' names were Harvey Hop and Guy Howard, of Patrol Wing 10, from the USS *Heron*, operating to the east of Timor Island. See Dwight R. Messimer, *In the Hands of Fate: The Story of Patrol Wing Ten, 8 December 1941–11 May 1942* (Annapolis, MD: Naval Institute Press, 1985), pp. 224–25.

[3] Sjahrir, *Out of Exile*, p. 226.

Sjahrir, Hatta, and four children were overweight by 130 kilograms. The Captain said that if everybody wanted to go we would have to leave most of the luggage behind. Lily and Mimi left one bag, Sjahrir took out his typewriter, and Hatta left two cartons of books, taking out a map of the Netherlands East Indies so that he could check where we were going. We were still about seventy kilograms overweight.

Suddenly I, a boy of fourteen who weighed fifty-one kilograms, decided to stay behind. I felt that I wasn't really prepared to leave beautiful Banda Neira; also, I was worried because the tail of the Catalina plane was full of bullet holes. Then my mother asked Uncle Rir if I could stay behind; she didn't like me to go by plane in such a dangerous time with the Japanese controlling the Moluccan skies. Uncle Rir nodded, and Uncle Kaca Mata said, "You look after my books and come to Java as soon as you can."

Hatta said that the Dutch had promised to send a boat to pick us up, and added that I could bring all the luggage left behind if I went by boat. Of course he meant the thousand books he had left behind plus the two boxes he left at the pier. My mother held me tight; she also agreed that I should stay. I was crying, *setengah senang, setengah sedih* (half happy, half sad).

The tall American flyer asked those who were leaving to step into the *orambai* to proceed to the Catalina. People began to cry and shout. I, too, began to cry, having said I would stay, but half wanting to go. I had the urge to jump into the water and swim after them, but it was too late. So the uncles left with little Ali, Lily, and Mimi.

When the plane's engines began to roar the people at the *los*, Muslims as well as Christians, started praying for its safe arrival in Java. Then the plane took off and flew past the Papenberg hill, and disappeared from Banda's sky. I felt lonely and unhappy. My young friends embraced me as I walked back to the house. I didn't know what to do, but I realized that my life had changed.

An hour after the departure of the Catalina a sudden hurricane swept over Banda and blew away many large trees and the roofs of several large houses. No Bandanese lost their lives during that storm, but it was followed by an earthquake that shook Neira and other Banda islands, and by torrential rain. Many people lost their houses and some were wounded by fallen trees. At the *rumah besar* the crystal chandelier crashed down during the earthquake. It was one of the most violent storms and earthquakes Banda had had for a decade. Some Bandanese believed that it was the work of *orang halus* and the *orang tua-tua* because the spirits were angry at the colonial government for taking Hatta and Sjahrir away in such a hurry and without consulting them. Further, the exiles had left without first sending an offering of flowers to the Papenburg *kramat* and other holy places. Some people also believed that the violent storm, earthquake, and heavy rain were warnings by the "protectors" of Banda that bad days lay ahead for the people. In the afternoon the torrential rain stopped suddenly, but the sky looked grizzly and soon ash rain fell on Banda. "There must be a volcanic eruption somewhere near our islands," said Uncle Mat, the non-*foe-foe* believer.

CHAPTER SEVEN

JAPANESE OCCUPATION IN BANDA

On the morning of February 1, 1942, the day after the Catalina took Hatta and Sjahrir away, while I was eating breakfast at a friend's house, gongs and *tifas* started beating. We heard the roaring of plane engines, and soon saw six double-winged fast planes with Japan's red-sun insignia on their wings above our heads. Before we could say anything each of the planes in turn dived toward old Fort Nassau and dropped their bombs on the radio station near the fort. All hell broke loose. People ran to look for shelter. Twelve big bangs were heard, followed by the clattering of the planes' machine guns. After about fifteen minutes the planes roared off.

After the bombing, the radio-telegraph station at Neira, although undamaged, ceased operation. Therefore, we had no way of knowing whether Hatta, Sjahrir, and the three children had arrived safely in Java. Radio stations in Java hadn't mentioned their arrival there. Presumably the colonial government had blocked the news to prevent the Indonesian people and the Japanese from knowing about the arrival of the two nationalist leaders in Java. I was worried about their safety, and thought that perhaps the Americans had taken them to Australia instead of to Java.

Anyway, the world was now at war and even Banda was mixed up in it. Japanese planes kept visiting Banda, either to drop a bomb or two at the radio station or just to fly above us on their patrols. The Bandanese slowly began to get used to the sound of the air-raid alarm, and only hid when one or two planes were already overhead. So far there had been no hits on the small radio station and its two tall aerials were still standing.

We kids began to like the war because the schools were closed and the rich *perkeniers* evacuated to their plantations, leaving their town houses with their fruit trees unprotected. It was really a free life for us: roaming around the bush and rowing to Gunung Api and Banda Besar to visit relatives and friends who had fled there for fear of the bombs. Kloosterhuis and his police were nowhere to be seen. Kloosterhuis had gone to stay at the Mangku Batu nutmeg plantation at the other end of Neira Island. His family had been evacuated to Java soon after the outbreak of the war in Europe.

The nutmeg trees grew undisturbed, but their expensive fruits were no longer collected, they just dropped to the ground and rotted. The tapioca roots, corn, sweet potatoes, and the other vegetables planted on the fertile soil of Banda began to yield enough food. Rice and flour, however, were nowhere to be obtained. Sugar disappeared from Banda, and people began to drink their coffee using brown palm sugar made from the blossoms of the Aren tree. If palm sugar were put directly into coffee it would taste rather sour. So, first you had to chew a bit of the brown sugar then sip some coffee, and repeat the process until your cup was empty. The Bandanese produced their own salt since the white salt from Madura Island, which before the war was a monopoly of the colonial government, could no longer be obtained. We kids helped our mothers make salt by boiling seawater, adding more seawater to the pan for several hours until we saw some grayish looking salt on the bottom of the pan.

Halik didn't sell fried bananas anymore. He was too old for that, and besides the cheap coconut oil from Seram had ceased to come. He changed his profession and became a maker of salt. With his twin brothers, Putih and Hitam, he opened a salt "factory," which consisted of about six large empty kerosene cans in which to boil the seawater, on Kola Rottan beach, a distance away from the radio station, where firewood was plentiful. Soon Halik and his brothers began to sell their Banda-made salt, putting it into small plaited baskets that they made themselves from the *nipa* palms that grew along the coast. They also sold mangoes and pickled nutmeg fruit that they placed in old jam jars. Halik's salt was whiter than that of his competitors, the hard-working salt-producing housewives. Halik didn't tell us his secret of how to produce white salt, but later we learned that he turned his gray salt into white by mixing it with egg whites. Not being able to sell all the salt he produced, Halik bartered it for tapioca roots, and soon his mother and sister started selling bread made of tapioca mixed with grated fresh coconut.

There was one snag with Halik's salt factory, however. Every time the gongs and *tifa*s started beating the air-raid alarm, Halik and his younger brothers had to put out their fire. They were afraid that the Japanese planes might see the smoke and bomb their factory, thinking it was a kind of signal to point out the location of something important.

The afternoon of February 28, 1942, after the Japanese had landed in Java, a large Japanese seaplane circled low above Neira. Many people thought that the plane was going to land on the bay, and some even thought it was the plane that had taken Hatta and Sjahrir away. It dropped two large bombs; one fell near Fort Nassau, and the other a few yards from the church. The blast shook Kampong China, but luckily nobody was hurt.

The plane had been trying to bomb the radio station, but missed again. By now the Bandanese could no longer ignore the nonworking, inactive, small radio-telegraph station. Young and old Neira people attended a meeting where it was decided that the two large radio aerials must go—to show the Japanese planes that the radio station was idle, and to make it look as if the recent Japanese bombing had destroyed it. The people no longer asked Kloosterhuis for his opinion. They just went ahead and demolished the two aerials. The two large aerials crashed down into an open field of tapioca plants behind old Fort Nassau. A few days later a Japanese patrol plane flew above Neira, but there was nothing else to be bombed and the Japanese planes did not disturb us anymore.

The Netherlands East Indies government surrendered to the Japanese on March 9, 1942, three months after the attack on Pearl Harbor. The so-called Dutch military bastion on Ambon Island had already fallen to the Japanese on February 2, 1942, after just two days of fighting. In fact, the Australian battalion stationed there did most of the fighting.[1] The Japanese didn't come to Banda until March 1942.

---

[1] Stanley Woodburn Kirby, *The War Against Japan* (London: H. M. Statonery Office, 1969), Vol. 6, p. 349, describes the Japanese attack on Ambon and the role of the Australians.

"REVOLUTION" IN BANDA

In early March, praus from Seram began to arrive at Neira, bringing the first cargoes of sago, coconut oil, and other foodstuff. Life started to turn normal again, but the old colonial officials, thinking they still controlled Banda, began to take charge of the incoming cargoes for the Central Food Distribution Office, which Kloosterhuis had created soon after the outbreak of the Pacific War. The Bandanese didn't like this corrupt system, which benefited the officials more than the people. When the second prau from Seram arrived at the *los* with a cargo of sago biscuits, and the entire cargo was again brought to the Central Food Distribution Office, the usually tolerant and peaceful Bandanese lost their patience. They tried to prevent the transaction by grabbing the customs officials, headed by Manubulu, and the harbor master. During the scuffle, Manubulu pulled out his pistol and shot into the air. One man jumped at him to try to take the pistol away. The pistol went off, injuring Manubulu's right hand. Manubulu, bleeding, jumped on his bicycle to go to warn Kloosterhuis of the incident and to get some first aid for his hand.

Shortly Kloosterhuis came to the *los* with two armed policemen. But the crowd turned against them. The native policemen surrendered their weapons to the people, instead of shooting them. The angry crowd tied up Kloosterhuis and marched him off to jail. At the jail, the crowd released all the prisoners and placed Kloosterhuis behind bars.

Hearing about the "coup d'état" and the "revolution" at Neira, the Lonthor people of Banda Besar dispatched ten *orambai* with armed reinforcements to Neira, some carrying old shotguns, hunting rifles, hatchets, spears, and sticks. Since Kloosterhuis had already been put in jail, the Lonthor brigade of about 150 men wanted to attack the police station and the police camp at Kampong Baru. The Manadonese police unit commander warned the Lonthor crowd that the police would not surrender if attacked, but would instead shoot at them. At last some sense was put into the hotheads of Lonthor, and they consulted with "their brothers in arms" of Neira. After a few hours of conferring, the Bandanese decided to elect a new officer in charge, who must be an Indonesian.

The local Javanese medical doctor, Sarwono, was then elected as Banda's new district head. Dr. Sarwono ordered new elections for village heads, but asked that the former colonial officials remain because Banda had no experienced civil servants. The Central Food Distribution Office was disbanded, and a new Cooperative Center of Banda was formed, under Uncle Hatta's three Sumatran students. The Bandanese Chinese and some *perkeniers* were required to donate to the fund of the Cooperative Center. Theo Kok refused to donate to the fund, so one afternoon a group of Bandanese Chinese marched to his house to ask for his donation. He still refused, so they beat him up. After that Theo Kok donated five hundred guilders to the fund.

In Kampong China and Negreh the local soccer star, Evert, was elected the new head, replacing Uncle Baltazaar. I witnessed the quick and spontaneous election. One older man, facing a huge crowd in front of Uncle Baltazaar's, stood up on a shaky chair and shouted, "Those in favor of Evert raise your hands."

Nearly the whole crowd raised their hands. So Evert, a young *burger* of Dutch descent, replaced Uncle Baltazaar, the *burger* of Spanish or Portuguese descent.

After spending a night in the local jail, Kloosterhuis was released and sent to Ambon. The delegation to see the Japanese commander of Ambon and to deliver Kloosterhuis consisted of six newly elected Banda Neira village heads. They left by prau, and got to Ambon a week later. On their arrival at Ambon harbor, the Japanese marine guard mistook them for the surrender of a Dutch officer and six native soldiers. He slapped them and then took them to the Japanese harbor master. Kloosterhuis was arrested at once and sent to a prison camp. The delegation did not see the Japanese commander of Ambon, but instead the harbor master told them to return to Banda Neira and wait for the arrival of the Japanese. (Kloosterhuis survived the war, and soon thereafter was pensioned and returned to Holland.)

The Bandanese became a bit restless because the Japanese hadn't yet come. They had already made Japanese flags to welcome them, and hoped they would soon come bringing food and cheap clothing. The Butonese working in the foreign-owned coconut plantations on Gunung Api refused to deliver their coconuts and other crops to the owners. The police commander, when requested by Dr. Sarwono, asked the Butonese to deliver some of their crops to the newly established Cooperative Center, but they refused. Instead they attacked the Manadonese police commander. The police opened fire, killing one and wounding several of the Butonese.

The situation at Banda Neira was again hot. The Butonese gathered along the Tita beach, in front of the empty *controleur*'s office. Lonthor again dispatched their "armed warriors." Dr. Sarwono had completely lost control of the situation. He didn't realize that the Bandanese hated the ex-colonial police he had used to establish law and order. After this incident Sarwono sacked the non-Bandanese police force and quickly formed a new police force consisting of unarmed and untrained Bandanese. It didn't help much because Warouw, the police unit commander, refused to surrender their weapons. Instead his police force took an oath of loyalty to the Japanese Empire, and put Japanese flags as insignia on their shirts. They also took strategic positions in front of their camps. Seeing the Japanese flag flying in front of the police compound, the Butonese and Lonthor warriors pulled back and went home. The police stayed in their compound until the first Japanese arrived in mid-March.

The Japanese in Banda

I remember the morning that Uncle Mat woke me up and told me that a big Japanese ship was landing Japanese troops on the beach in front of Aunt Willy's school. Half an hour later we saw Japanese marines, heavily armed and dressed in jungle-green battle uniforms, marching by our house. The very same morning the Japanese ordered the entire population of Neira to assemble in front of what had been the *controleur*'s office. The soldiers mingled with the crowd and ordered all the white people to gather in a nearby field. The Dutch population of Banda Neira consisted mainly of plantation owners, planters, and estate administrators. They were, in fact, prepared for their arrest and had brought with them bags of clothing and food. Two female schoolteachers from my school were also there, but none of my class teachers because as soon as the Pacific War broke out they had been conscripted and sent to Ambon.

While the white people were being arrested, two albino Bandanese were mistaken for white men, and were also arrested. These two men protested, shouting in Indonesian that they should not be arrested. However, the Japanese could not understand what they were saying, and slapped them for resisting arrest. Suddenly Uncle Mat emerged from the crowd and went straight to the Japanese sergeant who was in charge of the Dutch prisoners. The Japanese sergeant slapped Uncle Mat for not bowing down to him before speaking. Uncle Mat tried to explain to the Japanese about the mistaken identity of the two albinos, but was again slapped for having spoken in English. Uncle Mat then spoke in what little Japanese he had learned from the Japanese pearl divers who had worked for him. The sergeant became a little friendlier, having at last found an Indonesian who could speak some Japanese. However, as Uncle Mat was not too conversant with the Japanese language, he could not express the word "albino." The sergeant then summoned an interpreter, through whose efforts the albinos were released.

Immediately after this incident the interpreter made a speech in which he said that the Japanese came to Indonesia to liberate the Indonesians from 350 years of Dutch colonialism and slavery. Before the crowd dispersed they were ordered to shout three times *"tenno heika bansai"* [long live the emperor].

Soon after the Japanese landing, the Minseibu [Japanese Navy Civil Administration] ordered the arrest of all Dutch nationals in Banda, including the ELS teachers, the van den Broeke family, *perkeniers*, and Theo Kok. Several Butonese who had attacked the police commander were also arrested. The next day the Japanese marines left Banda Neira for their base at Ambon, and took with them the Dutch prisoners.

One platoon of Japanese marines remained in Neira to maintain law and order. Later, after their officers had left for Ambon, this platoon of Japanese marines left at Neira released the Butonese and disbanded the police force.

The Japanese marine force at Banda was headed by Lieutenant Masimoto, a stocky Japanese around forty years of age. He was very kind and polite, and walked around Neira carrying a small Japanese-Indonesian dictionary. He often stopped at the *rumah besar* to sip coffee with Uncle Mat and my father. Uncle Mat had probably explained the situation in Neira to him in his pidgin Japanese. Masimoto must have thought that Uncle Mat and my father were learned men when he saw all the books Hatta and Sjahrir had left at the *rumah besar*. Uncle Hatta left more than one thousand books, and Uncle Sjahrir around three hundred books. We didn't tell Masimoto that those books belonged to Hatta and Sjahrir since we didn't know their fate, whether the Dutch had taken them to Australia [where the NEI government-in-exile had been established] or whether the Japanese had arrested them in Java.

The second in command of the marine force was Sergeant Major Maeda. Six feet tall and handsome, Maeda was probably the tallest Japanese in the whole Japanese naval force in the Moluccas. He spoke a little English and made friends with the Bandanese; he was always invited to join house parties at Kampong Ratu and Kampong China. He soon found a *piara* (mistress), a *burger* widow with five children.

One of Maeda's bad habits was that when he got drunk he would wake up his Bandanese friends at night to ask for coffee or *makan kecil* [snacks]. The Bandanese didn't have much food, and the Japanese had brought only their weapons and rations for themselves. The Japanese liked eggs and bananas, and Banda had plenty of both to barter for Japanese rations, which consisted of barley, *taucho* (crushed soybeans), and some sugar. With Masimoto and Maeda in the hands of the Bandanese, soon the whole Japanese contingent at Neira mixed freely with the local population. They also learned to eat tapioca bread, which they bartered with Halik for sugar.

Koon and I became friends of Masimoto and Maeda. Using a dictionary and Koon's knowledge of Chinese characters, we were able to communicate with them. We invited them to go fishing, and suggested that we use Theo Kok's motor boat for the occasion, since Theo Kok had already been arrested by the Japanese and sent to

Ambon. We went deep sea fishing with Masimoto and Maeda and caught many tuna. We also took them to shoot *walor* at Banda Besar. They gave us Japanese cigarettes and some of their sugar in exchange for our eggs and bananas. We taught them to eat durian and jackfruit, and soon the whole Japanese platoon became durian and jackfruit lovers.

Then one morning in early April 1942 a large troopship arrived at Neira with about five hundred men of the Japanese marines and naval air force. Neira suddenly changed from a peaceful island to a militarized Japanese naval headquarters. Anti-aircraft guns and heavy machine guns were placed in the open fields where tapioca and corn were planted. Japanese navy planes, destroyers, minesweepers, and submarines were everywhere in Banda Bay and the harbor. The *los* was turned into the naval air-force headquarters. Neira streets were crowded with Japanese sailors, marines, naval air-force personnel, marine police, and Japanese officers with small moustaches. Some Bandanese with young daughters evacuated to Gunung Api, Banda Besar, and even to Ai and Run Islands. Large cargo ships arrived every day to unload war materials and supplies for the Japanese forces. The Bandanese were surprised to see the Japanese working from six in the morning to six in the evening with only a half hour break for lunch.

These new arrivals were totally different from the Masimoto group. They were hard-looking types with many gold teeth. They didn't mix with us or others in the local population; they only bought our eggs with their new paper money, printed especially for Indonesia, with a banana motif. They bought tuna fish by the hundreds and Bandanese couldn't buy tuna or other fish because all went to the Japanese. Bandanese male teenagers were picked up on the streets to work in the Japanese kitchens. Halik was also forced to work in the Japanese kitchen when he went there to sell his mango pickles.

Masimoto was no longer the chief of Banda. There were too many high-ranking officers above him, so he and his contingent were no longer so friendly. When Koon and I went to visit Masimoto at his compound at Kompong Ratu, his guards, with bayonets fixed on their rifles, chased us away. We ran for our lives.

ALLIED BOMB ATTACKS

A week after the Japanese reinforcements arrived, Allied bombers attacked the Japanese ships in the bay and the harbor but only one small ship was hit. Every Japanese gun on land or at sea shot at the planes. Neira became such a dangerous and noisy place that most of the population still there left for Gunung Api or another more peaceful island. A few Allied bombs fell on Neira, but didn't kill anybody. While most people hid during the Allied air attacks, Koon and I watched the aerial combat between Allied light bombers and Japanese fighters from the roof of the *rumah besar*. To our surprise, the Allied planes often fled to the south, toward Australia.

One day at twilight, Allied planes staged a surprise attack on the Japanese ships anchored at Banda Bay. Some bombs fell on Banda Besar's nutmeg forest and burned several *kanari* trees. Now that Banda Besar no longer seemed safe, the evacuees from Neira who had taken refuge there moved to the back part of the island, as far as possible from the bay. During every Allied air attack the Japanese shot back with everything they had, including rifles carried by individual marines. For about a month the Allied planes kept visiting Banda to attack the Japanese ships. Luckily, not a single Bandanese was hurt during these attacks (although Uncle Mat was killed in an Allied raid in 1944). A bomb fell in the backyard of a *perkenier* at Kampong Ratu, but, fortunately, it was a dud.

One morning in early May most of the Japanese military suddenly packed up and left Neira, leaving behind the Masimoto crowd. Two Allied planes arrived a few days later and bombed the *los*, killing thousands of fish. We boys had a wonderful time picking them out of the water. It was probably the first fish we had tasted in about two months.

The Allied bombing, although without a score except for plenty of dead fish, was too much for the people still living near the harbor. Some evacuated to Gunung Api and some to Lonthor and other places on Banda Besar. The planes, presumably from bases in Australia, kept coming regularly to check on Japanese movements. As there were no more Japanese ships or planes to be spotted, the Allied planes did not drop their bombs.

We moved to stay at my cousin's place on Gunung Api, where most of the Kampong China people sought refuge. We only came to Neira to get tapioca roots, which we planted in the open fields, or to barter eggs and bananas from Gunung Api for sugar and rice from the remaining Japanese stationed at Neira.

AN INCIDENT DURING THE JAPANESE OCCUPATION

Once a friend of ours was beaten by one of Masimoto's marines in a disagreement over the exchange of eggs for sugar. The young marine, by the name of Sato, took a basket full of eggs and gave our friend, Aman, only a cup of sugar. When Aman objected, Sato settled the argument by slapping him several times. A crowd of us boys went to see Masimoto to bring a charge against Sato because he had beaten people before, including an old jackfruit seller who Sato beat until the old man fainted.

When we arrived at Masimoto's headquarters, the marine guard stopped us at the gate. We told him that we wanted to see the commander; he told us to wait near the guardhouse. A few minutes later he returned, not with Masimoto, but with Sato. Seeing Aman, Sato knew the intention of our mission and went for Aman. Seeing Sato coming at him with a stick, Aman "took a thousand steps" (Bandanese slang for "running away"), and fled toward the fish market with Sato chasing after him. Some of the boys left quickly, but Koon and I remained near the guardhouse, not knowing whether to go or to stay. Luckily, before Sato returned, Maeda came out and asked us why we wanted to see the commander. I told him about the incident with Sato. He called us into his office, and angrily told us that the commander was a very high person whom we should not bother with such a small thing. He also explained to us that if Sato or any other Japanese soldier beat us up that meant they liked us because Nippon and Indonesia are *sama-sama* (equal). The Japanese, Maeda said, fought for us and even died for us to kick the white man out of Indonesia, and to establish Great Asia under the leadership of "older brother Nippon." "In fact," Maeda said, "you should give food to the Japanese troops instead of exchanging it for something else."

Had the Japanese marines of Masimoto and Maeda known that their marine forefathers helped the Dutch conquer the Banda Islands, and that those Japanese warriors in the service of the Dutch East India Company had executed the chiefs of Banda, forty *Orang Kaya* and the *syahbandar* [harbor master], they wouldn't have told us that they came to Banda to free us from the slavery of the white men when they themselves had assisted in murdering and colonizing the Bandanese. However, that was a long time ago, and most present-day Bandanese do not know that the Japanese helped the Dutch conquer and kill us. At the time of the Japanese Occupation some older Bandanese, who learned Banda's history by reading old documents, Dutch history books, and, of course, Banda's own relics and history, did know.[2]

Koon and I left the headquarters after the "indoctrination." To our surprise, Sato was waiting for us near the guardhouse, still holding a stick. I thought to myself, "now is the time for Sato to show how much he 'likes' us by beating us up." Seeing us coming, Sato blocked our way by standing in the middle of the gate. We bowed several times in his direction, to show him how much we "liked" him, and how polite we were to our "elder brother." When we came face-to-face with Sato-san, he yelled, *"bagero"* (stupid fools), followed by another Japanese phrase that meant something like "I hope I don't see your stupid faces in this area again."

I felt cold and stiff, and Koon was in a worse condition. At first he didn't move when I nudged him with my elbow when Sato moved away from the gate. On our way home we discussed why Sato didn't beat us up. Koon's opinion was that probably Sato realized that we were friends with Maeda and Masimoto, and he didn't want to touch us in front of the headquarters, but would probably settle with us if he came across us in town. The boys didn't believe us when we told them that Sato didn't touch us. They said that Sato hadn't caught Aman because Aman was too quick. They said that Aman had left for Lonthor and had sworn that he would not come to Neira as long as Sato was there.

I also didn't feel safe at Neira, and spent most of my time on Gunung Api or at Lonthor. Halik had disappeared long ago, after having been forced to work fourteen hours a day at the Japanese kitchen. Neira was nearly empty. The *burgers*, the Eurasian *perkeniers*, the Kampong China, and the Negreh people had all moved to some other island. Some were afraid of the Japanese disturbing their nice daughters, and others were afraid of the Allied bombings.

When the two uncles hurriedly departed from Banda, the three Sumatran students sent by the Minangkabau Cooperative Bank to study with Uncle Hatta were left to look out for themselves. Munir, the youngest, was about twenty-one years old, handsome, intelligent—the brightest of the three. Daman, about twenty-five, was the eldest. The third was Bachtul Nazar, twenty-two years old, who had married a cousin of mine, and with his wife and daughter went to stay at Lonthor. Munir found a job at a Sumatran trading company in Ambon, where Daman was to join him.

Banda and Banda Besar during the Occupation

In early May 1942 I was at Lonthor. By now everyone realized that the Japanese didn't bring anything that we Bandanese had hoped for, but were even worse than the Dutch.

Food was scarce, and during the Occupation nutmeg was useless to the Bandanese because it could not be sold. The Bandanese had no other products that could be used as barter with Seram for sago. Even the Sarua and Kei islanders didn't bring their foodstuff to Banda anymore. They were afraid of the planes, Allied or

---

[2] Hanna, *Indonesian Banda*, pp. 49–50, 57.

Japanese, and they knew the Bandanese had nothing to exchange with them. However, tapioca roots were plentiful, as tapioca and sweet potatoes were now grown on the open ground between the nutmeg and *kanari* trees, where the Dutch *perkeniers* had not allowed anything to be planted. We became used to eating tapioca root and sweet potatoes made into all kinds of cakes or bread, or just plain boiled. Digestion took a bit longer, though, and many times our stomachs remained hard as stones. The Bandanese had been rice eaters, even when we did not grow our own rice. Fish were plentiful in Banda, but the material to catch fish, such as string for the nets, hooks, and lines were getting scarce. Only the fish traps, made of material found in Banda, such as bamboo and rattan, could still be used.

Nobody knew what was going on in the world, although occasionally some people brought some old Indonesian newspapers printed in Ambon by the Japanese. We did know that Japan had not occupied Australia, although they had bombed Darwin, and had occupied the whole of New Guinea and the Solomon Islands.

Already three months had passed since the departure of the Catalina, and still there was no news about Hatta, Sjahrir, and the children. I gave some of Uncle Hatta's clothes that were still in my possession to some folks at Lonthor, where the exiles had many friends, and even many followers. The solidly Malay–Indonesian population at Lonthor was more politically conscious than the mixed population of Neira. They were very kind to me, treating me as a kind of representative left behind by Hatta and Sjahrir.

CHAPTER EIGHT

LEAVING BANDA

Finally in late April 1942 a prau came from Ambon bringing some Bandanese passengers and a letter from Uncle Sjahrir and the adopted children, saying that they had arrived safely in Java and were now staying in Jakarta. There was even a photograph of them enclosed with the letter.

The letter had been sent from Jakarta to a Bandanese family in Surabaya, who got hold of cousin Wachi, who was at that time working as a ship's engineer on one of the nonmilitary Japanese ships that sailed between Surabaya, Makassar, and Ambon. (The ship was a former KPM vessel, which the Japanese had seized from the Dutch when they occupied Java.) When Wachi reached Ambon in March, he gave the letter to another Bandanese, who finally brought the letter to Banda at the end of April. The letter asked me to come to Java, and to bring Uncle Hatta's books, but it did not mention how to travel to Java, or who would pay for it. But it gave me courage and moral support to prepare for my journey, although I had not a single cent in my pocket.

To get money to go to Java I sold all my chickens to merchants from Ambon, and made a few guilders. I doubled my money at cockfighting. The game had been banned by the Dutch, but during the Japanese time it flourished. Maeda liked to watch cockfighting, although he didn't gamble himself. Some of the Japanese marines loved to watch cockfights, but didn't realize that heavy betting was involved. The Bandanese gambled using sign language or Bandanese slang to place their bets. Most of the cockfights were held on Gunung Api. If any Japanese arrived to watch, a warning was given, and people kept their money inside their pockets or in their sarong knots.

Looking to start my trip to Java, I asked Koon if I could come along with him to Ambon in his prau. He agreed, but as he was planning a month's trip to Seram, I declined his invitation. I wanted to go to Ambon as soon as possible, and once there I would look for a way to proceed to Java. I was hoping to meet cousin Wachi's ship at Ambon, because folks from Ambon said that he would be back there in a month or so.

So I prepared to go as a paying passenger on another prau direct to Ambon. The passage cost five guilders, and the passengers had to bring their own food. After paying the fare, I had only a few guilders left from my chicken and cockfighting money. My mother gave me another five guilders after selling her last piece of jewelry, a gold bracelet, for eight guilders.

On May 17, 1942, with only a small metal case, two boxes of Uncle Hatta's books, and about fifteen guilders in my pocket, I left Banda Neira for Ambon. The prau, called the *Tenggiri* (the Indonesian name for horse-mackerel), had four passengers: myself; Does, a distant cousin of mine who had studied with the exiles, but was prevented by his family from going with them to Java; Daman, one of the uncles' Sumatran students, who was escorting the fourth passenger, Miss van der Poll, a

Eurasian school teacher, who had been my classroom teacher, and was engaged to marry one of the other Sumatran students, Munir, who was already in Ambon.

We left the *los* in the late afternoon. Before we reached Lautaka a large *orambai* approached, carrying my father, his friend Ho, and several rowers. The two men climbed into the prau to give me a tin of biscuits, and to give the *nakhoda* (the prau captain) some navigational suggestions on the quickest and safest way to reach Seram. After saying, *"Selamat Tioo"* (goodbye for a sea journey), my father and Ho jumped back in their *orambai* and paddled back to Neira.

From left: Munir (one of Hatta's Sumatran students), with his child;
Miss van der Poll (Munir's wife); Oen (Des's younger sister); Alwi, Des's father;
Moem (Ali's father, Des's cousin)

SAILING TO AMBON

On the way to Ambon, the prau stopped at Pasir Besar, the home of the *nachoda*, to load some large clay pots containing "mouse brand," a cargo meant for the liquor-loving Christian Ambonese. We also stopped for nearly a week at Tahoro in Seram, where the prau owner gathered more cargo to sell in Ambon. Finally, after another two days' sail we arrived at the beautiful Bay of Ambon, famous for its heavy swells. Once we entered the bay the sea was mirror-like. A fast Japanese fighter plane, probably a Zero, flew very low above the *Tenggiri* several times, probably wanting to make sure that our prau was a real prau and not an Allied submarine. The prau captain told us to put on our *songkok* to show the patrolling plane that we were Indonesian.

About five o'clock the *Tenggiri* reached the prau harbor, near the market. Praus from every part of the Moluccas were there, all of them carrying foodstuff to the busy town of Ambon, with its many Japanese marines and sailors.

When the *nakhoda* moored the *Tenggiri*, two Ambonese harbor policemen came on board to check the cargo and our luggage. They didn't pay much attention to the mouse-brand, but were a bit surprised to see Miss van der Poll. They asked her several questions: where she came from, what she was going to do in Ambon, and so on. She answered them in mixed Dutch and Indonesian. One policeman found some letters addressed to Hatta and Sjahrir in Java in Daman's bag, and told him that it was prohibited to carry letters. Instead of apologizing to the policemen, and getting away with it, Daman tried to argue with them, saying that the Japanese had not yet opened a post office in Banda and that was why his friends asked him to pass these letters to people going to Java. The policemen took the letters and told Daman to report to their office by the following morning. I discovered that one of the two policemen had been one of those who brought the Japanese civilian prisoners to Banda Neira in the early months of the Pacific War. He had served with the Dutch before, and now with the Japanese.

News traveled fast in Ambon, and half an hour after our arrival, Munir came to the *Tenggiri*. He was very happy to see Miss van der Poll, and she smiled broadly when she saw him. A cousin of mine, by the name of Saleh, who worked with Munir, told me that I could stay with him and the crowd at Munir's house at Kampong Batu Merah. Does had left us earlier without even saying goodbye. It was drizzling when we came out of the harbor compound. Still, I was happy to reach Ambon, the first leg of my long journey to Java. I was also rather astonished to see so many cars in the busy streets of Ambon town. Through the shower, and carrying my metal case, I walked with my cousin Saleh through the bustling streets of Ambon to Batu Merah.

OCCUPIED AMBON

Ambon town in 1942 was busy and crowded. The Dutch had militarized the island in 1940, and when the Japanese occupied it, they used it as a strategic base for the South Pacific campaign. The Japanese found the Dutch naval installation at Halong practically intact, as was the military airfield at Laha, across the bay from Ambon town. Most of the mixed Dutch and native troops defending Ambon Island panicked even before they came face-to-face with the attacking Japanese. When the Japanese landed, chaos ensued, and the invaders encountered very little resistance. Only the Australian battalion stationed at Halong, near the naval base at Rumah Tiga, and those at Laha airfield put up a stiff resistance. However, they had to surrender on February 4, 1942, after two days of fighting, because of the lack of ammunition, food, and medical supplies.

In Ambon town I found many newly rich people, who before the Japanese arrival were only harbor workers and small traders. When the Dutch military fled Ambon, the town's poor people saw a chance to loot the commercial center and the godowns in the harbor area, and to break into the banks. The stiff Australian resistance at Halong, about eight miles from the town, gave those people—including prisoners who broke out of the local jail—enough time to harvest the rich loot before the arrival of the Japanese troops. They then took the war-loot back to their homes, often burying it in their backyards.

In the year after the Japanese arrival, Ambon was probably the most prosperous and well-stocked town in the whole archipelago. Nearly every family had at least an ex-Dutch-Army bicycle. Canned food, cigarettes, khaki material, and army surplus left by the Dutch were plentiful. Many Dutch silver guilders remained in circulation, and were even used by the Japanese in addition to their banana-motif paper money.

During my stay in Ambon I saw many prisoners of war: Dutch, Eurasians, and Australian military personnel. Indonesian soldiers who had served in the Dutch colonial army had been released a few months after the Japanese landing. I saw Dutch military prisoners being used by the Japanese to load and unload ships at the wharves and to repair streets. Every morning at seven the prisoners were marched from their camps outside the town to work in the town, and at six in the afternoon they were marched back. I even saw two of my former school teachers working on the road near the harbor. I looked at them, but they pretended that they didn't recognize me. They were probably afraid of the Japanese marines who guarded them with a rifle and fixed bayonet. They had certainly lost weight. I pitied them, and nearly cried.

The Japanese treated the Australian prisoners much better than the Dutch or Eurasians. Australians worked in the harbor and at the airfield of Laha, and were allowed to use their military trucks. They could also keep fish and vegetables for themselves. People said that the Australians were treated much better because the Australians had fought bravely against the Japanese, and the Japanese respected them for that. Some friends said that the Australians were even paid by the Japanese for their work.

The local people liked the members of the Australian battalion, who had been stationed on Ambon Island for about a year before the outbreak of the Pacific War. Unlike the Dutch soldiers, the Australians mixed freely with the native population. They attended their parties, gave them some of their rations, and, in their free time, carried small brown children on their shoulders. When they became Japanese prisoners, the local people returned their goodwill. I saw market sellers give them free cigarettes and fish.

Ambon was so strongly militarized that when I was there no Allied planes attacked it. One night after my arrival in Ambon, the Japanese organized a torch parade with the local population. Through the loud speakers the Japanese had placed on street corners the population was told to proceed to the field in front of the old Dutch fort, Fort Victoria. The purpose, they said, was to celebrate the Japanese victory in the battle of the Solomon Islands. At the Fort Victoria field the children were given lighted kerosene torches, and were told to march through the town singing Japanese songs while accompanied by the Japanese marine music corps playing navy marches.

During my first days in Ambon, I assisted Saleh in selling merchandise in the store he ran at the town market, which was owned by Munir and some Sumatran politicians who had fled Boven Digul concentration camp soon after the outbreak of the Pacific War. They arrived in Ambon on a small prau just after the Japanese occupied New Guinea. With the aid of some Sumatran traders who had been settled in Ambon for a long time, these ex-political prisoners and Munir organized a trading company. The house where I stayed was sort of a mess for this company. The ex-political prisoners and Munir and Miss van der Poll also stayed there. Munir and Miss van der Poll had already been married by an imam. There wasn't much of a celebration; only the people in the house witnessed the occasion.

A Dutch Prisoner

Every morning going to the company's store in the center of the town, I had to pass Fort Victoria, which the Japanese used as their headquarters. The fort was in a military camp, which also contained some barracks for Dutch civilian prisoners. Early one morning, soon after my arrival in Ambon, as I was about to enter the street in front of the fort, to my horror I saw a Dutchman tied to a palm tree facing the street. Nearby was a board nailed on a stout bamboo pole, with this message written in Indonesian:

> Anybody passing this man must stop and slap him. Do you know who he is? He is Mr. Wolf, former *controleur* of Dobo on Aru Island. He killed fourteen Indonesians there. Indonesian brothers, this is a chance for you to take revenge against what he did to your fellow countrymen. This is your chance to take revenge against the Dutch who colonized you for three hundred years and turned you into slaves.

I didn't notice a Japanese marine guard standing a distance away behind a large *kanari* tree. As I started to move on, walking as fast as possible, I heard someone shout, "*Kora!*" [halt!].

When I looked back the guard ordered me to come to him. I bowed to greet him, but when I stood up, the guard slapped me violently. I stumbled, but didn't fall, although I felt dizzy. The guard pointed at the Dutchman, and said something to me in Japanese that must have meant, "You stupid boy! Why didn't you slap him?"

The guard forced me to face the Dutchman, and by a hand sign told me to slap Mr. Wolf. My hands shook. I didn't know what to do. I had no heart to slap this man, but I didn't want to be slapped by the guard for not slapping Mr. Wolf. The marine guard became annoyed. He again shouted at me in Japanese.

So I raised my arm and hit Mr. Wolf. It was a soft blow. As Mr. Wolf was a tall Dutchman, I was too short to reach his face and my arm only reached his left shoulder. The guard laughed at me sarcastically as I walked away. I could hear him saying in Japanese, "*Nani, yo?*" (What's that?, meaning, what kind of a blow is that?) I had never felt so sick as I did that morning. I still remember the sad face of Mr. Wolf, looking at me. At least he must have realized that I did not slap him of my own free will, but had been forced to do it by the Japanese guard. And I'm sure my blow did not hurt him a bit.

Mr. Wolf was tied in front of Fort Victoria for two days. When his punishment became known, many people took different roads to avoid passing Fort Victoria and being forced to slap him. Some intentionally passed near the fort to slap Mr. Wolf; others passed by out of curiosity, just to see the fate of the Dutchman. Later some said that by the first afternoon Mr. Wolf was already bleeding because some anti-Dutch fanatics hit him with their leather sandals because he was too tall for them to reach otherwise. Then the Japanese guard put a chair in front of Mr. Wolf so that people could climb up to reach the Dutchman's face.

Two days later Mr. Wolf was no longer there. Some said that that he had died where he had been tied up. Others said that he was not yet dead when the Japanese took him away, and that they later shot him behind the Fort. Still others said that Mr. Wolf had survived his punishment. I never learned what really happened.

The same afternoon as the incident with the Japanese guard and Mr. Wolf, I visited the *Tenggiri*. The Butonese crew told me the story of Mr. Wolf, which they had heard from the crew of the sailing vessel that had brought him to Ambon.

They said that when Ambon Island fell to the Japanese, the local Muslim population at Dobo, knowing that the central administration of the Moluccas no longer existed, staged a sort of coup against the *controleur*, Mr. Wolf, to run the local administration while awaiting the Japanese. However, a few weeks later, a small coaster arrived bringing some Ambonese soldiers from New Guinea. With the help of these soldiers the *controleur* restored the previous administration and put every adult male Muslim behind bars. According to the Butonese, Mr. Wolf had then ordered the execution of several prisoners, whom he charged with being pro-Japanese. Just when he and the soldiers were celebrating their victory at Dobo, and prepared to flee to Darwin, Australia, the Japanese staged a surprise attack and landed at Dobo.

The Ambonese soldiers fled the island in *orambai*s toward the main island of Aru, but the *controleur* was left behind. The Japanese attack party didn't stay long at Dobo, but before chasing after the Ambonese soldiers, they told the local people to take the *controleur* to the Japanese in Ambon. Some local people took Mr. Wolf to Ambon by sailing prau, which took more than a month. Mr. Wolf behaved very well on the journey, according to the crew of the prau. He was rather quiet, and spent his time reading a Bible. He admitted his guilt to the crew, and was prepared to receive his punishment.

LIVING AND WORKING IN AMBON

The store owned by the Sumatran company was inside the Ambon town market, in a sort of compartmentalized row of shops, selling nearly the same kind of general merchandise, rather like a bazaar. We sold large and small towels, shirts, socks, toothbrushes, pots and pans, and all sorts of colonial army surplus goods such as aluminum forks and spoons. (The Japanese administering Ambon and the Moluccas didn't seem to mind that people sold ex-Dutch colonial army stuff, even though they damn well knew it must have been stolen.) Our shop was very popular because cousin Saleh, who ran it, was young (twenty) and handsome, and had a pleasant manner. Besides, he had already mastered sufficient Japanese to please the customers, who were mostly Japanese: off-duty Japanese sailors, local Kaigun [Japanese Navy] people, and petite Japanese women of the Japanese-only brothels and clubs in Ambon.

I was Saleh's voluntary unpaid assistant. Knowing only a few Japanese words, I wasn't popular with the Japanese male customers because I couldn't understand them properly. However, I was rather popular with the Japanese women customers, who used to giggle among themselves and point at me, saying things I couldn't understand. Some of the Japanese women were rather pretty, especially those from the officers-only clubs and brothels. The rest wore too much make-up to cover their pale faces, which presumably were pale because of overwork. (There were a few thousand Japanese marines in Ambon, and no more than a hundred Japanese women.) Most of these pale-faced women had gold teeth, and until now I hate to see women with gold teeth.

The Japanese had several brothels in Ambon. One was in a house in the Batu Gajah residential area where once the Dutch Assistant *Resident* of the South Moluccas lived. This brothel was for the officers. Others were scattered around town, and were stocked with Japanese and Korean women. The Ambonese called the Japanese women "*ona-ona*," from the Japanese word for a girl or woman, *ona*, using the

Indonesian plural form. For the first time in my life I realized that such women existed to please men. We didn't have such houses in Banda. Later on the Japanese brought Indonesian girls from Sulawesi and Java for their brothels and clubs in Ambon. Most were good girls from nurses' training schools, whom the Japanese either by force or by cheating brought to Ambon. Some had been told that they were being recruited for further education in Tokyo, but were instead taken by boat to brothels in eastern Indonesia for the pleasure of the Japanese soldiers and sailors returning from New Guinea.

The day after the incident with Mr. Wolf, not wanting to have to pass Fort Victoria again, I moved to the home of a distant cousin of mine. This cousin was considered a sort of outcast by the Ambon Baadillas because she had married an ordinary barber against the will of her family. That was before the war, and things changed after the arrival of the Japanese. The so-called "good Baadillas" didn't even bother to invite me to stay at their homes, although I had visited them on my arrival to pay my respects. After that I didn't bother to visit them again.

My cousin's husband, Muhasim, was a kind man. While staying with them I helped him in his busy barbershop, which was near the harbor, distributing hot towels to the Japanese customers, brushing up the hair on the floor, and heating water on the electric stove. One day my friend Koon came by. He said I should quit because the job wasn't good enough for me. "Des, it is a coolie job," he said. Before he left, Koon gave me three guilders and two pairs of shorts that he bought at the shop in the market.

I had no heart to quit because the Muhasims were kind folks. Muhasim hadn't even asked me to do the job; I did it voluntarily because Muhasim was too busy just cutting hair. Customers paid only fifteen cents for a haircut, and Muhasim couldn't afford to hire an assistant. Ambon was short of laborers, and people would rather work in the Japanese military camps, the wharves, or the marine offices that paid more than as an assistant in a one-man barbershop.

One day a Japanese naval pilot by the name of Morakame, whom I had met in Neira, came in for a haircut. He had been stationed at Neira a few months ago, with a Japanese seaplane squadron. When he was in Banda, Morakame visited the *rumah besar* several times, and we treated him with coffee and fried bananas. He was surprised to see me in Ambon, especially working as an assistant in a barbershop. Using a Japanese-Indonesian dictionary and some broken English, he tried to ask me why I was there and why I was working in a barbershop. He tried, as best he could, to explain to me that, coming from a good family, I shouldn't work in such a place. I told him that I intended to go to Java for further education, but got stuck in Ambon.

The next day Morakame returned to the barbershop and invited me to go to Halong, the Japanese naval base. There he introduced me to a sergeant who was in charge of the kitchen and the canteen. Morakame told me that if I wanted to, I could work in the canteen as some sort of assistant for fifteen guilders a month plus food. He then treated me for lunch with the other naval pilots. They talked among themselves, and I could hear the word "Banda" mentioned in their conversation, and occasionally the word "Java." They must have been talking about me. I accepted the job at once, and only returned to Ambon town in the afternoon, riding in the Japanese truck.

Morakame was a nice guy, about twenty-five years old, and rather tall for a Japanese. I didn't know what his rank was. He was probably in charge of base supplies, or was some sort of administrative officer in charge of the seaplanes' personnel. He was a big shot all right at the Halong base. The supply sergeant in charge of the canteen and the kitchen always bowed when he came across Morakame.

Why Morakame was good to me I didn't know. He only came to the *rumah besar* two or three times during his stay at Neira. On his first visit my mother gave him some eggs. The next day he returned with a large packet of cream crackers and some sugar, which my mother turned into cracker pudding. She then invited Morakame back for coffee to go with the pudding. We were probably the only Indonesian family in Neira who invited Morakame to our home, and he must have enjoyed it. He told us that he was going to write his wife about our hospitality.

Morakame showed me a photograph taken in Japan of himself in civilian clothes, with his wife and their small son, and one taken in front of a factory, which he said his father owned, and where he worked before he joined the navy. He told me that he came from Tokyo and longed to go back; he was very homesick. He gave me a photograph of himself in his pilot's uniform. I guessed that Morakame was not a professional pilot, but had been conscripted into the naval air force just before the Pacific War broke out.

When he visited my family in Banda, Morakame had taken an interest in the books of Uncle Hatta and Uncle Rir, still kept in the *rumah besar*. He may have thought that those books belonged to my real father, who must have been a learned man. So it was no wonder that he did his best to help me to go to Java for my further education.

When I told the Muhasims about my new job, they told me that I could still stay with them. A Japanese truck picked up the workers for Halong at six in the morning in front of the market, and brought us back at six in the afternoon. My job at the Japanese canteen was rather light, just counting beer bottles in the incoming supply, and removing empty bottles from the tables.

The Japanese crowd visiting the canteen seemed very friendly. Their usual lunch consisted of a bowl of rice with dried vegetables, *taucho*, grilled tuna, and salted ginger. All of these meals were cooked by Ambonese kitchen assistants under the supervision of a fat sergeant and some low-ranking, plump marines. The Japanese joked much of the time with the Ambonese cooks, using some awful Indonesian phrases, such as: *babi bodoh* (stupid pig), *celaka tigabelas* (unlucky thirteen), and *sundal jalan* (street prostitute).

Because of Morakame's kindness and the nice behavior of the Japanese seaplane crowd at Halong, I began to think that not all Japanese were as rough as some of the Masimoto crowd in Neira, or the marine guard who slapped me for not slapping Mr. Wolf. However, in Ambon town every day I saw some Japanese noncoms [noncommissioned officers] slap or beat up lower ranks on the street. Some of the marines were so badly beaten that they had to be carried away by ambulance, or by their friends. Saleh told me that those who were beaten had forgotten to salute or were drunk, but I never saw drunken Japanese fighting among themselves in a bar.

PREPARATIONS TO LEAVE FOR JAVA

After I had worked at Halong for a week, cousin Saleh told me that although his brother Wachi wasn't yet back in Ambon as scheduled, if I wanted to go to Java, I could go on the *Dai Ichi Tora Maru*, the Japanese ship that used to come to Banda in the pre-war days, which was due to leave Ambon in about ten days. He laughed when he told me that the passage would cost thirty guilders, because he knew that I didn't have that much money. I told him that I had only a few guilders, not even ten. He suggested that I go around to people from Banda and our family members in Ambon, and request donations. That evening we went to visit some Bandanese to explain my situation and ask for a donation. We succeeded in getting five guilders.

One Bandanese, who worked for the Minseibu, told me that I had to apply for an exit permit from the naval authorities before I could leave Ambon. He gave me the addresses of Japanese offices where I must collect the "chops" [official approvals conveyed by a personalized stamp], such as the navy territorial commander, the police, the harbor master, and the Minseibu.

The next day cousin Saleh came with me to Halong to explain to Morakame about my chance to go to Java and to ask if he could help me get the necessary chops. Morakame promised that he would do his best, but could only help when he was off duty in three days. So I continued to work at Halong until then. The sergeant paid me five guilders for working ten days at the canteen, and gave me a carton of cigarettes.

With Morakame I went to the office of the territorial commander and got a chop in five minutes. Then we went to other offices, and the police gave me another chop on my application. Now that I had the two most important chops, Morakame said, the rest would be easy. But it took me about a week to get the other five chops, because some of the officers in charge of approving exit permits were hard to find.

Besides helping me to get the two most important chops, Morakame gave me three guilders toward my passage. My main problem in preparing to leave Ambon was to get the balance of seven guilders I needed to pay for my passage. Another Bandanese cousin, by the name of Moem, suggested that I ask Does for a loan. We went to visit Does, but he said he had no money because all his money had been pooled in a new company run by his uncle. The uncle was on his way to Java, also on the *Dai Ichi Tora Maru*, to sell cloves and to bring back badly needed sugar to Ambon. We then went to see an old friend of my father's who had just arrived from Ternate. After lecturing me for half an hour, he gave me five guilders.

The two remaining guilders were still a problem. I was too stubborn to ask the Ambon Baadillas. Even Moem advised me not to because he understood the old feud between the Baadilla clans of Banda and of Ambon. The poorer Bandanese Baadillas were very proud, and would never beg from the Ambonese Baadillas. (Most of the Ambonese Baadillas were the descendants of the two brothers of my grandfather.)

While Moem and I were sitting on the porch of the Muhasim's house, Munir came with a letter for Uncle Hatta. He was surprised to learn that I hadn't yet bought my ticket. I told him that I was short two guilders. He opened his wallet and gave me three guilders. That night I couldn't sleep because I still needed another Japanese chop before I could buy my ticket.

Early the next morning I borrowed Muhasim's bicycle to go to the house of the Japanese officer in charge of civilian transport ships to get the final chop. The stocky Japanese officer, wearing heavy spectacles, looked at me across his breakfast table, looked at my papers, and then looked at his watch. Then he walked to his room to collect his chop, came back to the table, blew on the small round wooden chop with Japanese characters, and stamped my paper. "Go!" he said, "Hurry up or you'll miss the boat."

I rushed back to the Muhasim's house to collect my metal suitcase, to arrange to have Uncle Hatta's books delivered to the ship, and to say goodbye to the Muhasims.

I tied my suitcase behind me on the bike, and told Muhasim that I would leave the bicycle with Moem at the quay. When I arrived at the quay crew members of the *Tenggiri* had already brought Uncle Hatta's books. I rushed aboard the ship, bought my passage in the purser's office, and then gasped for breath when everything was settled.

The *Dai Ichi Tora Maru* departed exactly at eight in the morning on June 21, 1942, for Makassar and Surabaya. That was her last journey to Java. She returned to Ambon a month later, and on the voyage back to Surabaya, was torpedoed by an Allied submarine and sank near South Sulawesi. After that, there were no more Japanese ships carrying civilian passengers between Ambon and Surabaya.

FROM AMBON TO MAKASSAR

The *Dai Ichi Tora Maru* had only four cabins, exclusively for Japanese. Others traveled as deck passengers, at a cost of thirty guilders, the same as the KPM charged in pre-war days. There were seven Indonesian passengers: myself; Does's uncle, an older man of about fifty; an Ambonese clerk who worked for the Minseibu at Ambon, and was being sent to Java to bring about twenty tons of cloves; a Javanese telegrapher from Manokwari; an Ambonese Muslim merchant; and a woman with two children on her way to Makassar to join her husband. The other passengers were about fifteen Japanese workers, who wore green uniforms without military insignia. I later realized that these workers were Koreans. They seemed to stick together and didn't mix with the Japanese; they spoke a language that didn't sound at all like Japanese, and their food was served separately from that of the Japanese. There were also two Japanese interpreters, who had lived in Surabaya for years and spoke fluent Indonesian, and an Ambon-born Japanese who spoke fluent Dutch and had studied at the Jakarta Medical School pre-war. This medical student was on his way to Jakarta to continue his education. He was one of the cabin passengers because his father was a senior official of the Minseibu in Ambon.

We had good weather during the journey to Makassar. However, soon after we passed Selayar Island an alarm was sounded—a submarine periscope was sighted a distance away. It was a Japanese submarine patrolling the Makassar Strait. We entered Makassar harbor, and were told that the ship would stop for a day or two and that we were allowed to go ashore. The once-busy international harbor was rather empty; only a few small Japanese cargo ships were moored along the quays.

In Makassar a distant cousin, Achmat, who had lived there for years, invited me to stay the night with his family, although he was surprised to see me. He stayed in a large house on Pisang Road that belonged to his boss, a Swiss by the name of Weber, who was a well-known person in Makassar, and had been a friend of my grandfather. Weber was probably the only white person not arrested by the Japanese, but that was because Switzerland was a neutral country.

Achmat worked as a rent collector for Weber, who owned many houses. Although Achmat's salary was small, life in Makassar was easy and cheap. Rice was plentiful. In the past South Sulawesi had supplied rice to the outlying regions of eastern Indonesia, but could no longer do so because of lack of transport. The Japanese were using all the ships in their military campaigns.

Life seemed to be normal in Makassar, although at night there was a blackout. Like Ambon, Makassar was under the Kaigun. Dutch civilian prisoners of war were doing repair work on the roads of the city.

At my cousin Achmat's house I met several of his Makassar friends, who were rather anti-Japanese. They said bad things about the Japanese regime, and that they hoped that the Allies would soon chase the Japanese away from Indonesia. This surprised me because in Ambon, nobody dared to say such bad things about the Japanese.

VOYAGE TO SURABAYA

The journey from Makassar to Surabaya was uneventful. Most of the Japanese passengers had disembarked in Makassar, but the two Japanese interpreters remained on the ship. They talked about *Dai Nippon's* victory over the Dutch and the British in the Far East, and told us that everything would be normal again when the Japanese occupied Australia. After that, they said, the United States would seek a peace agreement. The interpreters talked about the East Asia Co-Prosperity Sphere, and how the elder brother, Japan, would lead that movement to prosperity. I listened to them with interest, and in fact, I believed some of their propaganda, such as: Indonesians would now have opportunities to advance themselves in science and technology, Indonesians would be sent to Japan for further education, Indonesians would now have a chance to run their own country with the help of the elder brother.

The first mate of the *Dai Ichi Tora Maru* was a pleasant young Japanese who had sailed with the ship pre-war to Banda and Babo. He told me that at that time he was only third mate, that he knew Neira very well, and that he remembered my face, although I had grown up. I asked him where the ship was at the outbreak of the Pacific War. He told me that he was with the ship at Hainan Island, and only after the fall of the Indies was the ship ordered to return to Makassar to be used as a replacement for the KPM on the Moluccas–Java run. He spoke Indonesian with me, and told me that he would look me up in Surabaya. He asked for my address, but was surprised when I told him that I didn't know where I would stay. Looking a bit puzzled, he asked me, "You mean, you don't have any friends in Surabaya? How do you dare to travel to Java without knowing anybody there? Java is not Banda, you know."

I thought that if I were stranded in Surabaya I might ask the police for help. But the thought of asking the police for assistance worried me because to most of us in Uncle Rir's circle the police in colonial days, or even under the Japanese Occupation, were more enemy than friend. Luckily I did have the street address of two aunties in Surabaya, who had forwarded the letters from Hatta and Sjahrir through cousin Wachi to us in Neira.

ARRIVING IN SURABAYA

Early in the morning on June 30, 1942, we entered Surabaya's Tanjung Perak harbor. The first mate told us that the ship would anchor far away from the wharves and that the civilian passengers must disembark right away because the wharves were a military zone. From our distance I could see clearly the war materials on the quay: howitzers, barrels, and other military items being loaded onto several Japanese cargo ships moored there. It took nearly an hour for us to find a sampan. After much bargaining, the sampan man agreed to take us to the mouth of the river, Kali Mas, for a guilder. The sea and the river around Tanjung Perak looked brown and dirty. I longed for the blue sea of the Moluccas and the clean streams of Banda Besar and Ambon Island.

Still, I was excited to arrive at the well-known city of Surabaya, and even forgot that I had only twenty cents in my pocket. The other four passengers pooled twenty-five cents each to pay for the sampan. I kept my distance, afraid they would ask me for my share of the cost. They didn't; how could they ask a boy to pay twenty cents for the ride?

The Surabaya customs officer inspected my travel papers, boxes, and my unlocked traveling case. "Is that all you have?" he asked, in good Indonesian.

"Yes," I told him.

"What is your address in Surabaya?" he asked.

"Reiners Boulevard," I said, giving the address cousin Saleh had given me of the two Moluccan aunties.

"What number?" he asked.

Gosh, I thought to myself, I didn't even have the house number. In Banda it would have been a silly question; we paid no attention to house numbers, and the postman knew everybody in town. I told the customs man that I didn't know the number.

"How will you find the house? Have you ever been here before?" he asked me.

I shook my head. He looked at me, and shook his head, seeming to pity me. He then shouted, "Wim! Wim! Come here."

A dark-skinned chap appeared, and by looking at him I knew that this Wim was an Ambonese. They talked in mixed Dutch and Indonesian about me, about Reiners Boulevard, and about the two Moluccan aunties.

"Oh, yes," said the Ambonese. "I know the ladies and I know where they live, but I don't remember their house number. Reiners Boulevard is more than four kilometers in length. I will tell you tomorrow, boss."

The customs man nodded and chopped my travel documents.

There I was, in the customs house among strangers. Hungry and too exhausted to move, I sat on my small trunk in a corner of the customs house, praying and hoping for a miracle. A policeman came up to me and asked whether I was an *Indo* (Eurasian). I shook my head.

"Can't you reply with your mouth?" he asked in a nasty tone.

I stood up and showed him my travel papers. He then left me alone.

An elderly lady selling cakes entered the customs house, but the mean policeman chased her out. I took my case and followed her, intending to buy some of her cakes. She stopped near where the *dokar* [horse carts] were waiting. The *dokar* drivers ran toward me when they saw me coming out of the customs house, hoping to carry my case so that I would take their horse cart for a ride to town. I shook my head and walked past them. Coming to the old lady selling the boiled banana and rice cakes, I took two cakes, and asked her, "How much?"

She mentioned the price in Javanese, which I didn't understand, so I gave her a ten-cent coin. She took the money and gave me eight cents change. Gosh, it costs only one cent per cake; how cheap it is in Java, I thought to myself.

I returned to the customs house, it was cooler there than outside, and the area near where the *dokar*s were parked had a terrible smell. After eating the two cakes I felt better. I opened my case, took out my black *songkok*, and put it on my head. At least by wearing a *songkok* no one would think that I was Eurasian. Who would help a stranded Eurasian? I wondered what made the policeman think I was an *Indo*. Did I look Eurasian? Or hadn't he seen a Bandanese before?

It was now about three in the afternoon, and Wim didn't seem to be as busy as before. I approached him and using Ambonese slang asked him how much it would cost to take a *dokar* to Reiners Boulevard. Instead of replying to my question, he asked, "Are you still here?"

When I replied that I was new to Surabaya and didn't know my way around, he said, "Reiners Boulevard is a distance from here, near Wonokromo, not far from the zoo. A *dokar* wouldn't take you that far. It is at the other end of the city. You can probably take a *dokar* to Jambatan Merah, and go from there by tram to Darmo, and then by *becak* [pedicab] to Reiners Boulevard."

Typical of an Ambonese, Wim talked very fast, and I only half remembered what he told me. One of the places he mentioned, Wonokromo, I recognized from geography lessons we had at school as the location of oil wells and refineries in Surabaya. Wim told me that all together it would cost me about forty-five cents to get to Reiners Boulevard. I nearly fainted. The eighteen cents I had in my pocket would not even take me halfway there. All my hope was gone, and tears came to my eyes. I felt so alone in the world.

At last, shyly, I told Wim that I didn't have enough money to go to Reiners Boulevard, and asked whether he could help take me there. "I'm sorry," he said, "I live in Gubeng, far from Wonokromo, and besides I have to work until five o'clock. Also, I don't have much money, and I ride a bicycle to the office. I could carry you on my bike, but what about your case and boxes? It is a long way. Reiners Boulevard is about eight miles from here."

He paused for a moment. Then he said, "Wait. I will call a friend of mine who works in a trading office near here, and will ask him to take you to Reiners Boulevard. He also knows this family where you want to go."

Wim phoned his friend, and jokingly told him that some cargo from Madura had just arrived and if he wanted to buy it, he should come quickly. Ten minutes later a young man arrived, and believe it or not, he was a real cousin of mine, whom I hadn't seen for years. His mother was an older sister of my mother, who had married a Mr. Surati from Surabaya, and with their son, Jim, had gone to East Java about eight years ago. Wim was even more surprised than I. He said, "The world is small isn't it? If I had known you were Jim's cousin, I would have called him earlier."

Jim called me an "*anak dusun*" [village child], and after asking how I came to be in Surabaya, promised to take me to the aunties. But first Jim took me to the firm where he worked as a clerk, earning about twenty guilders per month, fifteen guilders in salary and five as commission. He agreed to keep the two boxes of Hatta's books there until I could leave for Jakarta. The firm belonged to an Ambonese Muslim and specialized in goods from Madura Island. Several young Moluccans working at the office were glad to see me, their newly arrived compatriot, who brought them news from Ambon and Banda. Most of them had studied in Surabaya before the war, but now their parents in the Moluccas couldn't support them. I was probably the first person from the Moluccas they had met since the outbreak of the war. I told them about the situation in Ambon and in Banda since the Japanese landing. It was so nice to meet compatriots in a place where I was a stranger. When Moluccans met each other in Java, we always talked about our beautiful islands, our blue sea filled with many kinds of fish, our lovely birds, our turtle eggs, our *kanari* nuts, our *papeda* (sago porridge) eaten with fish-head soup, our *orambai*, the *foe-foe*, our music that is popular across the archipelago, and our star soccer players who came to Java and become famous. With Jim and his Moluccan co-workers I felt quite at home, and forgot that I had only a few cents in my pocket.

SURABAYA STOPOVER

Late that afternoon Jim brought me to the aunties' house at Reiners Boulevard, in a beautiful residential area, known as Darmo. The trip took about half an hour, and cost Jim about twenty cents for a *becak* and another twenty for two tram tickets. When we arrived at the aunties' house, rather than being glad, they kept pinching me because they thought I had run away from Banda. But when I explained that I had come to Java by myself because the plane that had taken Uncles Hatta and Sjahrir to Java was overweight, they let me stay with them until I could contact the two uncles.

The aunties were surprised to see me. They hadn't seen me in about ten years and remembered me as a small boy. They asked me about my family, some of the Banda folks, and the behavior of the Japanese. They said that Uncle Rir, Hatta, and the three children had visited them in February.

The house at 101 Reiners Boulevard was a nice place with a small pavilion in the compound, where I stayed. The aunties were not rich. One worked in a cake shop in Tunjungan, the city center, and the other stayed at home to take care of the household. They seemed not to notice that I had not enough clothing, and I was too shy to tell them. I still had only three pairs of shorts, three shirts, a sarong, and my black *songkok*.

Because I was out of money, I sent telegrams right away to Uncles Sjahrir and Hatta in Jakarta. From the two aunties and from the Surabaya newspapers, I learned that Uncle Hatta was working with the Japanese and was now a big shot. Jim also told me that he had seen Uncle Hatta riding in a beautiful cream-colored car when he visited Surabaya recently. I didn't know what Uncle Sjahrir was doing, but knowing him and his anti-fascist views, I doubted very much that he would cooperate with the Japanese. And knowing the Japanese attitude toward those who opposed them or refused to work for them, I was worried about Uncle Rir's fate.

While waiting for a reply, and money, from Jakarta, I spent my first week in Surabaya doing little. Occasionally one of the aunties would give me a ten-cent coin for a tram ride to town. Jim came to see me a few times, and took me to the zoo in Wonokromo, and to visit several Bandanese families in Surabaya. While in Surabaya I was very surprised to see Dutch women and children in the town, not having been sent to camps as the Japanese had done in the Moluccas and Sulawesi. The Darmo residential area was full of Dutch families living in large, beautiful houses. Life seemed to be quite normal for many young Dutch women, even though their husbands were in prison camp, and they had taken in Japanese boarders or were the *piara* of high-ranking Japanese officers or officials. Except at Tanjung Perak harbor, very few Kaigun were seen in Surabaya because Java was under the army authorities.

Uncle Hatta was the first to reply; he sent a money order for twelve and a half guilders. The train fare to Jakarta was nine guilders. With the remaining money I bought a pair of shoes and a pair of long trousers for fifty cents each. Jim saw me off at Gubeng station, bringing the two boxes of books he had stored for me in his office.

CHAPTER NINE

ARRIVAL IN JAKARTA

The train journey from Surabaya to Jakarta was interesting, passing through towns in Java that I knew from geography lessons at school. The train was very clean. In the early stages of the Japanese Occupation everything ran normally. There was only one class on the trains, the third class. Japanese passengers, military or civilian, mixed together with Indonesian passengers in the compartments. It was pitch-dark outside, so I couldn't see the countryside of Java until we reached West Java early the next morning. Then I was able to see the rice fields of Priangen and the West Javanese countryside, which I admired very much. It was just like a dream come true to see the water buffaloes swimming in *sawah* [rice paddies] with little kids on their backs.

On July 1, 1942, at about eleven in the morning, I arrived at Jakarta's Gambir Station. No one was there to meet me, so I took a *becak* to Uncle Hatta's house at Jalan Diponegoro 57 (which was Oranje Boulevard under the Dutch). By bargaining, I was able to pay just *setalen* (twenty-five cents) for the fare. When I arrived at the house it was clear that Uncle Hatta was ready for his *sholat Jumat* [Friday prayers]. He shook my hand and praised me for traveling such a long distance in war time. He was very happy to see his important books that I had brought with me. I'd had an opportunity to peep at those books, and they included one entitled *Cain and Abel*, a book by Eddy du Perron,[1] and several philosophy books by Bertrand Russell, Plato, and Paul Deussen, which were heavy for the arms to carry as well as for the brain.

Longing to see my siblings and Uncle Rir, I very much hoped to see them soon. Uncle Hatta promised that we would go to Uncle Rir's that afternoon. We went in Uncle Hatta's cream-colored DeSoto, driven by his chauffeur, Angku Razak, a *jago silat* [martial-arts expert] who was also Minangkabau. Uncle Rir then lived at number 19 Jalan Latuharhari [formerly Jalan Dambrink]. We hadn't given advance notice of our visit, so the siblings and Uncle Rir were surprised and happy to see us. Also living there were Sulaiman, Uncle Rir's younger brother; Chairil Anwar (who I later learned was a famous young poet) and his mother, Saleha, who stayed in the guest pavilion. Sulaiman had his own room, while little Ali stayed in one room with Uncle Rir. Mimi and Lily also had one room. It had been planned that I would share a room with Sulaiman, but Uncle Hatta said, "For now, Des can stay with me." He had a large house, and only his niece, the daughter of his older sister, was staying with him.

Everyone had questions about the situation in Banda, my family, and the friends who had been left behind. They also asked about the Japanese planes that had

---

[1] Born in the Netherlands Indies in 1899, du Perron was an important literary figure in the Netherlands before his return to the Indies in 1936. There he became a mentor to a number of young Indonesian intellectuals, and introduced them to the journal *Kritiek en Opbouw*, where he himself worked. Rudolf Mrázek, *Sjahrir: Politics and Exile in Indonesia* (Ithaca, NY: Cornell Southeast Asia Program, 1994), pp. 162–63.

chased the Catalina that took them to Java, and about Uncle Hatta's books and effects that were still in Banda. I convinced them that everything was safe, and that the remaining books were in good hands at the *rumah besar*. For more than two hours the uncles asked me questions about the situation in Banda and the other Moluccan islands. They also asked about the three Minangkabau students, Munir, Bachtul Nazar, and Daman, and I explained everything. I also told them the story of my journey, and how I managed to scrape together the money to pay for the trip. We ate Bandanese food, grilled fish, and *ulang-ulang* (raw vegetables with vinegar-fish-peanut sauce; peanuts were substituted for *kanari* nuts, because *kanari* nuts were not obtainable in Java during the war). Uncle Hatta liked Bandanese food; he loved good food.

Uncle Hatta asked me what school I wanted to attend. When I said I would like to attend an engineering school, he laughed. "Why do you Bandanese want to study engineering? You don't even have electricity in Banda." We all laughed, Uncle Rir most loudly. Uncle Hatta left before I did, because I wanted to spend more time with Lily and Mimi. That afternoon, toward *maghrib* [sunset prayer], I borrowed Mimi's bicycle to return to Uncle Hatta's house.

Within a few days Uncle Rir suggested that I move to his house, explaining that his younger brother, Sulaiman, had moved and there was now space for me. My first week in Jakarta was spent visiting Bandanese friends and acquaintances, and getting myself acquainted with the large town of Jakarta. Often Lily or Ibu Saleha sent me to the shops or the market to buy kitchen supplies.

Sjahrir's small cozy house faced the Ciliwung River on one side, and the railway track of the Manggarai–Tanah Abang line on the other. Only an occasional passing train disturbed the quiet. The house belonged to a Dutch lady, who was interned in the Salemba camp with other Dutch women. Although most of the Dutch-owned houses were confiscated by the Japanese authorities, this one was skipped over. Somehow the owner managed to come out of the camp once a month to collect her sixty guilders rent, and always chatted with Uncle Rir when she did so. The rent was quite cheap, especially for a fully furnished house, probably because Uncle Rir promised the Dutch lady that he would look after the house and the furniture as if they were his own.

The house also had a garage, where Chairil Anwar was supposed to stay. However, the Dutch owner had stored two large liftvans [large wooden crates used for shipping] inside the garage, and they were too heavy to move. In any case, there was no space inside the house to put them.

We had only one servant at the house, a laundress. Ibu Saleha and Lily did the cooking. My job was to take little Ali to the kindergarten at seven in the morning, using Lily's bicycle, and then to do some marketing for the household.

SCHOOL

The weekend after I arrived in Jakarta Uncle Hatta invited his nephew Amar to his house. Amar brought application forms for admission to a technical school, and we discussed which courses we were interested in. Amar chose mechanical engineering, while I chose electrical and radio. Uncle Hatta then instructed us both to enter the IVEVO (Instituut Voor Electro Vak Onderwijs), the Institute for Electro-Science, located on Jalan Salemba. It was considered the best technical school in Jakarta and followed the German system. It had six months per semester, while other schools had one opportunity per year to be promoted to a higher class. School began at 7:30 in the morning, and ended precisely at 1:30 in the afternoon.

As the IVEVO was a private school which received no Japanese government subsidy, the school was very expensive: seven guilders and fifty cents per month, plus fifty cents for text books. Uncle Hatta paid my school fees because Uncle Rir said that he was too poor to spend that much money for my education. Every month I went to collect my eight guilders allowance from Uncle Hatta, who also gave us money when we needed it to buy school necessities, such as school uniforms, tools, and so forth.

We had to wear school uniforms even when clothing materials were already hard to get. The school uniform was white, with the school logo on the shirt pocket. One good thing about the school regulations was that we weren't required to shave our heads, as children in the Japanese government-run schools had to do. And instead of wearing Japanese school caps, we wore black berets with a red lining, copied from the German polytechnic attended by one of the teachers, Engineer Ho.

The school was run by Drs. Tjoa, who had been a college friend of Hatta's in Rotterdam. The teachers were good; most were academicians who taught at the school to avoid working for the Japanese. Among them were Engineer Ho, who had qualified at a German university before the war; Engineer Tung, who had studied at the Bandung Institute of Technology (as did Sukarno); Engineer Parlindungan, also from the Bandung Institute of Technology; and Mr. Samudjo, a former officer in the KNIL. I knew several of the teachers: Mr. Abubakar, who had been the machinist on a KPM ship that often came to Banda; Mr. Ko, the drawing teacher, from Ambon; Mr. Adam, the former first mate on the *Kapal Putih*, before the war; Engineer Suhud, who later became minister of industry during the New Order. (Mr. Adam was the first Indonesian to attain the rank of first mate; he actually had a captain's qualifications, but was not given a chance to become one, probably because he was Indonesian, not Dutch.) The teachers also included Engineer Tambunan and Mr. Rinjani, the teacher for applied electronics. All the teachers generally kept quiet that they didn't want to work with the Japanese.

The school had five different sections: Mechanical Engineering, Electrical Engineering, Radio Engineering, Architecture, and Telegraphy. All the first-year students followed the same course, with a lot of math, drafting, and practical workshop experience. The lessons were in Indonesian, with some Dutch technical terms mixed in. We also studied English, German, bookkeeping, and—of course—Japanese. Although the Japanese authorities banned the use of English, somehow our school continued to teach it without the knowledge of the Japanese. If I remember correctly, the Japanese only allowed the telegraphy section to continue teaching English—because the Japanese News Service, *Domei*, badly needed English-speaking radio telegraphers.

The curriculum at the technical school was quite substantive, unlike that at the Japanese government-run schools, which was filled mostly with gymnastics, military exercises, *Nippon-go* (Japanese language), and Japanese songs. We started every day with *taiso* (gymnastics), which were accompanied by Japanese music and instruction that were broadcast from Jakarta radio and relayed to all the other broadcasting stations in Java. Our teachers stuffed us with math, chemistry, science, two hours a week of English, and only an hour a week of *Nippon-go*. Besides these lessons, twice a week we had workshop training, such as blacksmithing.

I worked hard at school, but was weak in Japanese grammar. Uncle Rir occasionally helped me with math, but if he spotted me learning *Nippon-go* he would comment, "Why don't you learn English instead? It is more useful than Japanese. The Japanese won't be here long, and if you know English we might need you when the Americans come."

I also realized that Uncle Rir wasn't so interested in my schooling. Possibly this was because the Japanese always picked graduates from technical schools to use in their *Dai Toa Senso* (Great War) against the Allies.

We had a school band consisting of wind instruments, such as trumpets and clarinets, and many drums. Just to show the Japanese that we were as active in military exercises as their schools, every Saturday afternoon our school organized a ten-mile marching parade around the main roads of Jakarta. The parade, headed by the school band playing march music and students marching in their white uniforms and black berets, became a famous sight during the somber years of the Japanese Occupation. "Here comes the IVEVO parade!" people would shout when they heard our band.

The atmosphere at the school was rather pro-Western, which the Japanese termed in their propaganda *"ke-barat-baratan"* ("Westernisms," such as women wearing shorts or using lipstick, speaking Dutch at home, Western dancing, listening to jazz). The teachers and students had various levels of anti-Japanese feelings. For example, Drs. Tjoa had a Eurasian wife, and he obviously wanted the war to end with the Allies as victors. Samudjo, my math teacher, had been a first lieutenant in the KNIL, and was obviously anti-Japanese. Engineer Ho was a qualified aeronautical engineer who earned over five hundred guilders per month before the Japanese arrival, but who now earned only one hundred and fifty guilders and wasn't sure about his future.

One of the teachers was Mr. M. R. Dajoh, who taught Indonesian and was a self-styled poet.[2] He was rather pro-Japanese at the beginning, but later on realized that the Japanese were no better than the Dutch, and he slowly began to abandon his pro-East Asia Co-Prosperity Sphere lectures and concentrated more on Indonesian grammar. When I told Chairil Anwar that my Indonesian language teacher was a certain Mr. Dajoh, he laughed and said, "Oh! That Celebes legend writer!"

During the Indonesian language lessons Dajoh's favorite subject was to tell us how he had "suffered" during the Dutch colonial time because of his "activities" in the *pergerakan* [nationalist movement]. Once I interrupted him and asked, "Sir, were you exiled to Boven Digul?" He shook his head, but said that most of his friends had been. Later, when Dajoh found out that my school fees were paid by Uncle Hatta and that he was my guardian, he never again mentioned anything about his difficulties during the Dutch colonial period. Dajoh was never considered a real *pergerakan* chap, although he joined some sort of Indonesian writers' club. Later, in 1952, Dajoh became an active member of the Communist-inspired peace movement, and traveled to Moscow, Prague, London, etc., to attend peace meetings.

My drawing teacher, Mr. Ko, at once recognized me as coming from the Baadilla stock of Banda. He knew most of the Ambon and Banda Baadillas, including my family, but was a bit surprised to learn that Hatta was my guardian. I didn't explain much to him, but with Mr. Ko around, I felt at home at school. The Kos, now completely assimilated, were descendants of the first Chinese settlers in Ambon,

---

[2] A poet and writer from Minahasa, North Sulawesi, and a contributor to *Pudjangga Baru*.

about three hundred years ago. Mr. Ko spoke to me in Bandanese slang, as most Ambonese try to do when they meet Bandanese outside Banda. They do it as a sort of teasing—as though the Ambonese slang sounds much better and more superior to ours. Usually in such encounters, the Bandanese would react by answering with funny Ambonese expressions, such as, *"Ees, Tuang Ala! Ada papeda dingin"* (Oh, my God! Here is cold sago porridge). You see, the Ambonese are very fond of hot sago porridge, eaten with fish soup and chili-vinegar sauce. Cold *papeda* is usually used as a paste to stick papers together. Giving someone cold *papeda* is an insult, as if you were giving the person some sticky gum to chew. The expression *papeda dingin* was used by the Bandanese to tease talkative Ambonese. *Papeda* is not a Bandanese dish, and we consider it cheap stuff, though some of us love it. Because Bandanese are proud people, we would only eat *papeda* in the kitchen where we could not be seen by others.

WELCOMING SUKARNO

On July 7, 1942, I borrowed Mimi's bicycle and began school. That same morning Uncle Hatta sent a letter to the director of the school, his friend Drs. Tjoa, to ask that the school's pupils participate in welcoming Bung Karno, as Sukarno was called informally,[3] who would soon arrive from Palembang after several years in exile. So on July 11, together with the other students, I took a tram to Stasion Kota, and then continued on foot to Pasar Ikan. We all gathered at the *Setinjau Laut* restaurant, where hundreds of people were waiting for Bung Karno, among them Shimizu, the chief of propaganda for the Japanese military regime, and Lieutenant General Imamura, the first Japanese commander in chief on Java. Among the various prominent Indonesian nationalists who attended were Mr. Samsoedin, Ki Hadjar Dewantoro, Kiai Haji Mansur, Sukarni, Hanafi, Johan Sjahruzah, Mohammad Yamin, and many *rakyat Betawi* [Jakarta people].[4]

Finally the person for whom we were all waiting arrived, in a motor boat, with his wife, Inggit, and several other ladies. Uncle Hatta gave the first speech to welcome Bung Karno, saying in essence that the Indonesian people had been yearning for Bung Karno, who had been exiled by the Dutch for about ten years. The return of Bung Karno to Jakarta, according to Hatta, was at the right moment, when the Dutch had been removed from the land of Indonesia by the Japanese military. It

---

[3] On the use of "bung," a contraction of the Javanese word for older brother, see Kahin, *Nationalism and Revolution*, pp.138–39.

[4] Mr. Samsoedin had been a founder and leader of the pre-war cooperating nationalist party Parindra; Ki Hadjar Dewantoro was famous for having founded the nationalist Taman Siswa school system, which provided an alternative to both the limited Dutch system and Islamic schools; Kiai Haji Mansur was a prominent leader of the modernist Islamic organization, Muhammadiyah; Sukarni had been active in a number of nationalist youth organizations, and played a prominent role during the Japanese Occupation; Hanafi had been a protégé of Sukarno during the latter's exile in South Sumatra; Johan Sjahruzah was a nephew of Sjahrir; and Mohammad Yamin had been active in a number of nationalist organizations in the 1930s, and after internal rivalries, was a founder of Gerindo, which had a leftist and internationalist orientation. For information on Indonesian nationalists, see Kahin, *Nationalism and Revolution*, passim, and J. D. Legge, *Intellectuals and Nationalism in Indonesia: A Study of the Following Recruited by Sutan Sjahrir in Occupation Jakarta* (Ithaca, New York: Cornell Modern Indonesia Project, 1988). The variety of people demonstrating support for Sukarno is an indication of his broad acceptance as the leading Indonesian nationalist.

is to be hoped, Hatta continued, that by working together with the Japanese, we will greet a better future for Indonesia.

Then Bung Karno spoke in a very clear, firm voice, and presented a handsome appearance. He sounded quite revolutionary when he said "*Asia Raya tidak bisa raya kalau Indonesia belum raya*" [Greater Asia cannot be great if Indonesia is not yet great].

The Japanese propaganda chief, Shimizu, spoke next, acknowledging Bung Karno's statement that Indonesia must thank Japan for its service in ousting the Dutch from Indonesian soil. In essence, he said, Indonesia owed a debt of honor to Japan, and must listen to the words of Japan as an elder brother.

The ceremony was accompanied by songs that were pro-Asia Raya Japan. When it concluded, Bung Karno was given a luxurious dark-blue sedan. Later he was given a house at Pegangsaan Timur 56 (now the Proclamation Building).

Uncle Rir didn't attend the ceremony to welcome Bung Karno. This was deliberate because Uncle Rir's political position from the beginning was that he was not prepared to work together with the Japanese. Uncle Rir also didn't want to appear in public if Japanese were present. In reality, neither Bung Karno nor Bung Hatta wanted to be made "*kuda penarik kereta Jepang*" [a horse drawing the Japanese cart].

Soon after Sukarno's return, he, Hatta, and Sjahrir met to discuss future steps. From the start Hatta had agreed to work with the Japanese, so it was not possible for him to withdraw, or disappear, as he was automatically being watched by the Japanese. It was agreed that for the time being Sukarno and Hatta would cooperate with the Japanese, while Sjahrir and his friends, who were anti-fascist democrats, would be active in the underground,[5] with the goal of resurrecting the nationalist movement. Sukarno and Hatta agreed to keep Sjahrir's name secret from the Japanese, and from the group of Indonesians who were working with the Japanese.

Uncle Hatta headed the Advisory Office of the Japanese military government, located at the corner of Pegangsaan Timur and Jalan Diponegoro. Among the officials in the Advisory Office were Professor Supomo, an adviser to the Justice Department;[6] Engineer Surachman,[7] and Mr. Margono [the father of Professor Soemitro Djojohadikusumo].[8] The secretary was Mr. Karim Pringgodigdo, who had been a member of the organization of students from the Indies studying in the Netherlands, Perhimpunan Indonesia [Indonesian Union], at the same time as Hatta and Sjahrir. Later, Johan Sjahruzah, Sjahrir's nephew, and several people who were active in the underground movement also joined the Advisory Office. Colonel Miyoshi, from the Gunseikanbu, the Japanese military administration, became the liaison between Hatta and the Japanese military.

---

[5] As noted in the introduction, the "underground" did not carry out active resistance to the Japanese Occupation, but it was illegal, and therefore dangerous to some extent. The members shared news of the progress of the war, and actively sought young cadre in preparation for eventual independence.

[6] A graduate of the Jakarta Law Faculty and Leiden University, Professor Supomo had been a judge and worked in the Justice Department during the colonial period.

[7] Surachman Tjokroadisoerjo's engineering degree was from the Technical College in Delft. He had worked in economic offices of the colonial government and was not active in politics.

[8] Margono Djojohadikusumo was known as a protégé of Hatta's, and later played a role in financing the Revolution. Professor Soemitro was a leading economist in independent Indonesia.

JAPANESE POLICIES

On the morning that Bung Karno returned, the Japanese announced the change of the calendar from Christian to Japanese years; thus, 1942 became 2602.

Following the Dutch surrender to Japanese troops, it appeared that the repressive strategy of the Dutch through their PID [Politieke Inlichting Dienst— Political Intelligence Service] was copied by the Japanese through their Kenpeitai. Their agents represented a frightening threat to the community of freedom fighters. Most feared were the accomplices of the Japanese, that is the Kenpeiho, Indonesians who had become spies for the Japanese regime and worked for their interests.

Japanese policies were based on their experience in Korea and several areas under their control in China, namely the dangerous potential of an underground movement. Japan created a body to analyze all movements in the community, hoping to be able to activate and combine all the strength of the Indonesian people for its own interests. To that end Japan established the "Gerakan Tiga-A" (Triple-A Movement) on April 29, 1942,[9] with Mr. Samsoedin, the Parindra man, as its head. The Triple-A Movement only existed in the urban areas, because it was feared that it might be used by the peasants to rebel as a result of their suffering caused by the exploitation carried out by the Japanese.

LIFE IN JAKARTA

My first month in Java changed me from a village boy—or rather an island boy— to a modern city boy. The process was not so easy, especially when the educated group surrounding me mostly spoke Dutch. Even after the Japanese government banned the use of Dutch, the so-called middle-class Indonesians still conversed in it, only changing into Indonesian if a Japanese were present. Telephone conversations had to be in Indonesian or the connection would be cut off, as sometimes happened when in the heat of a conversation the speaker would suddenly switch to Dutch. My Indonesian did not improve much because we either spoke Bandanese Indonesian or Dutch at home. Only at school was I able to use standard Indonesian, although most of the boys, except in the class room, preferred to speak Dutch or mixed Dutch/Indonesian. The boys at school came from many parts of Indonesia, but mostly from West Java. Thus, I came to realize that people living in West Java were not called Javanese, but Sundanese, and that their language is different from Javanese. We had boys from Tapanuli, in northern Sumatra (which we had never heard of in Banda); Padang, in West Sumatra; Aceh (which we had heard of because of their heroic war against the Dutch); Sunda; Java; a few boys from Ambon; some Eurasians; and Indonesian Chinese.

Mimi studied at the Japanese-government high school, where she was registered as Mimi Sjahrir. One day a Japanese officer interviewed her about her father, Sjahrir, and what he did at home and why he didn't work in a Japanese office. When Mimi finished her third form, Uncle Rir told her to quit school. He didn't explain to Mimi what it was all about, but he told her that he would teach her at home. In any case, Mimi was glad to be free from being taught the *odori* (Japanese dancing), marching several times a week, and mending the socks and uniforms of Japanese soldiers.

---

[9] "Japan the Leader of Asia, Japan the Protector of Asia, and Japan the Light of Asia"; Kahin, *Nationalism and Revolution*, p. 103.

VISITS TO UNCLE TJIP

One rainy afternoon soon after my arrival, Uncle Hatta took Uncle Rir and me in his beautiful car to visit Uncle Tjipto Mangunkusumo in Jatinegara, a satellite town of Jakarta. The Mangunkusumos were surprised to see me. Uncle Tjip recognized me at once and embraced me. In Dutch, with his heavy Javanese accent, he asked "Duwes (as he pronounced Des), how is your family, and how is Banda?"

Uncle Tjip looked rather old and sick, and still smelled of tobacco. He still wore a white suit with a high-collared jacket. Auntie Mie was wearing a sarong and white *kebaya* and looked more gray. The boys, Donald and Louis, came out to greet us; I was glad to see them again. They brought me to their study and showed me their small boats and ships, and the small steam engines that Donald made himself. Louis still had asthma, but was as cheerful as ever.

The three older gentlemen sat on the large veranda in front of the house talking politics, until it began to rain heavily. Then they moved from the front veranda to the sitting room to sip tea. Auntie Mie came into the study to ask me about Banda, which she missed very much. She was worried about the food conditions on the island, especially after the KPM ships no longer existed. I told her that the Bandanese people hadn't tasted rice since the Japanese arrived, but that we fed ourselves with sago and tapioca.

Uncle Tjip's house was quite large, but not as large as his residence in Neira. Donald and Louis told me that they had many *rambutan* trees in their yard, but that the fruit wasn't yet ripe. They still remembered my fruit-stealing ventures in Neira, where they occasionally joined me, and told me that I must come often to visit and stay the night with them so that we could organize a fruit-stealing gang. They said that Jatinegara was full of unprotected fruit trees in the gardens of the Dutch residences because the Dutch male adults had been arrested.

One other Sunday morning we went by *dokar* with Uncle Rir to visit Uncle Tjip. When we arrived, we saw Uncle Hatta and another gentleman whom I recognized as Sukarno. We were introduced to him as "*anak-anak Banda*" [the children from Banda]. Sukarno laughed and said to Uncle Rir, "I didn't know you had such big children."

That was the first time I came face-to-face with Bung Karno. We children went to the garden to enjoy the *rambutan*s, while the four politicians—Uncle Hatta, Sukarno, Uncle Rir, and Uncle Tjip—talked (in Dutch) about politics, the war, and things concerning the nationalist movement. Auntie Mie asked me to bring a basket of *rambutan*s to the gentlemen, and Uncle Hatta asked me to bring some knives and water so they could cut the fruit and clean their fingers. When I tried to pass the jug of water around to the four gentlemen, Uncle Hatta told me to leave the jug on the table and to go back to the garden. This was a typical Hatta attitude: keeping young people away from his neighborhood when he was discussing politics and other important things.

Uncle Hatta and Bung Karno left the house before lunchtime, but Uncle Rir and we children stayed to lunch with the Mangunkusumos. One of Uncle Tjip's admirer's, Lim Kun Hian, who lived in Glodok, Jakarta's Chinatown, not far from Pasar Ikan, had sent a huge tuna, which Auntie Mie, a vegetarian (as were Donald and Louis), prepared the Bandanese way with some advice from Lily. Uncle Tjip, a non-vegetarian, took his lunch together with us on the front verandah, but he ate very little and didn't seem to enjoy the food at all. He lit his pipe and watched us eat. Pointing his pipe at me, he said, "No wonder Duwes grows so fast—he eats like a horse."

After smoking his pipe for a moment, he turned to me again and said, "Duwes, you better not go to a Japanese school. They won't teach you anything except marching with a wooden gun, and *Nippon-go*. You would do better to stay with us and let Donald and Louis teach you how to build engines."

Auntie Mie interrupted, and said, "It is not a Japanese school he is going to. It was formerly a Dutch technical school and the teachers are all qualified Indonesian and Indonesian–Chinese engineers who do not want to work for the Japanese. Instead they work as teachers. This is a privately run polytechnic."

Auntie Mie knew of this school because at one time she tried to send Donald to study there, but Uncle Tjip objected because of his anti-Japanese attitude. The Japanese authorities knew of his attitude, but since he was a national leader and one of the pioneers of the Indonesian nationalist movement, they were a bit reluctant to arrest him. The Japanese also knew that Uncle Tjip was a sick man and probably would not live long.

While we were sitting on the front verandah after lunch under the shadow of huge *rambutan* trees and chit-chatting about Banda, suddenly Uncle Tjip had difficulty breathing. Donald rushed into the house and came back with a syringe of adrenaline from the medicine cupboard and injected it into Uncle Tjip's back. Uncle Tjip moved to his rattan arm chair, and lay there quietly. Uncle Rir pulled his chair to sit near him. We children went inside the house. Auntie Mie came to bring us tea, and said that Uncle Tjip was quite ill and often had this kind of an attack especially after they moved to Polonia. "This house is too damp," she said.

Before we left the Mangunkusumos, Uncle Rir and Auntie Mie discussed the possibility of moving, and Uncle Rir suggested finding a house in the Menteng residential area. However, Auntie Mie preferred to stay in the Jatinegara area where Uncle Tjip's sister, Mrs. Ranti, also lived, and not far from his younger brother, Sujitno, known to us as the kind Uncle Jit, who lived in Manggarai. In the late afternoon we returned to Jalan Latuharhari by *dokar* (there were no taxis during the Japanese Occupation), with little Ali sitting near the coachman. The ride cost seventy-five cents.

Early the next morning Auntie Mie came by *dokar* to Jalan Latuharhari. She was alone and looked very pale. She told Uncle Rir that Donald had been beaten up by the guard of the dormitory of the Seinan-Korenso, Japanese-trained Indonesian youth, a sort of paramilitary fascist youth. The dormitory was in Polonia, near Uncle Tjip's residence, and had a sentry with a wooden rifle in front. Donald happened to cycle past the guardhouse without bowing to the Japanese-trained Indonesian youth standing there. Acting like the Japanese guards, the fascist youth occasionally beat up Eurasian and Dutch youths who happened to pass in front of their dormitory without acknowledging them. Donald looked Eurasian, and being worried about his father's illness, forgot to get off his bicycle when passing the guardhouse. So the fascist youth guard beat him up with a wooden rifle.

Arriving home with a swollen face and torn clothing, Donald told the story to Auntie Mie and Uncle Tjip, who were sitting on the front verandah. Uncle Tjip was so annoyed that he tried to get up with the intention of lodging a forceful protest to the Japanese, through Sukarno or Hatta, but he was too weak and collapsed on the floor. He was very sick when Auntie Mie, Uncle Rir, and I reached Polonia. Donald had already injected Uncle Tjip with a dose of adrenaline. He was too weak to talk, but from his face I could see that he was very angry. Uncle Rir told Uncle Hatta about the behavior of the Seinan-Korenso the evening of the incident, but I don't think Uncle Hatta could do anything about it.

That same day the Tjiptos decided to move to another house away from the Seinan-Korenso. While Uncle Rir stayed with Uncle Tjip, Auntie Mie, escorted by Louis and me, went house-hunting in the Jatinegara area. Luckily we found a house in Rohobot Road, situated a short distance from the Rantis, Uncle Tjip's sister. The new house was smaller than the Polonia house, a sort of pavilion-type house, but seemed not to be as damp. In January 1943 the Mangunkusumos moved to the new address.

CHAPTER TEN

SJAHRIR AND THE UNDERGROUND

The underground group was led by educated people. The members consisted of *pejuang* [freedom fighters] who had been fighting since the Dutch era, and youngsters who had just begun to be involved in the struggle during the Japanese Occupation. These youngsters were not only those who had been taught by established nationalist leaders, but many whose concept of struggle was formed by their situation, or they had naturally learned it by themselves, and only later joined with a group, or even stayed independent. For all these people, the principal goal remained the independence of Indonesia, and the principal enemy was Dutch colonialism and Japanese militarism.

Several days after the ceremony at Pasar Ikan to welcome Sukarno, a meeting was held at Uncle Rir's house to discuss the current situation. Those who attended were the core of his underground group, although some worked as officials in the Japanese administration. Several members of the underground were friends of Sjahrir from Bandung, and many of these had been members of the organization he and Hatta founded on their return from the Netherlands in 1931 and 1932, Pendidikan Nasional Indonesia [Indonesian National Education].[1] Sjahrir's nephew, Johan Sjahruzah, was a key member of the underground and had links with many nationalist groups.[2] One of those he brought into contact with Sjahrir's underground was Maruto Nitimihardjo, a follower of the nationalist-communist Tan Malaka,[3]

---

[1] Often referred to as PNI-Baru (the new PNI), to distinguish it from the Partai Nasional Indonesia, founded by Sukarno in 1927. Members Des Alwi has identified include Hamdani from Bandung and Mr. Sastra from Garut. Prominent among them was Sugondo Djojopoespito, who was a student leader in Bandung with Sjahrir in the 1920s, and active in the Taman Siswa nationalist school movement; he was also chairman of the 1928 Youth Congress, which helped to define the nationalist movement as Indonesian by pledging to support *"satu bangsa, satu bahasa, satu tanah air"* (one people, one language, one homeland). During the Japanese Occupation he worked at the department of justice. Mr. Wijono, from Yogya, was a founder of the Barisan Tani Indonesia (Indonesian Peasants' League), and was a member of the Pendidikan in Malang, East Java. Mr. Kartamuhari was active in the cooperatives movement around Ciribon. Also from the Ciribon area were Dr. Sudarsono, a 1938 graduate of the Medical Faculty in Jakarta, who had been involved in nationalist youth organizations in the 1920s and 1930s, and his close friend, Dr. Toha Ronodipuro, who served as chairman of the general hospital there during the Occupation. Later he served as rector of Airlangga University in Surabaya, East Java.

[2] Sjahruzah was important in his own right, and was active in organizing labor unions as well as nurturing the underground network during the Occupation. He was actually close in age to Sjahrir, his uncle, as his mother was the daughter of Sjahrir's father's first wife, while Sjahrir was the son of the third wife. Legge, *Intellectuals*, pp. 60–65; and Mrazek, *Sjahrir*, pp. 242–43.

[3] Also from West Sumatra; in the 1920s, Tan Malaka was a member of the Dutch Communist Party and the Comintern (Communist International) representative in Southeast Asia. He advocated an alliance of Islam, nationalism, and communism. Quiescent during the Japanese Occupation, he became a leading critic of the policies of Sukarno, Hatta, and Sjahrir during the Revolution. For an assessment of Tan Malaka, and his role during the Revolution, see Benedict

Sjahrir's great rival. Mr. Amir Hamzah Sirigar[4] also had ties outside Sjahrir's circle, in this case to the prominent nationalist Amir Sjarifuddin,[5] who was incarcerated by the Japanese during the Occupation. Those who held official positions during the Japanese Occupation included Mr. Ali Budiardjo,[6] who had a senior position in the Department of Justice, and Mr. Takdir Alisjahbana,[7] who headed the Indonesian Language Commission, which, in addition to its formal function, served as a center for discussion among many nationalist youth. Another member of the group, Mr. Sujitno Mangunkusumo, a younger brother of Dr. Tjipto, worked in the office headed by Hatta.

We usually had visitors the whole day long, and some often invited themselves for lunch. They were usually Uncle Rir's friends, "*orang-orang pergerakan*" [people from the nationalist movement]. We always had visitors on Saturday afternoons, mostly Uncle Rir's politician friends and intellectuals.[8] Sjahrir's nephew Johan Sjahruzah was a frequent visitor. Once in a while Uncle Hatta came to the house, usually in the evening.

Sometimes we didn't see Uncle Rir for days, and automatically the visitors ceased coming. However, as soon as he returned so did the *pergerakan* chaps. Uncle

---

R. O'G. Anderson, *Java in a Time of Revolution: Occupation and Resistance, 1944–1946* (Ithaca, NY: Cornell University Press, 1972), passim.

[4] Described as a brilliant student at the Law Faculty in Jakarta, Amir Hamzah was a member of the Indonesian Students' Union before the war and, during the Occupation, of the study club to which many Medical Faculty students belonged. A poet and writer, he was a central figure in the group associated with the *Pudjangga Baru*, an important literary journal in the 1930s and early 1940s. Some accounts report that Amir Hamzah died of tuberculosis in 1943. Others say he died in 1946 during the killing of members of the aristocracy in an uprising in North Sumatra, often called a social revolution. Mrazek, *Sjahrir*, pp. 229–31; and Heather Sutherland, "Pudjangga Baru: Aspects of Indonesian Intellectual Life in the 1930s," *Indonesia* 6 (October 1968): 122–23.

[5] Amir Sjarifuddin studied in the Netherlands and graduated from the Jakarta Law Faculty. He was active in leftist nationalist organizations in the 1930s, and led the largest anti-Japanese movement at the start of the Japanese Occupation (with the support of van der Plas, an anti-Fascist Dutch colonial official). Sjarifuddin was arrested in early 1943, and was saved from execution when Sukarno intervened. He was a co-founder with Sjahrir of the Partai Sosialis (Socialist Party) in 1945, and served as deputy prime minister and defense minister before being appointed prime minister in July 1947. He broke with Sjahrir and the Sukarno/Hatta government in 1948, joined with the reincarnated Indonesian Communist Party and the Madiun revolt against the government in September 1948, and was executed by government troops in October 1948.

[6] A graduate of the Jakarta Law Faculty, he held one of the highest positions in the colonial civil service of any "native." He became a member of Sjahrir's Partai Sosialis Indonesia when it was founded during the Revolution.

[7] The leading figure in Indonesian language and literature, he was one of the founders of *Pudjangga Baru* (New Writer), the journal, written in Indonesian, that promoted cultural nationalism and was key to the development of Indonesian as the national language and as "a tool for sophisticated inellectual and technical usage." Robert Cribb and Audrey Kahin, eds. *Historical Dictionary of Indonesia*, 2d ed. (Lanham, MD: Scarecrow Press, Inc., 2004), p. 14; and Sutherland, *Pudjangga Baru*.

[8] Frequent visitors included the lawyers Ali Budiardjo and Sugondo Djojopoespito, who worked at the department of justice during the Japanese Occupation; Soemitro Reksodipuro, also a Law Faculty graduate, who was an official of the education bureau during the Occupation; and Andi Zainul Abidin, of Makassar, another graduate of the Law Faculty, who was a member of a study group with Amir Sjarifuddin.

Rir always returned with a small case. He told us that he was doing business buying and selling rice in West Java. But I didn't notice anything that concerned rice dealing.

I began to realize the Uncle Rir was up to something. One night I discovered him using headphones to listen to an unregistered and unsealed radio. During the Japanese Occupation all radios had to be registered and sealed, and the short-wave bands were cut off. Of course, I was interested, and knelt beside Uncle Rir, who put the headphones on my ears. The broadcast was in English, from Radio Australia, playing some Western music. Uncle Rir had already listened to the news, which he regularly followed on the BBC and other foreign broadcasts to learn about the progress of the war. He told me that I should keep to myself what he was doing. He warned me that if the Japanese came to know about it, he might be considered a spy and could be sentenced to death.

I was given the task of putting up the antenna and tuning that illegal radio. First I took apart the radio down to the components and tuning device, so that it could be easily moved in an emergency. Then I changed the speakers for headphones, so that the radio could not be heard when it was on. The most difficult job was putting up the antenna, because an outside antenna was forbidden by the Japanese. To avoid observation I set up the antenna inside the house, at the highest point just under the tile roof of the house.

The underground also obtained two thirty-two caliber Colt pistols. We oiled them and wrapped them in cloth and then buried them in the yard.

DEATH OF DR. TJIPTO MANGUNKUSUMO

In February 1943, I spent many weekends with the Mangunkusumos. Donald and Louis taught me algebra and geometry to help me with my studies at the polytechnic, and gave me some of the clothes they had outgrown. Life with the Mangunkusumos was a bit more organized than that with Uncle Rir. A mother looking after the household makes a big difference. I began to like the vegetarian food prepared by Auntie Mie, which mostly consisted of *tahu* [tofu, soybean curd], *tempe* [soybean cake], eggs, and lots of *gado-gado* [vegetable salad] with peanut sauce. The Mangunkusumos were supported financially by Uncle Hatta, Uncle Tjip's lawyer brother Sujitno, his sister Mrs. Ranti, and some *pergerakan* friends of Uncle Tjip.

Visitors often came from all over Java to see Uncle Tjip, and Auntie Mie, although she was tired from looking after her sick husband, always invited them to stay for lunch. Auntie Mie always spoke Dutch or Javanese to the visitors. She spoke Dutch with a very heavy Javanese accent, although she looked more European than Indonesian. No matter how heavy her duty was to care for her sick husband, she always prepared cakes for us for afternoon tea.

During my visits with the Mangunkusumos, I witnessed Uncle Tjip's almost daily asthma attacks. Every time he had difficulty breathing he would shout for Donald, who would rush to the medicine cabinet and then rush to Uncle Tjip with the syringe and adrenaline. This type of medicine began to be scarce during the Occupation, but some of Uncle Tjip's Indonesian–Chinese friends used to get it for him—at black-market prices.

When Donald ran out of adrenaline and Uncle Tjip was too sick to receive guests, Mr. Lim Kun Hian, an ethnic Chinese leftist, and Doctor Loo Ping Kian, of the Yang Seng Yee Hospital (the Jakarta Chinese Hospital), after consulting with Uncle

Hatta and Uncle Sjahrir, sent Uncle Tjip to Yang Seng Yee. Uncle Tjip died there early on the morning of March 8, 1943. He was fifty-eight years old, although he looked older.

Donald came that morning to Jalan Latuharhari to tell Uncle Rir that Uncle Tjip had died. Uncle Rir at once rushed to the hospital; we children went to Rohobot Lane, in Jatinegara. Mrs. Lim Kun Hian was directing household preparations to receive people who would want to take their last look at Uncle Tjip. About eleven o'clock the hospital car brought Uncle Tjip's mortal remains to the house. Uncle Hatta and many prominent Indonesians arrived by one o'clock. The house, the front yard, even the side yard were soon filled with people paying their last respects. There were *pergerakan* chaps, journalists, all sorts of people, but not a single Japanese. Wreaths by the hundreds arrived at the house, including one sent by Shimizu, head of the Japanese propaganda bureau, and a member of the notorious secret police. (In fact, soon after the Japanese occupied Java, Sukarno had brought Shimizu to visit Uncle Tjip to ask him to work with the Japanese. Uncle Tjip refused, giving the excuse that he was too old and too sick.)

I didn't recall seeing Bung Karno around that day, although he made a statement about the death of Uncle Tjip:

> Dr. Tjipto Mangunkusumo has died. Although I knew about his illness during these last days, the news of his death shocked me. I owe Brother Tjipto a moral obligation for what he did for me. He taught me many things when we were in Bandung. At that time I called him my chief. I am still grateful to him. Tjipto sacrificed for our people. The Indonesian people will always value his service and be grateful for what he has done for us. Even when there were differences of opinion, people who knew Tjipto admitted that he was honest. Tjip, I pray that God will give you peace.[9]

Lim Kun Hian, Uncle Hatta, and Mr. Ranti (Uncle Tjip's brother-in-law) financed Uncle Tjip's burial. The family decided to bury him at the family burial ground in Ambarawa, and to wait for another brother, Darmawan, an engineer based in Surabaya (although he did not arrive in time). Because he was officially a Muslim, Uncle Tjip had to be buried the day he died. So, through Lim Kun Hian, a Chinese embalming expert was asked to prepare a casket, and Uncle Tjip was officially buried inside the casket with a little earth put in it (a Muslim must be buried with the corpse touching the earth). The casket remained in the house until everything was arranged.

Most difficult was getting an extra coach for the train to bring the remains, accompanied by the family and friends, to Ambarawa. The Japanese needed coaches to transport war materials to harbor areas to supply their troops in the Pacific, and they knew that Tjipto Mangunkusumo was anti-fascist. But somehow Uncle Hatta managed to get Japanese consent to have a coach connected to the Jakarta–Surabaya express, and then to the Semarang train, which stopped at Ambarawa.

In the meantime, hundreds and hundreds of people wishing to extend condolences to the grieving family had to be fed. Rice was still plentiful during the first year of the Japanese Occupation, and many village people donated rice and

---

[9] Quote provided by Donald Mangunkusumo, Tjipto's nephew.

other food to honor the death of the great nationalist leader. We older children were busy serving the visitors, who arrived from every place and corner of Java. Uncle Rir passed word to us to be careful when talking because Indonesians who were Japanese spies were among the crowd, disguised as visitors from outside Jakarta.

On March 11, 1943, the day Uncle Tjip's casket was to leave for Ambarawa, we teenagers were mobilized to take the wreaths ahead of the cortege to the Jakarta Kota railway station, a distance of about eight miles. We left the house exactly at noon, each of us traveling in a separate *dokar* with several wreaths. We were each given one guilder to pay the coachman, and twenty-five cents to return by tram. When we arrived at the railway station at about one-thirty, I was surprised to see a crowd of well-dressed Indonesians, all wearing *picis* (black caps [worn by many nationalists]), waiting on the open station platform. Boy Scouts, serving as guards of honor, were already waiting in front of the station, and some had also assembled at Jatinegara to follow the cortege. The cortege, with the casket in a black hearse, arrived around three o'clock, and the casket was placed on the platform where the well-dressed people wearing *picis* had assembled.

One of the *pici*-wearing men made a speech, praising Uncle Tjip for his part in attacking the Dutch colonialists. Donald told me that the ugly looking man who made the speech was a fellow by the name of Mohammad Yamin. I was too new to Jakarta to know who Yamin was, but Donald told me that he was a famous writer who now worked with Shimizu, the bad guy of the Japanese propaganda and cultural office. After Yamin's speech, another man, who was wearing a sarong, a white high-collared jacket, and a black *pici*, said some prayers. I recognized him as Kiai Haji Mansur, one of the *"empat serangkai"* [the "Four-Leaf Clover"], as the four nationalist leaders who were then cooperating with the Japanese were called.[10] After the speech and prayers, the casket was carried to the waiting coach. Uncle Rir seemed to avoid the Yamin–*pici* crowd at the platform, although he accompanied Uncle Tjip's casket to Ambarawa.

Four days later, when Uncle Rir returned from Ambarawa, I asked him why he had avoided the *pici*-wearing crowd at the train station. He told me that some of them were Japanese collaborators. Uncle Rir was also angry about Sukarno's behavior at the time of Uncle Tjip's death. Although Sukarno's black American car was seen when the cortege left Jatinegara, he was not seen paying his respects at the Kota railway station. Probably he was busy celebrating the one-year anniversary of the Japanese Occupation. At a rally at Gambir celebrating the anniversary, Sukarno began to hit out at the Americans and the British by shouting: *"Amerika kita setrika, Inggeris kita linggis"* (We will iron America, we will crowbar Britain [We will crush America, we will smash England]). If I am not mistaken, that was when the underground realized that Sukarno was being used by the Japanese. In public rallies Sukarno shouted, *"Sehidup semati dengan Dai Nippon"* (to live and die with Japan). He attacked the Allies as imperialists and bloodsuckers of the people of Asia. The last meeting between Sjahrir and Sukarno until after the Japanese surrender was when Sukarno came with Hatta to Uncle Tjip's house in early February 1943.

---

[10] Sukarno, Hatta, and the educator Ki Hadjar Dewantoro were the other three. Mansur was the former chairman of the important Islamic organization, Muhammadiyah. See Harry J. Benda, *The Crescent and the Rising Sun* (The Hague: W. van Hoeve Ltd, 1958), p. 117.

SURVIVAL IN JAKARTA

In early 1943 we had enough to eat. Rice was still easy to get, and cheap compared to a year later. The *pergerakan* chaps living in the interior often sent us food, such as rice, coconuts, vegetables, and dried fish. Auntie Sujitno, Uncle Sujitno Mangunkusumo's wife, often sent us cooked dishes, and some friends even sent us ice cubes at noontime because we had no refrigerator. On Sundays the whole family often had lunch at Uncle Haji Agus Salim's place.[11] We often went to Uncle Hatta's house in the afternoon, but he seldom invited us for lunch as he used to do in Banda. There he was on his own, but in Jakarta he had enough relatives to look after him.

By the end of 1943 life was getting hard for us at Jalan Latuharhari. One of our neighbors, a Czech who worked for the now Japanese-controlled Bata shoe factory, was arrested. A Japanese colonel moved into a large house next to ours. In the evenings, he had wild parties with many other Japanese officers and giggling Dutch or Indo–European women. Later on more Japanese officers came to stay on Latuharhari, which faced the railway line to Tanah Abang, Tengarang, and Merak. Trains loaded with troops and war material passed our house day and night. One morning we received a notice from the Kanrikodan (office of the Japanese administration responsible for houses of the Dutch internees) to move from 19 Jalan Latuharhari within three days. By now we knew that the Japanese were going to zone the area only for the military.

We managed to pack within three days, but were unable to take all the furniture belonging to the Dutch owner because we couldn't find a house to move into. Donald, Iwan Ranti (his cousin), and their Jatinegara teenage friends assisted us in moving to a temporary lodging in the house of Uncle Rir's sister and her medical doctor husband, the Djoehanas. We quietly took the unsealed, unregistered radio to Donald's house in Jatinegara, a temporary shelter. For three weeks we lived with the Djoehanas in their crowded house. At last, through the influence of Uncle Hatta, we found an old-fashioned-looking house on Jalan Maluku, although at a much higher rent (ninety guilders a month).

During the removal from Jalan Latuharhari, I managed to open the large crates in the garage and removed some old clothes and sold them at Senen market for a handsome price. I used the money to buy textbooks for school, and some extra food from the vendors in front of our school. It was probably from eating this food that I landed in Jakarta's General Hospital. For three days I ran a high fever. Dr. Djoehana suspected malaria, but when he later diagnosed me as having typhoid, he sent a hospital car to take me to ward three, the typhoid ward. I was wild when the fever was high, and extra male nurses had to guard me because I would jump out of bed and run to look for drinking water. For two days I was in a coma. Every day a few people died in ward three. Thank goodness Uncle Djoehana was one of the top doctors at the hospital, and I received special care. The chief doctor of ward three, Dr. Badar Djohan, was Uncle Djoehana's best friend. I spent about two months in the hospital, and was fed only thin rice porridge, and occasionally some milk. When I recovered I had lost all my hair and weighed only seventy pounds. I looked like a skeleton, and even had to learn to walk again.

---

[11] One of the older nationalist leaders, Haji Agus Salim was one of the leaders of the first nationalist organization, the Sarekat Islam. After its demise he led other Islamic nationalist organizations. He was one of Sjahrir's father's cousins and Johan Sjahruzah's father-in-law.

Dr. Djohan asked me if I would mind being shown as a typical typhoid case at the medical college where advanced students gathered to hear his lecture. I agreed because he was so nice to me during my illness. One by one the students inspected me. They opened my eyelids, touched all parts of my body, asked me to walk around the lecture hall, and told me to climb stairs. This I could not do, because I had no strength to pull myself up without holding on to something. I really felt embarrassed, and wished that I hadn't agreed to Dr. Djohan's request.

Among the crowd of students I recognized the Ambon-born, Dutch-educated Japanese student who had come on the same boat with me from Ambon to Surabaya. When his turn came to examine me, I spoke to him. He didn't recognize me, but when I mentioned the boat trip on the *Dai Ichi Tora Maru* he was very surprised. Later in the day he visited me and brought me some bananas. Not many people visited me during my illness; I guessed that they were a bit scared to enter the typhoid ward. Lily visited me once a week, Uncle Rir showed up once, and Mimi came a few times to bring some books. Uncle Djoehana often came to see me, and when I was recovering he ordered the chief nurse to move me to another room, away from ward three where patients died every day. Uncle Hatta didn't visit me at all, but he did send some mandarin oranges.

I was released from the hospital in the middle of January 1944. Uncle Rir was not at home; he was busy with his underground movement, and was often away traveling to East Java and the Bandung area. Once he went with Uncle Hatta in the cream-colored DeSoto to Bandung.

When Uncle Djoehana came to the house to check on me two weeks after I came home from the hospital, he was worried by my weak condition. I wasn't able to climb even a few stairs. He ordered me to eat lots of papaya, and gave Lily some money to buy soy milk for me. Uncle Djoehana was a fine and very kind man. He also paid my hospital bill of about seventy-five guilders.

Food was getting expensive and hard to find. At home we lived on the two hundred and fifty grams of rice for each person that was collected from the Menteng district distribution office. The price was fifty cents per thousand grams, while rice on the black market was three times as much. We seldom had meat, but ate rice with vegetables cooked in coconut milk, fried *tempe*, and *tahu*. I was hungry all the time, but there was not enough food at home. I ate papayas from the two trees in our backyard, but I couldn't find ripe papaya everyday. So I ate unripe papayas boiled with salt. After one month, the trees were bare of fruit. When he was at home, Uncle Rir didn't seem to worry much about me. Although he knew that two hundred and fifty grams of rice was not enough for me, he refused to buy expensive rice on the black market. Slowly I recovered and gained more weight, thanks to the soy milk donated by Uncle Djoehana and my visits to their house to get some extra food. I had to walk to visit friends, because the bicycle that had been lent to me was taken away while I was in the hospital. Uncle Rir didn't buy me another secondhand bicycle because he didn't have much money. When I was fully recovered, Uncle Hatta lent me a used women's bike that belonged to his niece, and sent me back to school.

SCHOOL AGAIN

When I returned to school I was behind in all subjects after nearly three months' absence. I studied hard to catch up with my other classmates. The atmosphere at the polytechnic had slowly changed from pleasant to unpleasant. English and German language study was now banned, and Japanese language study was increased from one hour per week to five hours.

Military drill started soon after the morning gymnastics until about ten o'clock. When we returned to school from the athletic field we were too tired to learn. I was in such bad shape after my typhoid, plus lack of nutritious food at home, that I often vomited and fainted on the field. I began to wish that I had stayed in Banda to fish and pick *kanari* nuts. I was becoming fed up with school, but I didn't know what to do.

Our school, the only private middle school in Jakarta, was under Kenpeitai observation, but they couldn't discover anything because we were just harmless school children who were enrolled in this school because our parents or guardians were of the opinion that the teachers in our school were better than the teachers in the Japanese-controlled schools. To test our loyalty to the Dai-Nippon, one morning a notice was placed at the school for volunteers to join PETA (Pembela Tanah Air, Army for the Defense of the Fatherland).[12] Not a single final-year student at the school enlisted in the PETA. The Japanese authorities ordered the students in the senior grades to work as non-salaried volunteers for the railway, at Priok harbor, and at the electricity works. But not many showed up. During the celebration of the birthday of the Japanese Emperor on April 28, the Kenpeitai required all the school children and students in Jakarta to gather at Merdeka Square to parade and dance before the Japanese authorities and to listen to anti-Allied speeches by the Seiko Seikikan (Japanese military governor of Java) and by Bung Karno. When the celebration was over, and while we were marching with our banners and musical instruments back to school, a group of Kenpeitai soldiers with Japanese characters printed in red on their sleeves, stopped us and broke several school banners and trumpets, pulled off the school beret from the heads of several students and stepped on them or threw them away. Then they told us that we were *ke-barat-baratan* (westernized) sons of bitches. We did not panic when the Kenpeitai broke up our parade, but after that incident I never returned to the Salemba polytechnical school.

LIFE WITH UNCLE RIR

By this time I had become more interested in Uncle Rir's underground movement. When they had meetings at home I listened to their conversations, either hiding behind the door or sitting in the corner of the room pretending to read a book, but actually listening eagerly to their talk. The regular visitors included the core members of Sjahrir's circle, including his nephew Johan Sjahruzah and members of his network from Semarang and Surabaya.[13] A number who were later active in

---

[12] PETA was formed by the Japanese in October 1943. By 1945, PETA comprised 37,000 Indonesians in 65 battalions under the command of locally prominent Indonesians, trained by Japanese instructors with the intention of opposing any Allied invasion.

[13] Des remembers Pak Sastra, a faithful follower of Sjahrir's from Garut; Ali Budiardjo; Dr. Sudarsono; Pak Wirjono, a teacher of the Taman Siswa senior high school in Jogjakarta; Sundjojo, a Taman Siswa graduate who headed a student *asrama* in Jogjakarta; Suparnadi, a Taman Siswa graduate who served as a liaison to a number of the underground cells in Java; Miss Musiah, a Madurese girl who later married Dr. Sja'afril and who was well-known for establishing cooperatives and social-welfare programs in Malang, East Java; and Sister Kemi, whose husband, Maskun, had been at Boven Digul with Hatta and Sjahrir, and who was still there when the Pacific War broke out.

Sjahrir's Partai Sosialis Indonesia [PSI] came frequently: Subadio Sastrosatomo, who worked in the Komisi Bahasa under Takdir Alisjahbana during the Occupation and stressed the social responsibility of intellectuals;[14] Hamid Algadri, a member of the executive of the Persatuan Arab Indonesia [Indonesian Arab Association];[15] and Miss Soesilowati, a teacher who headed Pemuda Putri Indonesia [Young Women of Indonesia].[16] Other visitors included several young men who were later leaders of the Indonesian Communist Party: D. N. Aidit, a dynamic young man, who led the PKI from 1951 until his and its demise in 1966; Lukman, later the second in command of the PKI, whose father had died in exile at Boven Digul; Ibnuparna; and Munir.

Life at home became irregular, especially when Uncle Rir wasn't at home. A teenage boy and girl from Garut, cousins of Pak Sastra, came to stay with us while going to school in Jakarta. Their families sometimes sent us rice and dried fish. Uncle Rir trained us to live economically, and to lead a hard life. "We are the people," he said. "If the *rakyat* [people] suffer because of the Japanese suppression, we must suffer too. We cannot lead a happy life in the present circumstances."

We had no servant, and had to do our own cooking and laundry. Lily cooked lunch until she got a job at the electricity office. Then another of us would cook the rice, and we would have cooked food delivered in a *rantang* from a family who delivered food for a monthly payment. The small boys, about the age of twelve, who delivered the *rantang* almost always arrived late, and once or twice didn't show up at all and couldn't be located. Either the poor boy had an accident and spilled the food on the street, or he had taken the *rantang* home to feed his hungry brothers and sisters.

Sendenbu, the Japanese propaganda office, began to campaign for the establishment of *tonarigumi*, a Japanese system of neighborhood associations. Every street had a *tonarigumi* society, with a *tonarigumi-cho* as head, chosen from the household heads. The *tonarigumi-cho* was responsible for food distribution, if there was any, and for sweeping the streets, cleaning the drains, air-raid training, etc.

Uncle Rir was reluctant to take part in any *tonarigumi* activities, and I used to represent him. He said that the Japanese organized this system to check on the movements of underground members, because every visitor who stayed with a family should be reported to the *tonarigumi-cho*. Thus, it was very easy for the Japanese intelligence or the Kenpeitai to know the movements of the "undesirable" persons.

---

[14] Active in nationalist student and youth groups in Jogjakarta and Jakarta, including the Indonesian Student Union (USI), Subadio first studied at the Medical Faculty, then switched to Law. He retained contact with medical students, many of whom were politically active during the Occupation, partly through his brother Soedarpo Sastrosatomo, who was a Medical Faculty student. Subadio later led the PSI faction in Parliament.

[15] Algadri's father was head of the Arab community in Pasuruan, East Java, and Hamid founded a welcoming organization in the moderate nationalist Indonesian Arab Association. He was editor of USI's journal. While a student at the Law Faculty, he was a member of Amir Sjarifuddin's study group. He returned to Surabaya after Amir's arrest, and formed a youth group there.

[16] During the Revolution, Miss Soesilowati was a member of the executive board of the KNIP (Komite Nasional Indonesia Pusat, Central Indonesian National Committee), which functioned as a sort of parliament.

PAK SASTRA OF THE UNDERGROUND

One of Sjahrir's most faithful followers was Pak Sastra, whom I first saw in Surabaya, the morning after my arrival from Ambon. I was sitting on the front porch of the aunties' house observing the activities of the city, when the OJS train rolled past the house on its way to the harbor. It was crowded with people, chickens, ducks, and baskets of vegetables. On the last coach I caught a glimpse of a well-dressed man wearing a black *pici*, who waved at me. I was surprised—who could that be?

About a month later I saw Pak Sastra again when he came to visit Uncle Rir in Jakarta. Then I knew who Pak Sastra was and why he had waved to me in Surabaya. Uncle Rir and the children had stayed with the aunties just before the Japanese landing in Java. Pak Sastra had realized that I must be related to Uncle Rir's Bandanese children.

Pak Sastra followed Uncle Rir wherever he went; he had been a staunch follower since the days of Pendidikan Nasional Indonesia in Bandung. Pak Sastra came from Garut, a hilly town in the Priangan, West Java. Compared with the other *pergerakan* chaps, Pak Sastra was considered quite rich. He and his younger brother owned some *jeruk* [citrus fruit] plantations in the cool climate of Garut, and cultivated fresh-water fish in their ponds. While his younger brother took care of the fish and the fruit, Pak Sastra traveled all over Java to organize the anti-colonialist movement under the Hatta–Sjahrir banner in the early 1930s.

When Sjahrir was jailed at Cipinang prison, in Jakarta, and later, together with Hatta, banished to Boven Digul, and then to Banda, Pak Sastra continued with the independence movement. He was never caught by the PID because he looked too harmless and too well-dressed for a *pergerakan* chap, or he was too quick for them.

During the Occupation, Pak Sastra often stayed in our house when he came to Jakarta. Whenever he came, he brought some rice, dried fish, or something edible for the family. Such items were always welcome in the economically minded Sjahrir household.

If Uncle Rir was not at home, Pak Sastra would talk with us children. He would tell us how bad the Japanese fascists were, and how stupid and chickenhearted Bung Karno was. When Uncle Hatta and some of the intellectual crowd visited the house and discussed politics with Uncle Rir, Pak Sastra never spoke a word. He couldn't speak Dutch, although he understood a bit of it, and if the discussion switched to Dutch, Pak Sastra would be left behind, unnoticed. As soon as the crowd disappeared, Pak Sastra would comment on the discussion to us children, using such difficult words as: *rasionalisasi, reaksioner, politik oportunis, doktrinasi fasisme, mentaliteit kolonial*, etc. I often noted down the difficult words, and later looked them up in the dictionary.

Lily often made jokes about those difficult political words during breakfast or lunch, by telling little Ali not to have a colonial mentality when refusing to eat *tempe* or native vegetables such as *kangkung*. To me Lily would say that, since I was a proletarian from Banda, I shouldn't ask for money to buy new shoes, but should walk shoeless on the street. Uncle Rir would laugh, and ask who taught Lily all these words. We would all answer, "Pak Sastra!" If Uncle Rir said that those words weren't for everyday terms, Lily would answer by calling him reactionary, and the whole family would laugh. *Pergerakan* chaps always used these political terms. If one wore a *pici* and used these words one would be recognized as a *pergerakan* chap.

At the later stage of the Japanese Occupation, when things became too hot, Pak Sastra only appeared occasionally at our house, but he often met Uncle Rir at some secluded place in Bandung or Jakarta. Later, after the proclamation of independence and beginning of the Revolution, Pak Sasta became very ill. The Garut *pemuda* [youth] guarded his house, and later on he led them to fight the Dutch. During the time Uncle Rir was prime minister, I never saw Pak Sastra around Uncle Rir in Jakarta or Jogjakarta. I only saw him again after the Revolution, in 1950, after I returned from London. At that time he looked old and gray. However, in the 1955 parliamentary elections, Pak Sastra's constituency in the Bandung and Garut areas gave Uncle Sjahrir's party nearly half the votes it received throughout Indonesia.[17]

---

[17] Although the PSI had provided many of the intellectual leaders of the early Republic, it received only 2 percent of the vote nationwide in the 1955 parliamentary elections.

CHAPTER ELEVEN

CHAIRIL ANWAR—THE POET

When I first came to Jakarta, Chairil Anwar and his mother were living at 19 Jalan Latuharhari with Uncle Rir. Later I realized that Chairil Anwar, whom we called Nini, was a brilliant poet. He had completed three years of the lower high school (MULO) when the Pacific War broke out. His Dutch and English were so good that even Uncle Rir was astonished. Nini was a real bookworm, and was so good in Western literature that he was able to discuss many subjects with Uncle Rir. Nini even spoke Bandanese with us, because at home our conversation with Uncle Rir was in Bandanese slang.

THE LITTLE ENTREPRENEUR

While Chairil Anwar (Nini) was living with us and was jobless, he asked Uncle Rir for a small loan that he could use as capital for doing some trade in secondhand goods. Nini's idea was to buy bicycles, radios, refrigerators, and crockery from Dutch and Eurasian families, and sell them to Indonesian friends. Uncle Rir agreed to lend Nini fifty guilders, but on the condition that I join Nini as a partner because I also belonged to the *kaum nganggur* [unemployed]. Uncle Rir told me to try to earn some money before my school started again in another two months. I agreed because I knew that Uncle Rir was also a member of the *kaum nganggur*, because he refused to work for the Japanese, and thus had to live from his meager savings and donations from his *pergerakan* chaps.

With the fifty guilders Nini and I went house to house among the husbandless, fatherless Dutch and Eurasian families, whose men were all in prison. We bought a bicycle for thirty-five guilders from a Dutch lady whose husband was interned in a Japanese prison camp. Two days later we sold it for thirty-seven guilders to Amir Hamzah Sirigar, a young lawyer friend of Uncle Rir. Nini bought books of the Multatuli[1] series, and I got the lamp and dynamo that we had removed from the bicycle.

Later we bought a Phillips radio from a fat Eurasian lady for one hundred and twenty-five guilders. Uncle Rir, the financier, came along to pay the money and to check the radio, which he wanted to use for his monitoring. He discovered that the radio, although registered and sealed by the Japanese, could be switched to short wave without breaking the seal by pushing the knob carefully.

Our trade in secondhand articles slowly turned into a nonprofit venture designed solely to help Uncle Rir get things he needed, such as unregistered radio tubes and spare parts, small electric dynamos, pistols, books, typewriters and ribbons, stationery, and wires. It was about this time that Nini discovered that the two large liftvans in the garage contained some interesting items that had sales

---

[1] "Multatuli" was the pen name of a Dutch colonial official, who wrote about the inequities of the colonial system and its Javanese aristocratic collaborators.

value. The first item we took out was a pair of large-size boots, which we sold at Pasar Senen for two guilders. A few days later Nini found some used 220 volt electric bulbs, which we sold for fifty cents each. Had they been 120 volt bulbs we could have made a lot of money since electric bulbs were hard to get during the Japanese Occupation, and were very expensive on the black market.

Nini spent his share of the loot on secondhand Dutch and English books. I spent mine on a tire for my bicycle. After our sales we always came home with fruit from Senen for the family. Uncle Rir was too busy with his underground to mind our venture. Nonetheless, I told Nini that we better tell Uncle Rir what we had done before he discovered it. Nini told me that he had told Uncle Rir many times about the crates, but Uncle Rir wasn't interested in them because the Dutch lady who owned them had told him that they contained only old household "rubbish."

One day Lily and Mimi came to the garage to see what we were doing, and asked us to open up the liftvans to see if there were curtains for the bedrooms, saying that the Dutch lady "told us to get anything we needed from the liftvans."

We found some old curtains inside the crate, and a roll of aerial wires for Uncle Rir's radio. He was very happy to have the wire, and that gave us courage to tell him that we had also taken other things. Surprisingly, he asked, "What kind of things?"

We replied, "Oh, a pair of old boots and some 220 volt light bulbs."

"What did you do with them?" he asked.

Nini replied, "We sold them at Pasar Senen and used the money for used books and a big meal at the Padang restaurant."

Uncle Rir looked very unhappy. Then he said, "Why don't you rob a bank? It's just the same whether you steal an old pair of boots or ten thousand guilders. Stealing is stealing."

I was hurt when Uncle Rir said the word "stealing," and I never forgot that sentence of his.

Uncle Rir then told us that if we needed money we should have asked him for it, not just open the crates for which he was responsible. The two girls also protested when they were told to return the curtains to the liftvan. Pointing at the radio aerial, Mimi said, "Mister, how about that wire?"

Uncle Rir smiled, and said he would return the wire some day, but that now he needed it.

The Intellectual

When Chairil Anwar found a job at the Kantor Statistik [Statistics Office], he and his mother moved to a house in Kampong Kwitang. The job didn't suit Nini at all, but brought in sixty guilders a month to support him and his mother. This was quite sufficient in the early stages of the Japanese Occupation. But after two months Nini had had enough of the Kantor Statistik, and stopped going to the office. He complained to Uncle Rir that he couldn't stand the work, especially when the Japanese twisted numbers to make propaganda. His absenteeism tactic brought him an extra few months' salary, which his mother collected for him.

Although Nini no longer stayed with us, he was at our house almost every day. If he was wearing clean clothes it meant that he had money, and that he would treat little Ali and me to ice cream and cakes that he bought in a shop near Pasar Cikini. When he was broke, his hair was uncombed and his clothes were dirty. He would sit in Uncle Rir's study and read a book while waiting for lunch.

Occasionally Nini received a thirty-guilder money order from his father in Medan. His father had separated from Nini's mother when Nini was a child. Being the only boy, Nini was very much spoiled by his mother. Nini used some of the money sent by his father to buy books or to treat us children to the cinema, which until the middle of 1943 still showed American films.

Nini mixed with all sorts of people: the *becak* drivers, *tukang loak* [scavengers or street vendors who sold secondhand goods], intellectuals, artists such as Affandi[2] and Emiria Sunassa,[3] and literary people such as H. B. Jassin[4] and the poet, Miss Nursjamsu Mochtar.[5] But he always kept a distance from the Japanese. Nini never borrowed money or books from his good friends, or people that were not so well-off. Rich people, snobs, opportunists, stingy people, and *penjilat Jepang* (Japanese lickers)—these people were usually his victims. It was quite odd, but those people who complained about Nini were mostly persons whom I myself didn't like, although I couldn't explain why.

When Nini was tired because of his irregular way of living—wandering all over town on foot to look for cheap secondhand books, visiting friends, and some Eurasian girl friends—his eyes turned blood red. With his small face, brown hair, and fair complexion, if one saw him on the street and didn't know him, one would think that he was Eurasian. Nini's individualism, easy-going nature, and artistic way of living made him the most talked about young man in Jakarta during the Japanese Occupation. Later I realized that his individualism was a logical reaction to the regimentation of the Occupation period.

Nini became quite interested in Banda and the Moluccas. The *foe-foe* stories of Banda and Ambon, and Ambonese names, interested him so much that he later wrote a poem incorporating them for Dien Tamaela, a young Ambonese girl who stayed not far from Jalan Latuharhari.[6] Another of Chairil Anwar's celebrated poems was entitled *When Death Comes.*[7] (See below.)

One Saturday afternoon Nini came to the house with a bundle of typewritten poems. He showed them to the visitors, who included poets and writers associated with the leading Indonesian cultural magazine, *Pudjangga Baru*, such as Takdir Alisjahbana and Amir Hamzah. Also present was Sujitno Mangunkusumo, Uncle Tjip's younger brother, who had been a frequent contributor to *Kritiek en Opbouw*

---

[2] Already recognized for his talent in the 1930s, Affandi became internationally known for his bold impressionistic style; his paintings are in museum collections in Europe and elsewhere.

[3] Emiria Sunassa was the sole female painter among Indonesian artists active in the 1930s and 1940s.

[4] Hans Bague Jassin, originally from Gorontalo, in North Sulawesi, was a leading author, literary critic, editor of several prominent cultural journals, and translator (including the Koran).

[5] Nursjamsu Mochtar was Professor Mochtar's adopted daughter (and niece of his wife). Professor Mochtar, who was head of the Jakarta Public Hospital, was executed by the Japanese in 1944 after they claimed that he poisoned Japanese officials by giving them blood transfusions.

[6] Included in the original Indonesian and in an English translation in *The Complete Poetry and Prose of Chairil Anwar*, ed. and trans. Burton Raffel (Albany, NY: State University of New York Press, 1970), pp. 98–101

[7] This text, which he says was translated by Burton Raffel, is in the possession of Des Alwi. A similar poem, with the title "Me" or "My Spirit," is included in *The Complete Poetry*, edited by Raffel, pp. 20–21.

[*Criticism and Construction*], edited by the progressive Dutch intellectual Eddy du Perron. If I am not mistaken, that was the period when Chairil Anwar started to write the poetry for which he became so famous.

<table>
<tr><td>

Tale for Dien Tamaela
                    by Chairil Anwar

I am Pattiradjawane[8]
When the Gods watch over
I alone.
I am Pattiradjawane
Foam of the sea.
The sea is my blood.
I am Pattiradjawane
When I was born
The Gods brought me an oar.
I am Pattiradjawane, guarding the
        nutmeg groves.
I am fire on the shore. Whoever comes
        near
Must call my name three times.
In the night time quiet,
        seaweed dances
To the sound of my drum,
Nutmeg trees become maidens'
        bodies
And live till dawn.
Dance!
Be Happy!
Forget everything!
But take care not to make me angry.
I'll kill the nutmeg trees,
        stiffen the maidens
I'll bring down the Gods!
I'm in the night, in the day
In the rhythm of the seaweed and in
        the fire that roasts the island.
I am Pattiradjawane
Whom the Gods watch over
I alone.

</td><td>

When Death Comes
                    by Chairil Anwar

When death comes
No one will mourn for me, I know
Not even you....
I do not need your grief
I am a wild animal
Wounded, one that the herd has left
In pain I turn challenging the wind
With the poisoned wound I'll fly
Until the wind has cauterized the pain
I shall bear the agony and live on
Another thousand years....

</td></tr>
</table>

---

[8] Patti = regent, radja = king, wano = daring: "the daring regent and king"

CHAPTER TWELVE

SURABAYA AND EAST JAVA

Finding life in Jakarta impossible, I left for Surabaya in May 1944. Uncle Rir wasn't at home when I departed, so I had no chance to tell him I was leaving. I had sold my metal case to a *tukang loak,* so used a small bag to carry two pairs of shorts and two shirts, my only possessions other than the clothes I wore. The night express to Surabaya still cost only Rp. 12.50, the same price I had paid when I went to Jakarta from Surabaya, although the value of the Japanese-issued paper *rupiah* was not as much as a year ago.

In Surabaya I went to see Jim, and he again took me to the Bandanese aunties, who had in the meantime moved from Reiners Boulevard to Darmo. Both aunties now worked at the cake shop in Tunjungan. They were glad to see me because they needed someone to watch their house while they were at work. Surabaya, like any of the larger towns of Java, was full of thieves during the hard times of the Japanese Occupation. However, life in Surabaya was better than Jakarta; food was much cheaper.

The aunties were very kind. Every morning before they went to work they gave me fifty cents, which was enough to keep me alive for the day. They also gave me clothes, and a pair of black and white leather shoes. Auntie Irma, who was about forty years old, and had been a classmate of my mother, was very strict, and told me that I must always appear clean and neat, especially in the afternoon. Her younger sister, Auntie Silva, who was about thirty-six, was the kinder of the two, and looked after me as if I were her own son. She had lost her own son years ago in Banda.

MR. HAYASHI

To my surprise, one evening a Japanese textile engineer by the name of Hayashi, whom I had met once at Uncle Hatta's house in Jakarta, came to visit the aunties. He was very friendly, and spoke good Indonesian and some Dutch. He had worked in Surabaya before the war, and was now director of the Japanese government office that looked after all the textile factories in East Java. He asked about my relationship to Hatta. I told him that I knew Hatta from Banda, and that he was a friend of my father's. I did not disclose much because from living with Uncle Rir, and belonging to a *pergerakan* family, we always suspected friendly Japanese of being secret-service agents. Anyway, I hoped it was just a coincidence that I met Hayashi again in Surabaya. Later on I realized that he was just a lonely human being, and probably in love with Auntie Silva.

When Hayashi came to visit the aunties in Surabaya, they served him tea and cakes from the shop. From their conversation I gathered that he had met them at the cake shop. He seemed to like the unsold cakes very much. The aunties told him that they were typical Bandanese cakes. Jokingly Hayashi asked, "Are they Bandanese or Belandanese (Dutch) cakes?" We all laughed.

Des Alwi in Surabaya, 1945

One Sunday morning Mr. Hayashi came to Darmo to pick me up for a visit to Pajet, a hill resort near the town of Mojokerto. It was a wonderful car trip, and my first chance to visit a mountain resort in Java. The climate in Pajet is very cool. We stopped at a rest house looked after by a Eurasian lady, who gave us a Dutch lunch that consisted of Pajet-grown potatoes and vegetables and some good beef steaks. After lunch, while Hayashi made love to the Eurasian lady, I went for a stroll in the village. There I admired the beauty of the countryside, and the lovely flowers, such as gladiola and large roses, and strawberries in the rest-house garden. The rest house only admitted Japanese, but because I was Hayashi's guest, I was also welcome.

On our return trip we stopped at Mojokerto because Hayashi needed a few brandy-sodas at a Chinese restaurant. He didn't talk much during the car trip; he only became talkative after a few brandy-sodas. He showed me photographs of his wife and two daughters. I guessed he must be homesick. He said to me that Japan must soon win the war so that he could go back to his wife and children. I didn't talk much to Hayashi becaause I wasn't sure about him or his motives. However, during our car ride he didn't ask me anything about Hatta, or any of the Indonesians that often visited Hatta.

One day Hayashi came to the house and gave me a Swiss-made, "Mido" brand watch, which was the most expensive and most-wanted watch by Japanese military and civilian personnel. It fetched a price of three hundred to five hundred *rupiah*, on which one could live for six months. I was quite astonished when Hayashi gave me a Mido watch, but he showed me two others he had, so I gladly received his present. Hayashi told me that some Chinese people had given him those watches.

I introduced Jim to Hayashi. One day Hayashi took us to *Darmo Kaikan*, one of the best Chinese restaurants in Surabaya. Mostly Japanese big brass came there to eat, while most Chinese avoided the place because there were too many Japanese. This was the first time in my life that I ate at a Chinese restaurant, and I thought that if my Bandanese relatives found out, Jim and I would be outcasts. We didn't eat much, except for fried crabs; we were afraid that the dishes were cooked with pork or pork fat.

THE UNDERGROUND IN SURABAYA

About the time I went to Surabaya, Uncle Rir sent his nephew Johan Sjahruzah to organize the underground there, starting with the workers at the oil company. Johan had been working at Uncle Hatta's office in Jakarta, so his move to Surabaya was obviously done with Uncle Hatta's agreement. Johan opened a sort of mess hall for the people working at the Japanese-controlled oil company, and at the same time used it as a place to train underground cadres. I moved from the aunties' place to stay at the *asrama* [dormitory] attached to the mess hall, which served as a center for the underground *pemuda*. The *asrama* was situated in Kampong Maspati, between the Surabaya railroad station and the oil company office.

The *asrama* chief was a man called Effendi, who lived there with his family—a wife and two little daughters. Effendi was one of the administrators of the oil company; he didn't seem much interested in politics or know much about what was going on in the *asrama* or what Johan was up to. The older boys who lived in the *asrama* worked at the oil company, and there were several young Javanese mechanics from the oil company who lived there as paying guests. The older boys all read books about the Russian Revolution and the French Revolution, and other revolutionary books. The *asrama* had a small library, probably Johan's collection, of books written by Indonesians, such as Hatta, Tan Malaka, and Takdir Alisjahbana. Other books came from a privately run library in Kampong Keputeran,[2] including Marx's *Das Capital* and works by Maxim Gorki, Hemingway, Pearl S. Buck, Steinbeck, Richard Wright, Lenin, Sun Yat-Sen, Mao Tse-tung, Hitler, and Gandhi. Most of the books were in Dutch. We also read old *pergerakan* magazines from the 1920s and 1930s. We often held political discussions and debates at the *asrama*, and Sukarno was often criticized for his collaboration with the Japanese. I listened to these discussions with interest, and began to read some of those political and revolutionary books.

---

[2] The inhabitants of this kampong were "known for their sullen, recalcitrant attitude and their refusal to obey city laws and officials," See William H. Frederick, *Visions and Heat: The Making of the Indonesian Revolution* (Athens, OH: Ohio University Press, 1989), p. 9.

Johan Sjahruzah, Sjahrir's nephew (facing the camera), with members of the
underground he established in East Java during the Japanese Occupation

Often we had visitors from Jakarta, such as the well-known nationalist youth
leader Sukarni. Old *pergerakan* chaps such as Pak Sastra occasionally came to visit
and led the political discussions. Many doctors, especially those from the oil
company hospital in Wonokromo, participated in this "underground" led by Johan.
Abang Johan didn't live at the *asrama*, but with his wife, the third daughter of the
nationalist leader Haji Agus Salim. She was very friendly and lively; we called her
Yu Yet.

RADIO SCHOOL

Abang Johan told me to enroll in a radio technical school, and so I did. This
school, located in Genteng Kali, was privately run. Although the Japanese provided
no assistance, they watched the school closely. Students had to provide their own
tools and equipment. The Japanese-controlled Radio Surabaya sent old radio sets

and broken equipment to us for repair. We also repaired the radios the Japanese placed in markets or other public places to broadcast their propaganda and the speeches of Sukarno.

It was really a poor school; only three subjects were taught: math, radio theory, and Japanese language. The rest of the time was spent repairing broken radio sets. From my studies in Jakarta I already knew how to examine and repair broken radios, and could change alternating to direct current. The school director, Sutedjo, owned the school and was more interested in making money from the students' fees than in their learning radio engineering. He also earned money from the students' repair of broken radio sets. Sutedjo was short and fat, bald, and talked a lot; he usually oversaw the students' work himself. Later on we learned that he worked with the Kenpeitai.

Surabaya was a pleasant city. The people, although provincial, were friendly. However, the students at the school spoke Javanese among themselves, and unless one spoke Javanese–Surabaya slang, one was considered a stranger. I also had difficulties at school because the students seemed to be pro-Japanese. It was very hard to influence them against the Japanese, even when they led a miserable life because of Japanese oppression.

ALLIED BOMBING ATTACKS

Surabaya was crowded with Japanese marines and sailors. There was also a group of German sailors and officers in Surabaya from the two German U-boats located at the Tanjung Perak harbor. The Germans had their own mess hall, and many Caucasian women from the internment camps were brought there by special buses.

One morning in the second half of 1944, Surabaya was attacked by low-flying Allied planes. This was the first daylight attack on Surabaya; previously there had been several attacks after dark. In this daylight attack the Wonokromo oil installation and the industrial area of Braga were severely damaged. Two of my Javanese mechanic friends who worked for the oil company, Kastam and Jojo, were killed during the attack. I was very upset, especially because these two were brothers and my good friends. A week later their old father, wearing traditional Javanese dress, came from Madiun to collect their belongings. He didn't say much, except to ask Effendi, the *asrama* supervisor, where the bodies of his sons were. Tears came into Effendi's eyes when he told the old man that most of the people killed at Wonokromo were burned beyond recognition. The old man then said a few prayers and left with his sons' belongings.

That is the tragedy of war. It was somebody else's war, but we Indonesians got hurt. A few hundred Indonesians were killed that morning in Wonokromo and elsewhere in Surabaya. Tanjung Perak harbor was also attacked, and a few dockyards were damaged. The two German U-boats were not hit. People working at the harbor told us that the submarines' antiaircraft guns were the only guns that fired at the attacking Allied planes. The Japanese were taken by surprise that morning.

Air-raid alarms sounded that same evening when larger bombers, using as their target and for their bearings the big fire at the Wonokromo oil installation, came to drop more flares and bombs. That evening I was at the aunties' place, which was only a mile or two away from Wonokromo, because they were a bit scared to be home alone without a male bodyguard. The bombing shook the house, and we fled to the garden and hid below a tree. Then, when we heard machine-gun fire, we fled back inside the house and hid under the beds. The Japanese ground defenses shot back at the attackers using ack-acks [antiaircraft guns] and searchlights. Small flares to guide the bombers were being fired from the ground, and it appeared that there were many Allied spies operating in Surabaya.

A few days after the attack the Japanese paraded four American flyers around town in a truck. A downed Allied plane was set up in front of the office of the city council, and thousands of Surabaya residents queued up in the blazing sun to see it.

THE VOLUNTEER BRIGADE

Soon after the daytime attack on Surabaya, we students were ordered to join the Kenrohoshi, a "volunteer" brigade to assist the Japanese by collecting scrap iron, growing castor seeds, and digging air raid shelters for the Japanese Army and Navy hospitals. We were called "Sukarela Barisan Belakang," something like "behind-the-lines volunteer corps." My school's Kenrohoshi consisted of five platoons of forty boys each: three to dig holes for air-raid shelters and two to collect scrap iron. Since I was quite tall and rather well-fed, thanks to Hayashi's Mido watch that I had sold to buy extra food, I was ordered to enlist in the scrap-iron platoon. Our duties were performed three times a week: Tuesday, Thursday, and Saturday, during the school hours of 7:30 AM to 2:00 PM.

Each platoon was commanded by an Indonesian *pemuda* who was Japanese-trained, -indoctrinated, and -militarized. My scrap-iron platoon was headed by a Javanese *pemuda* called Waluyo. His father was a traffic policeman, who had been in the police before the Japanese Occupation. Waluyo was about twenty-five years old, but looked about five years older. He was pale and rather tall for a Javanese, and looked like a typical *anak tangsi* (as children of native soldiers or police were called in the colonial days).[3] Waluyo had a shaved head, like any Japanese soldier or sailor, or anybody who had been trained in a semi-military commando unit by the Japanese. Our first introduction to Waluyo was when he made us march for one hour in the blazing sun and then ordered us to run back to school. Before he dismissed the platoon he told us to appear the next morning with our heads already shaven, just like him.

We went back to our classroom and discussed among ourselves whether to follow Waluyo's order. Those students who already had shaved heads supported Waluyo's order, but those of us with non-*botak* [bald] heads objected to it. I told the boys that Waluyo had no right to order us to shave our heads because we were not in the military. One boy said that Waluyo was our Kenrohoshi commander and therefore we must follow his command. Some boys wanted to quit school because they did not want to shave their heads, and were not in the mood to work in the Kenrohoshi platoon. But then somebody said that if they quit the Kenrohoshi, the Kenpeitai would arrest them. Although they changed their minds about leaving school, they still refused to have their heads shaved.

---

[3] *Tangsi* meant the camps or compounds of the police or military, and the children of native soldiers or police lived in these compounds and were brought up in the *tangsi* atmosphere.

I decided not to quit school because Johan asked me to continue my study of radio engineering, which might be useful for the underground. But I refused to have my head shaved.

When we assembled in the schoolyard the next morning, five boys didn't turn up. Waluyo noted down their names and addresses. A bunch of us boys didn't have *botak* heads, so Waluyo separated us from the others and lectured us on why shaved heads were necessary in wartime. He told us that having no hair was very practical, especially when you were in the front lines fighting the enemy: if you had no hair to comb you would not be distracted in an area infested with enemy soldiers; your hair would not block your view when you were shooting at the enemy; lice wouldn't bother you if you had no hair; you wouldn't feel warm if you had a bald head, especially if working in an open field; and you would feel very fresh with a clean-shaven head. Waluyo went on to talk about those gallant, hairless Japanese soldiers fighting to free Asia from the slavery of Western imperialism and Indonesia from Dutch colonialism. Suddenly Suwondo, the student with the sharpest sense of humor in the school, said, "But Captain, we are not on the front lines fighting the enemy, we only belong to the *barisan besi tua* (scrap-iron front), behind the lines."

Waluyo was angry at being interrupted, and by the asking of such a non-*semangat* [spirited] question. He told Suwondo to shut up, and said that if Suwondo didn't understand discipline, he, Waluyo, would drill him right away. However, after the lecture we managed to get away without shaving our heads the Japanese-soldier style.

THE SCRAP-IRON BRIGADE

Now everything was ready for us to collect scrap iron for building ships to speed the Japanese victory; more ships meant victory for the Japanese armada over the Allied navy. That was what Bung Karno had said when he inaugurated the first Kenrohoshi battalion in Jakarta in 1944.

First we marched to the office of the Surabaya Municipality to listen to more lectures about the *Dai Toa Senso*, and to collect tools to use to break down the iron fences around private houses. We were given a list of houses with iron fences, and started with the area nearest to our school, on Ketabang Boulevard. The first house with an iron fence had one that was nicely built in a pattern that looked like a row of spears. It reminded me of those sharp iron fences we had at our Banda houses, which we kids didn't dare to climb over into someone's yard when we wanted to steal fruit.

While we were hammering and poking with our iron bars and crowbars to break down that fence, a small Indonesian–Chinese boy came out of the house and shouted in Dutch, "Granny! They are breaking our fence!"

A few moments later an old lady came out on the porch. She asked us why we were breaking down her fence. Waluyo told her proudly that it was an order from the Gunseikanbu (Japanese Authority) because iron was needed to build more ships, and more ships meant a speedy downfall of the imperialist colonialist forces. Without saying anything, the old lady took her grandson by the arm and walked back into the house. Then she shut all the doors and windows, and didn't appear outside again. She was probably scared of Waluyo, who was wearing a khaki uniform and a Japanese soldier's cap, and of us boys with our iron tools.

Breaking iron fences with ordinary tools was not as simple as we had thought. By noon we had only managed to dismantle one of the six sections of the fence. Then we started with the gate, which was very easy to tackle, but was too heavy to carry to pile it with the first section we had dismantled. So we put it on the pavement. Knocking down iron fences from their concrete foundations was a heavy job. It was the dry season and the weather was very hot. We were thirsty, but the old lady didn't open her door when we knocked on it to ask for some drinking water. At 1:30 in the afternoon Waluyo ordered us to stop our work and return to school.

When we returned to the same house two days later to finish the job, the house was completely closed up. Either the occupants had gone away to avoid us, or they had left the house temporarily. We finished the job, and piled up the fence pieces on the pavement in front of the house. There was a special Kenrohoshi team whose job it was to collect scrap iron from the roadside, put it into trucks, and transport it to an unknown destination. We were not supposed to know where the scrap iron was sent. Waluyo said that it was a military secret, and therefore we must not ask too many questions. But he said optimistically, "It will be turned into good warships."

A few months later when I passed Ketabang Boulevard, those broken down iron fences were still lying on the pavement. Nobody had come to collect them.

The next house on our list was occupied by a Javanese high official from the East Java Public Works Department. When he came home on Saturday from his half day's work and saw us hammering at this fence, he turned pale with anger. But when Waluyo explained to him that we had been ordered to collect scrap iron to speed up Dai Nippon's victory, the Javanese official became very friendly, and even assisted us in breaking down his own fence.

The third house we tackled was occupied by a Eurasian family. The occupants didn't say anything when we started on the job, but one of them, a middle-aged lady I had met at the Banda aunties' house, recognized me. She motioned to me to come inside and said, "Shame on you for getting mixed up with these natives who are working as coolies for the Japanese."

I didn't say anything, but felt rather uneasy. A few days later when I visited the Bandanese aunties, they scolded me for breaking people's fences. The Eurasian lady must have told them about the fence-breaking operation on Ketabang Boulevard. I felt rather annoyed that they saw me as a coolie working for the Japanese. I thought that they wouldn't understand if I explained to them about the Kenrohoshi, why I had entered the radio school, and why I had to join the Kenrohoshi.

We had almost completed our iron-fence-breaking operation on Ketabang Boulevard when we ran into trouble with a Japanese naval officer who did not like having his iron fence knocked down by a bunch of Indonesian schoolboys. His mistress, a Eurasian woman, phoned him at his office when she saw us hammering at the fence. A little while later a green car stopped in front of the house and a Japanese officer emerged and at once started showering blows on the boys nearest him. Luckily Waluyo received most of the blows. The naval officer seemed to hit first and ask questions later. "What is the meaning of ruining my fence?" he shouted angrily.

Waluyo stood at attention and told him that we were ordered to collect scrap-iron for the *Dai Toa Senso*, in order to speed up the Nippon victory at sea.

"Who ordered you to do this?" shouted the naval officer.

Waluyo, still standing at attention, replied, "The Japanese at the municipality."

The naval officer then said, "So? The gentlemen at the municipality ordered you to do this. Why didn't you go first and break down their fences? What the hell are these rotten pieces of scrap-iron for? Do you think we will use them to build ships? You all must be crazy!"

We were glad to get away from that house. Waluyo didn't say anything; he didn't even answer when Suwondo asked where we were headed next. We just went back to school. The director was surprised to see us back in the middle of the Kenrohoshi hours. When we told him about the incident, he told us to avoid any Japanese-occupied houses.

When there were no more iron fences to be dismantled except at the houses occupied by Japanese, our Kenrohoshi platoon was detailed to dig air-raid shelters at Gubeng naval hospital. Digging deep holes was hard work; we got dirty and suffered from backaches. The naval hospital had been built by the Dutch just before the outbreak of the Pacific War, and was the largest hospital in Surabaya. Most of the people working there were Japanese, but there were some Indonesian nurses. The Japanese at the hospital gave us tea and bananas during break time.

FACTORY WORK

Next we were sent to work in factories at the Braga industrial area. Our jobs were mostly cleaning water tanks, mopping floors, and other unskilled coolie jobs. One beneficial thing about the Kenrohoshi factory work was that we got the chance to steal anything that was produced in the factory where we had been placed. Being so-called "student volunteers," we were not checked when we left the factory. When we worked in a Japanese-controlled coconut-oil factory near Wonokromo, which produced cooking oil available only to Japanese, some of us took the opportunity to fill our empty flasks with coconut oil. The Japanese guard at the factory exit was either too stupid to realize our game, or he was also stealing, but on a larger scale. Because of its scarcity, a bottle of coconut oil fetched a good price on Surabaya's black market. I used to see some *sakura* [civilian] Japanese going home carrying a five-gallon drum of coconut oil; it was certainly not their daily ration.

To get a Kenrohoshi job at the soap factory (probably one of the pre-war Lever Brothers' plants) was like getting a promotion, since soap was hardly obtainable during the Occupation. Two bars of toilet soap cost a week's allowance. We used to pocket one or two bars every time we worked there.

Some Kenrohoshi students got drunk when they worked in the former Heineken's brewery. After that episode students were no longer allowed to work there, although some of the Japanese factory officials were very much amused to see drunken students parading around the factory grounds as a punishment for drinking beer during working hours.

Stealing from a Japanese-controlled factory was a dangerous game because if you were caught, you would be beaten up and sent to jail. We were probably too young to realize the danger, especially when life was so hard during the Japanese Occupation.

I began to get fed up and tried to find a way to quit school. I didn't know the actual reason behind the Kenrohoshi. There were certainly enough laborers and jobless people in Surabaya to work in those factories. Why should the Japanese use students? It was probably a kind of *tambah semangat* [increase spirit, enthusiasm] stunt. Another such program was the *romusha* [forced labor]. At first these programs appeared harmless, based on voluntary participation, but as the war grew adverse to the Japanese, the *romusha* became coercive, and later turned into slave labor. Unfortunately, Bung Karno was associated with these programs.

When the Japanese authorities started sending Kenrohoshi teams to Madura Island for two-week working sessions on a secret project, I quit school. I did this as quietly as possible, giving as the reason that I had to return to Jakarta. The head of the school, Mr. Sutedjo, suggested that instead I work for the radio repair office of the Japanese Navy (Kaigun). I told him that I just wanted to return to Jakarta. Mr. Sutedjo threatened to report me to the Kenpeitai if I didn't want to work with the Kaigun. I told him, "Go ahead. I am not an evil person. I just want to return to Jakarta."

CHAPTER THIRTEEN

EAST JAVA AND THE UNDERGROUND

When I left the radio school, I didn't go to Jakarta but went to live in Kedurus, a small village about eight miles south of Surabaya, on the Surabaya–Mojokerto road. I stayed with Mr. Sudjono, who was on the staff of the Japanese-run oil company and one of Uncle Sjahrir's top underground workers in East Java. At night I slept at Mr. Sudjono's home, but in the daytime, together with many of my friends from the Surabaya *asrama*, we gathered at the home of Mr. Sunarjo, the Indonesian manager of the oil field near Kudurus, one of Mr. Sudjono's co-workers in the underground. We set up a six-watt radio receiver at Mr. Sunarjo's home so that we could listen to foreign broadcasts. According to his wife, a middle-class woman from Solo, Mr. Sunarjo had known Mr. Sudjono since the *pergerakan* years. The Sunarjos had named their son Mohammad Hatta Darusman; this was enough for me to trust Mr. Sunarjo.

Before the war the Kedurus oil field was owned by BPM, the Dutch Shell Oil company, and Mr. Sunarjo had been one of the Indonesian chief clerks. Now he was in charge of about two hundred workers and officials. Many workers of the oil company in Wonokromo lived in Kedurus because there was daily train service between the two locations.

When the Japanese army landed near the oil field in February 1942, the colonial army fled without setting fire to the oil installation. Mr. Sunarjo was the first Indonesian official of the BPM met by the Japanese army officer in charge of taking over the BPM and its oil fields around Surabaya. Although the Japanese officer spoke English, Mr. Sunarjo did not, so he took the officer to Mr. Sudjono. With his rather good English and a good general knowledge of the oil fields around Kedurus and Wonokromo, plus some bluffing, Mr. Sudjono not only translated the discussion between the Japanese officer and Mr. Sunarjo, but at the same time managed to be appointed as a high-ranking Indonesian official of the Japanese military-run oil company.

Within a year the whole East Java oil industry was managed by Sjahrir men as a cover for the underground movement that was being run by the Sudjono–Johan Sjahruzah combination. Courses for oil workers, seminars, management-training courses, guard-training courses, and the like were supplemented with political indoctrination and courses in nationalism. Even the intelligence body formed by the Japanese to protect the oil installations for the *Dai Toa Senso* was heavily infiltrated by the underground. The Sudjono–Johan men used traveling passes and free railway tickets meant for oil intelligence men and inspectors for their underground couriers. Mr. Sudjono was the man who suggested to the Japanese oil chief to form this intelligence body, which was meant to protect the Japanese-controlled oil industries. In fact his purpose was to have a legitimate security body to cover up certain work of the underground.

MR. SUDJONO

Mr. Sudjono, whom we called Uncle Jon, lived in Kedurus, about three miles from the main road. His house was a good hideout for the underground workers and those sought by the Kenpeitai. The *asrama* boys used to spend their weekends there. Fish and vegetables were plentiful in Kedurus, and the *asrama* boys fed themselves well, making up for the meager food they got at the *asrama* in Surabaya during the week.

Behind the house was a *ladang* (non-irrigated field) belonging to Auntie Jon and her family. Auntie Jon was a real *desa* [village] girl, about fifteen years younger than her husband. She didn't speak Dutch, but she knew how to read and write Indonesian. She was well-informed about the political situation, being a self-taught woman with Uncle Jon as her tutor. She was hard-working and was well-respected by the simple *desa* folks of Kedurus. Auntie Jon ran the business of selling crops from the *lading* around Kedurus to Surabaya traders. During the wet season *padi* [rice] was planted on the *ladang*, and during the dry season other crops were planted, such as tomatoes, eggplant, and chili peppers. Auntie Jon's influence and connections with the assistant *wedana* [local official] and petty *desa* officials of Kedurus were so good that, instead of delivering rice to the Japanese authorities at a very low price, the authorities gave Auntie Jon ten *piculs* of rice per month at a far-below-market price for distribution to the population of Kedurus. Only a few Kedurus people bought this rice. The rest of the *tani* [peasant or farmer] population didn't bother, as they were quite satisfied with the portion of their harvest that was not taken by the Japanese. This enabled Auntie Jon to deliver rice to her Surabaya friends and underground people at a very low price. During the Occupation the price of rice in the market was about two *rupiah*s per liter, while the rationed rice cost only thirty cents. However, the ration for one person was only two hundred grams a day.

The Japanese set up many public radios to broadcast propaganda in the villages. Every morning and evening the population was required to train for war and self-defense. This very much disrupted the *petani* who were needed to plant *padi* or, in the dry season, vegetables. All the *pemuda* were required to make wooden rifles. Fortunately, in Kedurus there was no semi-military training because almost the whole population of Kedurus, including the farmers, appeared to work under the direction of Uncle Sudjono and Uncle Sunarjo in oil production. The people of Kedurus also were not included in the *romusha* forced-labor program, in which many Javanese were used as military auxiliaries in the war by the Japanese. The Sudjono–Sunarjo duo was greatly respected; they were protected by the head of the Japanese oil enterprise in Surabaya, because oil was much needed for the Japanese war effort. At the same time, quietly they were members of the most important underground cell of independence fighters in the Surabaya area.

Uncle Jon was a jolly good fellow, fat and round, a two hundred pounder. But he had kidney trouble, and at night he snored like hell. When his kidney stones bothered him he moaned constantly, keeping the whole house awake. A German doctor who worked for the Japanese oil company used to come to the house to treat him. The doctor put him on a strict diet, restricting meat and eggs, to reduce his weight. Dr. Sutojo, a surgeon at Surabaya's Central Hospital, wanted to operate on Uncle Jon, but there was no film for his x-ray apparatus. Finally, after six months, through the help of Uncle Hatta, a doctor in Ceribon managed to obtain some x-ray film. After the x-ray, Dr. Sutojo told Auntie Jon that her husband must be operated on at once since the left kidney had so many stones that it wasn't functioning at all.

Although it was a very delicate operation, Auntie Jon agreed to it, and the next day Uncle Jon had his left kidney removed. When Uncle Jon came out of the hospital we used to joke that without a left kidney, Uncle Jon leaned too much to the right.

THE SUNARJO FAMILY

The Sunarjo house was located near the junction of the main road from Wonokromo and Sepandjang, about half a mile from that of the Sudjonos. The Sunarjos had three children: two daughters—Upi, eighteen years old, and Nining, sixteen—and a twelve-year-old son, Mohammad Hatta (named after Uncle Hatta). The two young girls were part of the attraction of Kedurus for the young men from the Maspati *asrama* in Surabaya. Nining was very pretty, with a mole on her right cheek. Some of the *asrama* boys were also drawn by Mr. Sunarjo's collection of books in Dutch and English about politics, such as those about the Long March of the Chinese Communist Party, Chu Te, Marx, Trotsky, Tan Malaka, and Hitler. Mr. Sunarjo also had other educational books and novels by well-known authors. I often spent the whole day reading to increase my political knowledge. On Saturdays and Sundays the *asrama* boys visited Kedurus to discuss politics and the activities of the underground.

Other than Nining and Upi there wasn't much to see in Kedurus. The area was flat with just a few village houses surrounded by bamboo. On the other side of the road were *sawah*. The area along the main road to Surabaya was rather busy because the local train stopped there to pick up passengers and vegetables for Surabaya. Behind the village flowed the wide Brantas River.

THE EURASIAN FAMILY NEXT-DOOR

Next door to the Sunarjos lived a Eurasian family: three boys below the age of ten; two girls, ten and fourteen; a pale-looking mother; and an old grandmother. They seldom went out, except the girl of about ten, who ran to the Chinese store to buy coconut oil and sweet soy sauce nearly every afternoon. Her name was Stien; she was rather tall for her age, but was pale, and had hollow cheeks, probably from malnutrition. Mrs. Sunarjo, who knew the family since the pre-war days, explained that the father and two older brothers had been interned by the Japanese. Before the war the family owned a chain of sugar factories near Mojokerto, about twenty miles from Kedurus. Their possessions, including *sawah*, everything but their house, were taken away by the Japanese. The family lived secluded from the outside world, as if they were afraid to mix with their neighbors. The women feared being sent to camps as had happened to other Dutch or Eurasian families. The Japanese authorities must have overlooked or forgotten about this particular family, which looked more European than Eurasian.

One afternoon while I was standing in front of the Sunarjo's house, Stien rushed out of her house with an empty bottle to buy some coconut oil. I tried to talk to her, but she was afraid and ran toward the store. When she returned, I spoke to her in Dutch. I told her not to be afraid of me, saying, "I am not a Japanese spy."

She responded, "My mother told me not to talk to strangers." Then she vanished inside her home, behind a small bamboo hedge.

For days I didn't see Stien or her young brothers going outside their house. Then one afternoon while I was walking nearby, a lady peeked her head out the garden door and waved me over. She first asked me whether I was an "Indies boy" (Eurasian). I replied that I was not an "Indies boy." "Well," she said, "you look like one."

I told her that I came from the Moluccas and was staying with the Sudjonos. She then asked if I could go to the Chinese store to get her a bottle of coconut oil. I agreed, and she handed me an empty bottle and some money. When I returned, she opened the garden door and let me in. I hesitated for a moment, but then she introduced herself as Stien's mother. "Come in," she said, "you look honest to me." Then she said, "Stien is ill, my older daughter is afraid to go outside the house, and my three sons are too small to be sent to the store. The people of Kedurus do not want to mix with or even talk to us."

I pitied her, and told her that I was prepared to do her shopping until Stien got better. When I left, Nining happened to see me coming out of the house. With a smile she asked, "Hey! What were you doing there? It's odd. They never let people come into the house, and they act very strange."

I told Nining what had happened. Then Nining asked, "Did you see Stien's beautiful sister?"

"No," I replied. But later, when I did see Tien, Stien's older sister, she was no longer beautiful. She was too pale and too thin.

Nining told me that before the war this Eurasian family never mixed with them. They were too proud to mix with natives, and now nobody bothered with them.

The next day when I went to their house to shop for them, I was shocked at how miserably they lived. To survive in the midst of "unfriendly" people they had sold nearly everything in the house. All that remained were a few pieces of old, broken-down furniture and some family albums with photos of the glorious and prosperous past. On hearing my voice, the grandmother, too old and too absent-minded to know what was going on, asked "Marie, Marie. Is that Jan?" Jan was her interned son, Marie's husband.

"No, *Oma* (grandma)," said one of the little boys. "It is not daddy."

The family, whose name I've forgotten, practically lived on tapioca and sweet potatoes, which they grew in a small plot in their backyard. Occasionally the Chinese shopkeeper allowed them to buy on credit, until the amount they owed reached the price of a large used bed sheet or a window curtain, which was then used to pay the bill.

One day when I was at the neighbors' house a teen-aged boy appeared and introduced himself as Teo. The mother was a bit startled, but hastily told me, "He is my son. Please don't tell anyone that he is here."

She told me that when the Japanese came, guided by some village folk, to arrest her husband and her eldest son, her second son, Teo, fled into the *sawah* fields. She said that if the Japanese discovered him in her house they would certainly punish her and Teo. I told her not to worry because I was also a fugitive. Surprised, she asked, "But why are you walking around outside?"

I told her that the Kedurus people were nice folks, and that Uncle Sudjono was respected by them. She told me that she had intended many times to ask Mr. Sudjono for help, but didn't because she was afraid of causing him difficulty.

Then she took me to see the little girl, Stien, who was in bed with fever. Stien greeted me politely in Dutch with "*Dag, meneer* [Good day, sir]."

From the way they spoke Dutch I could tell that they belonged to an upper-class Indies family, one that had lived in Indonesia only two or three generations, with only a little mixed blood. Had they been a hard-core average Eurasian family they would have been better off, since most of the Eurasians in Java had lived like Indonesians, could speak the local dialect, were used to hardship, and could continue to live as before.

When I told Uncle Sudjono about this family, he told me not to visit them too often or the *lurah* [village head] might suspect that we were in contact with the Dutch and he might inform his Japanese masters. However, one evening Uncle Sudjono asked me to take a few *katis* of rice, a bottle of coconut oil, and some sugar to the family. He instructed: "Tell them these presents are from you. Do not say they come from me. Also tell them that for the time being you cannot visit them because you are also hot."

I brought the presents to the Eurasian family and told the lady exactly what I had been told to say. Teo came out from his room. He was glad to see me.

I left their house in the darkness of the night and thought how awful the war was. I wished they were Indonesians, but asked myself if I would notice them if they were Indonesian. Yes, I thought, if they were an Indonesian family living in misery, I would pay attention to them. But if they were an Indonesian family they would not be in such a condition. They would have had their family and friends around to help them, they would still have had their *sawah*, their sugar factories. What? Sugar factories owned by Indonesians? Not likely in the colonial period.

PERGERAKAN FRIENDS

I was stuck in Kedurus for several months, afraid to go to Surabaya because friends said that the Kenpeitai was looking for students who didn't attend the Kenrohoshi. Bung Rambe, who had vanished from Jakarta because of his anti-Japanese attitude, also stayed at Kedurus, as did several other *bung*s of the *pergerakan*, and some of Johan Sjahruzah's underground couriers. I became quite close to Rambe, because he taught me English and mathematics during my voluntary exile in Kedurus. Rambe had been a civil engineering student during the pre-war period. He came from Nias Island, off the west coast of Sumatra, but he looked more like an Ambonese than the average Sumatran. Rambe knew a lot about the Moluccas because he had an Ambonese girl friend in Jakarta, and he liked to listen to my Bandanese stories. Rambe and I organized adult evening classes for the *buta huruf* [illiterate] young farmers' crowd, which led to friendlier relations with the local villagers. At first the Kedurus village folk considered us to be strangers, but they became nicer to us when they came to know us better and when we began to speak their local East Javanese dialect.

One of the other young men who often came to Kedurus was Karel Tobing. He had studied in the Dutch military academy in Bandung before the war and was a brilliant man, but rather lazy. He preferred to read leftist literature rather than bother much with the village folk. Tobing was a good friend of Aidit, later head of the Communist Party of Indonesia. Although Aidit was only nineteen in 1944, while Tobing was twenty-three, Tobing admired Aidit's courage, character, and his political knowledge. Tobing used to tell us that he considered Aidit to be a genuinely revolutionary *pemuda* with a leadership inclination. Although Tobing was himself a good debater, he thought that Aidit was better. I had met Aidit many times at our house in Jakarta, and when we talked about Aidit in Kedurus we always referred to the tiger-skin-like *songkok* he often wore.

For an Indonesian Tobing was rather tall. He looked very strong, and behind his unshaven face he looked fierce. In fact he looked quite handsome when he shaved. He didn't particularly like to have a beard and a seal-like moustache, but he was either too lazy to shave or too poor to own a razor. We noticed that Tobing had light green eyes, but out of respect nobody dared to ask him where he got them from.

Tobing's belongings consisted of a pair of khaki trousers and two patched-up shirts. Every time he arrived in Kedurus, he would borrow a sarong, and ask the housemaid to wash his only pair of trousers. In an afternoon stroll around the village, or when we visited the Sunarjo's house, Tobing would wear a pair of Bung Rambe's trousers and one of my three shirts. Despite his laziness, his bohemian way of life, his proletarian look, and his anti-bathing attitude, the boys respected him. Some of the Kedurus folks thought that Tobing was my older brother. I wasn't very enthusiastic about this, for although I admired his wisdom, I did not like his laziness.

Tobing's Dutch was quite good, and he read English, French, and German books. There was only one man in Surabaya that Tobing didn't try to debate with or say much to: Johan Sjahruzah. Sometimes we didn't see Tobing for weeks. He was probably somewhere in Java acting as Johan Sjahruzah's courier.

Among this group there was a very good man by the name of Ruslan Wijaya, who was born in Kuningan, a border town between West and Central Java. Ruslan worked with Johan Sjahruzah in the oil company, was one of the organizers of the oil cadres, and the man in charge of training the newly recruited *pemuda* for the underground. While Tobing read Maxim Gorky and Russian leftist books, Ruslan concentrated more on Mao's work, and other Communist Chinese books. The boys at the Maspati *asrama* called him "Chu Te," and he did look a bit Chinese. Ruslan often came to Kedurus, but unlike Tobing or Rambe, he didn't talk much, but would speak up occasionally when he disagreed with Rambe. For instance, when Rambe said that when the time came we should try to get Ambonese and those who served in the old colonial armed forces to join us, Ruslan disagreed. He said that those who had served with the colonial armed forces and fascist regimes should be wiped out when the revolution came. A long debate, using all the political phrases they got from those political revolutionary books, lasted until late at night. I got used to all these political debates and discussions, which often lasted until after midnight. As a Javanese lady, Auntie Sudjono was too polite to tell them to go to bed, but when the discussion was at Johan Sjahruzah's home, his wife, Yu Yet, would shout, "Hey, *bungs*! Go to bed! Continue it some other time. Don't you know it is already after midnight?"

UNCLE SIDIK

In addition to Kedurus, Johan Sjahruzah's house in Plampitan, and the Maspati *asrama*, another gathering place of the underground movement in Surabaya was at the house of Uncle Sidik, Kebangsren Gang (alley) III. Uncle Sidik was an old *pergerakan* man, who had been active in the nationalist movement since 1913. He was a simple and honest man who lived in a modest kampong house with his wife, Auntie Sri, and two grandchildren. His life was devoted to the *pergerakan*. At his house one could find all sorts of past *pergerakan* documents, such as: Sarekat Islam files; old newspaper clippings of nationalist conferences and congresses and the names of political activists arrested or banished by the colonial government; books, pamphlets, and other publications issued by the nationalist movement; records of court cases of political activists arrested by the colonial government; and, perhaps most importantly, the whole dossier of the Pendidikan Nasional Indonesia activities of the 1930s. Uncle Sidik was really a *rakyat* man. The whole population of Kampong Kebangsren respected him.

Kebangsren was sandwiched between the glistening shopping centers of Tunjungan and Embong Malang, the area of Surabaya where European hotels were located. Unlike Jakarta, where the kampongs were usually situated a distance away from the high-class residential areas, Surabaya's kampongs were usually sandwiched between the glittering high-class areas and famous main roads. A stranger to Surabaya would not know that behind all those large buildings and beautiful main roads lay kampongs with small alleys, known as *gangs*, where the *rakyat*, the ordinary people, lived.

I often visited Uncle Sidik's house to chat with the old man about the *pergerakan* activities of the 1920s and 1930s, and to read his collection of *pergerakan* publications. I could tell that he was a staunch follower of Uncle Sjahrir and Uncle Hatta, and their former Pendidikan Nasional Indonesia [PNI–Baru] organization. Although not working, Uncle Sidik was self-supporting. He owned a few acres of *sawah* near Mojokerto, and a few houses at Kebangsren that he rented out to some of the kampong folks.

Uncle Sidik told me about his youth in Surabaya. He got into politics when Dr. Sun Yat-sen proclaimed the Republic of China, and began a campaign to modernize China and to cut off the pigtails of male Chinese. Pro-Republican Chinese in Java started a pigtail-cutting campaign around 1913, supported by many Indonesians, and presumably agreed to by the colonial authorities. The campaign started off well enough, but the Indonesians in East Java made use of the opportunity not just to cut off pigtails, but to destroy or dismantle Chinese graveyards that interfered with landscapes around the kampongs. Uncle Sidik got into trouble for such activities, and spent several months in jail. From that time on he was active in the *pergerakan*, contributing his earnings to the cause of Indonesian independence. Many *pergerakan* chaps on the run from the Dutch—and later Japanese—political police hid in Uncle Sidik's house at Kebangsren.

Uncle Sidik prayed five times a day, but did not belong to a Muslim association. He had first joined the Partai Sarikat Islam Indonesia,[1] but later on became a member of the PNI–Baru of Sjahrir and Hatta. Uncle Sidik knew all of the *pergerakan* chaps, and would warn us beforehand about any unreliable and undesirable characters in our midst.

I often stayed at Uncle Sidik's house in Kampong Kebangsren, in whose yard was a rose-apple tree that bore the same, but slightly smaller, green rose-apples as in my backyard at Neira. Uncle Sidik's grandsons studied at the Taman Siswa school.

Often students of the Taman Siswa high school in Jogjakarta, who formed an underground group under the guidance of the head of the school, Uncle Wijono, came to Surabaya to exchange views with the group at the Maspati *asrama*, and with students at the Surabaya Taman Siswa school. The Jogjakarta group included Dimyati, who was responsible for recruiting *pemuda* for the underground; Miss Mursiah, a Madurese student; and Munir, who had been an organizer of transport workers in Jakarta and was recruited by Johan Sjahruzah to the underground. The

---

[1] Partai Sarikat Islam Indonesia was the successor to the original nationalist organization, Sarekat Islam; see Kahin, *Nationalism and Revolution*, p. 94.

Surabaya group included Suparnadi, an adopted son of Pak Sidik, who often traveled between Surabaya and Jogjakarta as a courier for Johan Sjahruzah; Oni Subiyakto, a very pretty girl whose mother was Dutch and whose father was the deputy mayor of Surabaya; Sjafei, the first of the group to be killed in the Battle of Surabaya in November 1945; and others. The meetings of the underground usually took place at Uncle Sidik's house, which was strategically located in the center of the city. Cooperation between the *pemuda* in Kebangsren and the underground leaders to oppose Japan was very close. The visits of the Taman Siswa students from Jogjakarta were very helpful in giving political courses to the Kebangsren *pemuda*.

Uncle Sidik had a great deal of influence in Kebangsren, not just because he had been a follower of Uncle Sjahrir since the 1930s, but because of the large role he played in the area around Surabaya. His *sawah* in Krian produced extra rice, which was needed by the *pejuang* in Surabaya as well as by deserters from PETA. Some remnants of those who had participated with Supriyadi in the PETA revolt in Blitar in February 1945[2] hid in the Kebangsren area, and were taken in by Uncle Sidik without the knowledge of the Japanese.

Occasionally when Uncle Sidik worked too hard or had too many worries, he suffered what was called *"penyakit ayam-ayam"* [chicken sickness], a rare sickness which made the patient jump uncontrollably, like a just-slaughtered chicken fighting to stay alive. I had seen this type of illness before in Banda Neira. People who suffered from it were not allowed to go to sea to avoid their falling overboard and drowning.

Auntie Sri, Uncle Sidik's wife, was a very nice lady although she was illiterate and spent most of her time in the kitchen cooking or doing laundry for her family and the *pergerakan* guests. Twice a year, during harvest time, she visited her village of Krian, near Mojokerto, to collect her share of the crops. She told me how happy she was when Uncle Sjahrir paid them a visit when he came to Surabaya about a year ago. She also told me that she was more afraid of the Japanese police than she had been of the Dutch. Although she trusted the kampong folks, she was always afraid that one day the Kenpeitai might raid her house.

SUFFERING DURING THE OCCUPATION AND ALLIED ATTACKS

By the end of 1944 the number of beggars in the streets of Surabaya increased, and many, especially those who lived under bridges, died of hunger. Some were as thin and emaciated as a skeleton, and wore clothes made of gunnysacks. The people began to understand that Japanese colonialism was worse than that of the Dutch. The people were frequently insulted by being slapped in public, only because they forgot to bow in respect to the Japanese. Such actions in themselves gave rise to the understanding that we did not want to be colonized any more, and that we had to oust all colonizers from Indonesia.

Surabaya was attacked by Allied planes almost every week by the end of 1944, and by early 1945 was attacked almost every night. We heard on our clandestine radio that American forces had already occupied Balikpapan and Tarakan on the east

---

[2] This brief revolt, one of the first significant instances of open opposition to the Japanese Occupation, was likely based on local grievances directed at the Japanese paramilitary organization. The uprising provided nationalist credentials to a number of PETA members who later formed a significant element in the Indonesian army. Described briefly in Benda, *Crescent*, p. 182; and in Anderson, *Java*, p. 36.

coast of Borneo. The closer the Allied forces came, the more frequently the Japanese military installations in Surabaya were attacked. One morning in January 1945, more than fifty Allied planes, B-25 and B-26 bombers accompanied by Mustang fighters, attacked Surabaya. The oil installations in Wonokromo and the industrial area of Ngagel were the primary targets, and many oil wells were set on fire. Some of my friends from the Maspati *asrama* died in the bombings.

We could see that attack from Kedurus. One plane was shot down, but the pilot survived. The next day he was tied on top of a truck, and, escorted by Japanese military trucks, was driven around the mayor's office and Ketabang, the headquarters of the Japanese navy. Then the pilot was shot dead, an action that was contrary to the Geneva Convention, of which Japan was a signatory. Because of the execution of several Allied pilots who had been downed in Surabaya, and other war crimes, an Allied military court that met in Jakarta after the war in 1946, sentenced to death Lieutenant General Harada, commander of the Japanese 16th Army in Java, who had signed the orders to execute those pilots.

The Allied bombing destroyed the electrical installation near Malang, the source of Surabaya's electricity. For more than three weeks Surabaya was dark, and the city's electric trams couldn't move. Only the OJS train, fueled by wood, connected Kedurus with Sepanjang or went toward Wonokromo, and as far as Ujung, near Tanjung Perak harbor. In other parts of the city, officials were forced to walk for kilometers to their offices. It took the Japanese three weeks to repair the damage to the power station.

During the power outage, I stayed with the Bandanese aunties in Surabaya. They told me that Mr. Hayashi had been arrested by the Kenpeitai because he was drunk most of the time. The non-Japanese staff of the textile office was also arrested because of corruption in textile distribution. Corrupt practices among Japanese civilian and military officials were common and well-known to the public, but when the Kenpeitai discovered corruption it was usually the Indonesian staff that they arrested. Cheap clothing for the people was not distributed to the villages because it had already been sold by Japanese civilian officials, with the help of corrupt city and village officials.

The aunties had also heard that the Japanese had arrested several Indonesian doctors in Jakarta, among them Uncle Sjahrir's brother-in-law, Dr. Djoehana, who had been so good to me when I was ill. Many students at the medical faculty in Jakarta were also arrested, as were several Indonesian intellectuals and writers, such as Takdir Alisjahbana. Even Chairil Anwar, the poet, was arrested, because he mixed with the anti-Japanese crowd headed by an Indonesian officer of the former KNIL.

SUKARNI VISITS SURABAYA

In about March 1945, Sukarni,[3] the leader of one of the underground groups, visited the Maspati *asrama*, staying for a week with his three-year-old son. He recognized me as one of the children who had taken him to meet Hatta and Sjahrir when he visited Banda Neira clandestinely in 1939. Sukarni was close to Ruslan Wijaya and Johan Sjahruzah. I didn't know Sukarni's connection with Uncle Rir in the underground, but Sukarni's wife was one of Uncle Rir's many nieces.

---

[3] Sukarni was a prominent pre-war nationalist youth leader and, during the Occupation, he was the leader of an underground nationalist group based within Sendenbu, the Japanese propaganda service. See Kahin, *Nationalism and Revolution*, pp. 86, 112–14.

Sukarni was rather short and thin, with a mustache *a la* Clark Gable. The way he spoke and the way he carried himself made a good impression. I was glad to meet Sukarni; I was always happy to meet someone who had visited my island. He said that his visit to Banda Neira was only for a few hours during the transit of a New Guinea-bound KPM ship, and that he had met Uncles Hatta and Sjahrir secretly at a place far from their residences because he was under surveillance by the colonial police. His descriptions of Banda Neira and its harbor, and of Gunung Api, were quite accurate.

Sukarni's little son, called Lulu, brought change to the *asrama*. He was a bright little boy, and made us happy with his three-year-old tricks, such as pretending to be an angry Japanese guard slapping people who did not bow to him.

Although Sukarni was working with the Sendenbu, the Japanese regime's propaganda outfit, he was actually a member of the underground. I was not included in the meetings between Sukarni, Johan, Uncle Sudjono, and some of the older boys of the network, because I was considered too young. Later it was decided that I should return to Jakarta to work at the Japanese radio station there, and should contact Sukarni in Jakarta to make the necessary arrangements.

CHAPTER FOURTEEN

END OF THE JAPANESE OCCUPATION AND START OF THE REVOLUTION

I arrived back in Jakarta in March 1945. When I got to the house, Uncle Sjahrir was away. Lily had obtained a job at the electricity office. Mimi didn't go to school anymore, but had joined English classes given by Mrs. Herawati Diah. I also enrolled in Mrs. Diah's English class. These classes were considered illegal, because the Japanese authorities prohibited anyone from studying imperialist languages. Herawati Diah had worked as an English announcer with the Japanese overseas broadcasting service, which is where she had met B. M. Diah, who also worked there. They married in 1943, and subsequently both resigned from the broadcast service. Mochtar Lubis and Charles Tambu also worked at the overseas broadcast service, as so-called censors.[1]

RADIO JAKARTA HOSOKYOKU

Soon after I arrived in Jakarta I contacted Jamal, one of Sukarni's people, and through him I obtained work as a control-room operator at the Japanese-run Radio Jakarta Hosokyoku, at a salary of thirty-five guilders a month. I had been told in Surabaya that the job was an important one—listening to Allied broadcasts on the unsealed radio sets at the station. We needed more of our group to work there; we now had only one person.

Mr. Achmad, who had worked at the Jakarta Nirom radio station, was the chief control-room operator. He trained me to operate the control desk, to place microphones for live musical programs, to work the switchboard that connected the studios with the control room, and to charge the batteries and other radio equipment needed for the broadcasts. Radio Jakarta had two programs: the home service and the external service. The home service was broadcast in Indonesian, with extra news and commentaries in Javanese and Sundanese. All the news programs were relayed to other stations in Java, as were the *taiso* gymnastic programs and propaganda broadcasts, including Sukarno's speeches at public rallies. The external service had three language programs: English, directed to Australia, America, and Europe; Arabic, directed to the Near East; and Japanese, directed to the Pacific, for the Japanese troops in the area.

---

[1] B. M. Diah was a prominent journalist who served as chief editor of the Japanese-sponsored newspaper *Asia Raya* during the Occupation. Later he was publisher and chief editor of *Merdeka*, for which his wife, Herawati, worked as a journalist. She was the first Indonesian woman to study in the United States, receiving a B.A. from Columbia University in 1941. Mochtar Lubis, an award-winning journalist and novelist, was also a reporter for *Merdeka*, then was publisher and editor of *Indonesia Raya*. Charles Tambu was a Ceylonese journalist who was captured in Singapore by the Japanese and then brought to Jakarta to monitor Allied radio broadcasts.

The home service was headed by a Mr. Nakayama, an Indonesian-speaking Japanese. Another Japanese and Dr. Utoyo Ramlan were the two assistant directors. The external service was headed by a Japanese graduate of Harvard, with Suryo Dipuro as chief announcer. Many Indonesians, mostly good English speakers, plus several Allied civilian prisoners of war worked at the external service.[2]

I was young and inexperienced, but had a strong will to learn new things that were foreign to me, such as classical music. The Japanese regime banned swing music and jazz, but allowed classical music on the home service. Many famous Western composers, such as Beethoven, Bach, Chopin, and Schumann were unknown to me, and at first I made many mistakes in playing their recordings by mixing up the movements. Once when playing Beethoven's Ninth Symphony I skipped from the first movement to the third, then back to the second, without realizing that I had made a fatal error. One of the Japanese censors, a Mr. Oka, who knew classical music well, was very annoyed. He came to the control room and shouted at me: "You fool! You stupid native!" That was a terrible and bitter lesson for me.

During my second week as a control-room operator I also blundered during the 7:00 AM *taiso* broadcast, which was relayed by all the stations in Java. School children, office workers, soldiers, and others followed this gymnastic session. Usually this program was broadcast live, with one person playing the *taiso* song on the piano and another shouting the exercise commands in Japanese. But one morning when I happened to be on duty, the *taiso* shouter, a certain Margono, did not show up. There was no substitute, and not a single Japanese was there of whom I could ask for advice. The duty announcer told me to play the *taiso* record as a substitute, but neglected to tell me that the *taiso* song was recorded on a finer disc using a different speed than other records, and had to be played on a different turntable with a different needle. Inexperienced as I was, I began to play the *taiso* record with an ordinary needle. For the first few minutes it went well, but suddenly—while the whole of Java was *taiso*-ing following the shouted commands and the *semangat*-sounding Japanese tune—the needle got stuck and the *taiso*-shouter on the record kept repeating his commands. When I tried to correct it, the needle went wild, slipping back and forth and cutting through the fine grooves of the record. Instead of just stopping, the duty announcer told me to play it again. But it just wouldn't work, and the on-air program went from bad to worse. Finally the announcer realized that we couldn't proceed, and he apologized on the air, saying that because of some technical difficulties that morning's *taiso* would be discontinued.

But it was too late. Japanese officials rushed from everywhere to the control room shouting "*bakero*" [fool] at me and the duty announcer. I thought they would send me to the Kenpeitai for sabotaging the most-hated *taiso* program. The director, Nakayama, lectured me for half an hour on how to be serious and more *semangat* while on duty. Margono was the one to be blamed, and when he arrived at the studio one hour after the whole incident was over, Nakayama and the other Japanese

---

[2] Among those Des Alwi remembers were a Miss Mary Henson, an Englishwoman; a Mr. Benson; and Mrs. de Knecht, the wife of a Dutch Air Force major. The Indonesian announcers included Rudy Gonta, who worked with van Mook (a relatively progressive colonial official largely responsible for the design of the attempted federalist system) after the war and later joined the Indonesian Foreign Service; Harris Sitompul, who later joined the *Merdeka* daily as a correspondent; and Budiman, who became an English-language newscaster in Jogjakarta.

officials were waiting for him. His reason for not arriving on time? A punctured bicycle tire.

This was a common ailment during the Japanese Occupation because bicycle tires and tubes were hard to obtain. The black-market price for a tire and tube were equivalent to two months' salary. The Japanese offices didn't provide their employees with tires and tubes, and except for electric trams that only ran on fixed routes, no other public transport was available. *Becak* were few, and most of them used *ban mati* (tubeless tires). Some people had begun to use *ban mati* on their bicycles, but they didn't last long. Either the person using such tires would become exhausted or the tire itself would jump from the rim of the wheel in the middle of the road. It was a common sight to see adults and school children stuck on the road because of *ban mati* or other bicycle troubles.

Poor Margono, I felt sorry for him. He had a heavy duty as a *taiso* shouter, three times a day at 7:00 AM, 12:00 noon, and 5:00 PM. His house in Salemba was about twenty minutes from the studio at Gambir Barat, and he had to make the round trip three times a day—for a salary of only forty guilders a month. Margono looked pale, and wore tight khaki shorts high above his knees. He was very pro-Japanese and *bersemangat*, and was an active member of the Barisan Pelopor, a fascist-like *pemuda* organization formed by Bung Karno, and blessed by the Japanese—or was it the other way around?

Margono spoke rather good Japanese. His *taiso* commands sounded so much like a Japanese soldier that even Uncle Rir didn't believe me when I told him that the daily *taiso* shouter was Indonesian. Margono's voice was only suitable for shouting *taiso* commands or commanding members of his Barisan Pelopor company. His voice was too light and *garing* (sharp) to be a radio announcer or a news reader, although he was quite good as a sports commentator. Some of the boys at the office called him *jangkrik* (cricket), and other called him *tukang teriak*, Jakarta slang for a shouter or screamer.

One thing I liked about Margono was that he was not a Japanese spy or informer, although he was heavily indoctrinated by the Japanese, and occasionally acted like a Japanese. (Well, we also had many Indonesians who copied Dutch manners and accents in the pre-war days.) Margono never let his friends down. If we pestered him by saying that the Japanese only came to bring misery, Margono would say, "Ah! Don't talk that way. Don't you know we are at war against the colonialists and imperialists?"

We would reply, "To hell with the war. It is not our war."

Then Margono would say, "*Saudara kurang semangat*" [You have little spirit]!

BROADCASTING AND LISTENING

My assignment at Radio Jakarta was as operator for foreign broadcasts, directed to the West, India, and Europe. These broadcasts, which were heavily censored by the Japanese, were relayed through Dayeuhkolot, in Bandung, with a ten kilowatt transmitter. They lasted from 11:00 PM until 1:00 AM. However, when they finished at 1:00 AM, and the Japanese supervisor went to bed, I quietly operated the radio and tuned in to Radio Australia or the BBC. Since I was the operator and the Japanese controllers were too lazy to work after 1:00 AM, I had many chances to listen to foreign radio broadcasts. The following day I would report the situation of the war to one of our underground contacts.

The safest time for my job was during the early morning broadcasts that the Japanese directed to Australia. Since the broadcast started at 6:00 AM, I would need be in the operating room at about 5:00 AM. This gave me time to prepare the amplifier and the microphone, and to switch on the lines to the transmitter, which gave me the opportunity to listen to the early morning broadcasts of Radio Australia. Should the Japanese supervisor enter the room, I would automatically switch to our transmitter beam. As I used headphones, he could not know that I was actually listening to outside broadcasts.

END OF THE WAR APPROACHES

By April 1945 the foreign radio broadcasts, especially Radio Australia and the BBC, reported that thousands of Japanese troops had been killed by American bombs and artillery fire from American warships in the Pacific. Saipan had fallen in July 1944, and Morotai and several other islands in the northern Moluccas were taken by American forces by September. The Americans had landed in the Philippines in October 1944, and from January 1945 until the city finally fell, attacked Manila. Iwo Jima fell to the Americans in March, after a month-long battle, and Okinawa fell in June, after another month-long fight. In Europe, Italy was in the hands of the Allies, who had liberated France and the Netherlands, and by May were nearing Berlin. (Later I learned that Tarakan and Balikpapan, in Borneo, were under Allied control by July 1945.)

We were surprised that Bung Karno still included in his speeches the phrase, *"Amerika kita seterika, Ingris kita linggis."* But there was no one brave enough to report the progress of the war to the nationalist leaders who were working with the Japanese. We even found it difficult to meet with Uncle Hatta, although Mimi, Lily, and I often took to his home some of his favorite Bandanese foods, such as grilled yellow-tail fish.

If I went to Hatta's house at midday, I could only meet with his younger sister, Aunt Giah, who lived there with her daughter, Ain, and I didn't feel that I could ask her to pass on to Uncle Hatta news of the defeats of the Germans and Japanese. The neighbors were Japanese who had the duty of monitoring Uncle Hatta's movements.

In about April 1945 the Japanese intelligence network began to close in on Sjahrir, yet he remained somewhat active in the underground. Reportedly this intelligence network was that of the Japanese Navy, which worked with Mr. Subardjo and Jusuf Hassan.[3] We had heard that the Kenpeitai had captured Chairil Anwar and Yam Idham,[4] who were both very close to Uncle Sjahrir. Sjahrir was asked to give a talk to the Indonesian *pemuda* who were following political seminars at Menteng 31. These *pemuda*, including Aidit, Lukman, and many others, had been sent to Menteng 31 after escaping the Japanese Navy intelligence net, thanks to help from Mr. Subardjo.

One morning in May 1945 Uncle Sjahrir gave me a piece of paper to give to Uncle Hatta, on which was written news of the advances of the American forces in

---

[3] Subardjo was an older politician who had a law degree from Leiden. He was close to Admiral Maeda, and was one of the directors of the Japanese navy-sponsored Asrama Indonesia Merdeka at Kebon Sirih 80. Jusuf Hassan had studied in Japan before the war, and during the Occupation worked for the Kenpeitai.

[4] During the Occupation Yam Idham was imprisoned in Bogor for two years by the Kenpeitai. He later represented the Republic in Pakistan from 1945 to 1950.

the Pacific. The note also included the news that Hitler had committed suicide on April 30, and that leading Nazis had been captured by the Allies. Sjahrir instructed me to deliver the note only into Uncle Hatta's hands, and that if I could not do that, I should burn it. In an emergency, if I were caught by surprise by Japanese spies, and I didn't have the opportunity to burn it, I should put it in my mouth, and if necessary, swallow it. I thought this was a difficult task, and I said jokingly to Uncle Sjahrir, "This note should have been written on *kerupuk* [shrimp chips] so that it would have been tasty to eat." (Fortunately I was able to give the note directly to Uncle Hatta.)

Mimi also frequently served as a courier to take letters from Uncle Sjahrir to Uncle Hatta. Once Uncle Hatta was angry at Mimi because she took a letter to him from one of her plump schoolteachers. The letter from the woman, whose name was Suwarni, began, "Oh, Tata. I love you."

When Uncle Hatta read this letter he became angry at Mimi and asked her why she had brought it to him. Mimi replied, "She said it was important."

He then returned the opened letter to the unsuccessful applicant. We children all read the letter, and even showed it to Uncle Sjahrir. Lily commented, "That letter was misaddressed. It should have been sent to Uncle Sjahrir."

Uncle Sjahrir replied, "*Bolletoet begitu, siapa yang mau?*" [Someone with chubby cheeks like that, who would be interested?]

Family by car. From left to right: Tati (a friend of Mimi's), Des Alwi, Sjahrir, Lily, Poppy (later married to Sjahrir), Mimi, and an unidentified man

THE SJAHRIR UNDERGROUND

The underground held its meetings at a number of different houses. Usually before a meeting, a bamboo ladder was put up in preparation to run away if the Kenpeitai came to arrest the participants. Once when a secret meeting was being held at the home of Mr. Kartamuhari, in Manggarai, some youngsters who wanted to steal fruit from the neighboring house took the escape ladder. Suddenly shouts of "Thief, thief" were heard from the direction of Kartamuhari's neighbor. In a second the secret meeting dissolved, and some participants hid and others fled any which way on their bicycles.

By early August 1945 the underground began to prepare for action. From foreign radio accounts I learned that an atom bomb was dropped on Hiroshima on August 6, and on Nagasaki on August 9. On August 10, almost all the cells of the underground movement gathered at the home of Wikana.[5] Many were students of the Medical Faculty.[6] The journalist Adam Malik, who worked for the Japanese News Agency *Domei*, and who was close to Tan Malaka, was present, as was Sukarni. Chaerul Saleh[7] led the meeting, and began by saying: "According to the August 9 foreign news broadcasts, which we received from Des Alwi, on August 10 the United States will give an ultimatum to Japan that they must surrender by August 15, or their cities will be bombed."

The underground members believed that before Japan surrendered we must seize power and proclaim Indonesia's independence. The way to carry this out was through the people's militias outside the city, helped by PETA and anyone who owned firearms. Our group was headed by Abubakar Lubis and was directly responsible to Chaerul Saleh.

Tasks were divided up. Mine was to prepare our network in the Radio Jakarta Hosokyoku station[8] to broadcast the proclamation of independence. We were given a pistol to use if necessary to enter the station.

On August 13 we began our action by seizing the automobile of the director of the Medical Faculty, whose driver was Deki Suharsono, a medical student. Our plan to enter the radio studio was ready, and the text of the proclamation was ready to be signed by Bung Karno, Bung Hatta, Sjahrir, Chaerul Saleh, and Sukarni (representing Tan Malaka), who were said to be already at Cepu.

However, on the night of August 14, the Kenpeitai, with the help of their Kenpeiho auxiliaries, were guarding the area around Radio Jakarta Hosokyoku. A number of our colleagues inside the studio were not able to leave because they did

---

[5] Wikana was a one-time protégé of Sukarno and had ties to Taman Siswa. Wikana had been an activist in the leftist nationalist party Gerindo and was associated with the Japanese navy-supported Asrama Indonesia Merdeka. At the start of the Revolution he became chairman of Angkatan Pemuda Indonesia (API—Younger Generation of Indonesia).

[6] Among them were Johar Nur and Darwis, prominent *pemuda* who became active in the youth group API; Abubakar Lubis; Ali Akbar; Ridwan, Rahardi Usman, and Subianto Djojohadikusumo, all of whom were killed during the Revolution; and Hari Supit, Eri Sudewo, and M. T. Haryono, who became officers in the Indonesian army.

[7] Chaerul Saleh was a prominent youth leader who had been one of the founders of the radical student association PPPI (Perhimpunan Peladjar-Peladjar Indonesia); he worked at the Sendenbu during the Occupation, and was associated with the Asrama Angkatan Baru at Menteng 31, which was established by the Sendenbu.

[8] Des says that the network included Suwardi, Irsan, and Tajuddin, and that he was also to work with the *pemuda* Ridwan, Rahardi Usman, Bowo Mukiman, and Mr. Jamil.

not have an identification arm band with Japanese letters issued by the Kenpeitai. Irsan and I, who worked at the station, went to the security office to get the arm bands. Then we lent those arm bands to the *pemuda* inside, so that they could leave.

Then we went to the medical students' dormitory at Prapatan 10, where I left one of the arm bands for Rahardi Usman, who had been assigned to read the text of the proclamation once it had been signed by Bung Karno. The four others had already signed that text, including Bung Hatta. I later learned that Sukarno was not prepared to sign because he did not believe that the Japanese had surrendered.

After evening prayers several friends and I headed for the Japanese garage in Cikini to steal one of the Japanese vehicles that were kept there. Kusnaeni, a *pejuang* who had been a student of the Law Faculty, already had the keys to that vehicle, and Deki Suharsono drove us to the garage in the automobile we had stolen from the director of the Medical Faculty. However, in front of the Miss Cicih theater in Kramat, we were ambushed by two Japanese vehicles occupied by Kenpeitai in civilian clothes and wearing *pici*, but armed with pistols. They threatened us and escorted us to the Kenpeitai office in Gambir to be interrogated.

Separately we were taken into different rooms by a Kenpeitai officer, and seated facing an interrogator, with a lamp shining in our eyes. From one side I could hear Bowo Mukiman's voice as he was being worked over, and from the other I heard Rahardi Usman yell whenever he was struck by the interrogator. I wasn't beaten, not because I was the youngest of the group, but because when we filled out the forms for the Kenpeitai, I noted that I was a nephew of Mohammad Hatta. The Japanese interrogator stopped questioning me and left the room, returning with his boss, a colonel in uniform with gold stars and four stripes. He asked, "Why did you meet with the students?"

"I wanted to meet with my friends," I replied.

"Who?"

I hesitated; it was clear that the Japanese already had a list of the students. The colonel took me to his office, and I was afraid I might be killed because I mentioned the name of Mohammad Hatta. The colonel told me to sit down and gave me a glass of ice water. Then a Japanese sergeant entered the room and bowed to the colonel, who then went to the adjoining room. When he left, the sergeant picked up the glass of ice water and threw the water in my face, shouting harshly, "Don't lie! Are you really a nephew of Hatta? If you are lying, you will not leave here alive!"

I said only, "If you don't believe me, just take me to Jalan Diponegoro 57."

The firmness with which I said that I stayed at the home of Mohammad Hatta seemed to convince the Japanese that I was not lying. The Kenpeitai colonel came back into the room and said that he would order an officer to take me to the home of Drs. Mohammad Hatta. Deki Suharsono was brought out of the interrogation room to drive the car. When we got to Hatta's house it was after one o'clock at night. The Japanese officer stood waiting outside the house. Inside, Aunt Giah, Hatta's sister, was preparing the *sahur* meal [meal eaten before daybreak during the fasting month] for her brother. I remember that it was a *malam jumat* [Friday eve] during the fasting month. Then Aunt Giah told Uncle Hatta, "Des is outside, brought by a Japanese officer."

Uncle Hatta came out. As soon as he saw Hatta, the Japanese officer bowed, and then left in the car we'd come in.

Hatta said to me, "Des, you are lucky that the Japanese have begun to lose their teeth. If not, you would have lost your head."

The following afternoon, August 15, the other five of my group were taken home, leaving behind their stolen vehicle. From their interrogations that night the Japanese certainly learned that many Indonesians already knew about the atom bombs dropped on Hiroshima and Nagasaki, and that Japan would soon surrender to the Allies.

At one o'clock in the afternoon (twelve noon in Tokyo) on August 15, 1945, Japanese officers gathered in the auditorium of Radio Jakarta Hosokyoku to listen to the speech of the Japanese Emperor. Only Radio Jakarta Hosokyoku could receive that broadcast because it was the only station equipped with relay equipment to receive long-distance broadcasts. In his speech the Emperor said that Japan had lost the war and surrendered to the Allied forces. After his speech I saw that many Japanese were crying.

PROCLAMATION OF INDEPENDENCE

At six o'clock on the morning of August 17, 1945, we gathered again, ready to broadcast the proclamation of independence. After having been kidnapped by *pemuda* and taken to Rengasdengklok, and made to listen to the broadcast of Japan's surrender, Bung Karno was ready to sign the proclamation.[9] (The text of the proclamation was not the same as that prepared four days earlier.[10])

We gathered at the medical students' *asrama* at Prapatan 10, bringing the text of the proclamation to be broadcast by radio and given out to the people. Oddly enough, many students were unaware of what was going on as they had not been following our activities. On that morning many of them were preparing to carry out their routine daily activities. They were not aware that on that day, August 17, 1945, Indonesia would change from a colony to an independent state, or that a bloody struggle would ensue for five years, with more than 500,000 victims, before the Netherlands recognized Indonesia's independence. They only understood after the proclamation was announced, and then they quickly immersed themselves in the Revolution.

By seven o'clock the morning of August 17, we were ready. The area around the radio station was tightly guarded by the Heiho, so we had to enter the station by jumping the back fence on the Tanah Abang side. I went in first, and all was quiet within. We were prepared to broadcast the text of the proclamation at 10:00 AM. However, when Rahardi Usman jumped the fence he accidentally dropped his pistol, which went off with a loud noise. The others jumped back over the fence and ran away, while being chased by several Heiho. I, who was already inside, quickly gave the text to Jusuf Ronodipuro,[11] but he only succeeded in broadcasting it that evening.

Because we thought that our effort to broadcast the proclamation had failed, Chaerul Saleh asked me to go to the *Domei* news service to ask Adam Malik to publish the news that Indonesia had proclaimed its independence. It was through *Domei*, sent by Morse code, that the news was successfully sent to all parts of the world. That evening the BBC broadcast the statement by Lord Louis Mountbatten,

---

[9] On the kidnapping and events surrounding the proclamation of independence, see Kahin, *Nationalism and Revolution*, pp. 134–36; and Anderson, *Java*, pp. 74–84.

[10] No copy of the earlier draft has been found.

[11] Jusuf Ronodipuro was director of Radio Jakarta and later a member of the Indonesian Foreign Service.

Allied commander in chief for Southeast Asia, who had been designated to occupy the Netherlands Indies: "I understand that the natives of Java have proclaimed their independence."

After our broadcast the Kenpeitai went to Radio Jakarta and arrested several people, but some friends and I fled through the back exit. However, during the Japanese raid that night at the medical students' camp, some of us were arrested and brought to Kenpeitai headquarters. We were beaten up during the interrogation, but since they had already surrendered the Japanese were not as fierce as they used to be. Two days later we were released, and I was sent back to Surabaya to prepare for a broadcast there.

START OF THE REVOLUTION IN SURABAYA

When I arrived in Surabaya I discovered that the independence proclamation was not as big an occasion there as it had been in Jakarta. Our underground links there were still preparing to establish an "aboveground" organization to obtain weapons from the Japanese, either by peaceful means or by force.

On September 13, 1945, an Allied plane flew over Surabaya and parachuted in several Dutch administrative officers to prepare for the entry of Allied forces and the NICA [Netherlands Indies Civil Administration]. We did not know at that time that the British were going to take the Japanese surrender and administer Indonesia. These parachutists were received officially by the Japanese, who behaved very nicely toward them, and accommodated them at the famous Oranje Hotel in Surabaya.

Six days later some Dutch youths hoisted the Dutch flag on top of the Oranje Hotel. That gave us a chance to strike and get the public with us. People from everywhere streamed to the hotel to haul down the Dutch flag. Several Dutch who were responsible for hoisting the flag were wounded.[12] The situation was tense in Surabaya, and we made use of it to organize a youth brigade, formed under the name Pemuda Republik Indonesia (PRI, Youth of the Indonesian Republic), to attack the Japanese as well as Dutch anti-independence forces.

The Japanese, especially the Japanese marines, who were quite willing to surrender their weapons to us, seemed to be only half-heartedly opposing our movement. Only the Japanese Kenpeitai were still hostile. However, on September 23, the population, which did not forget the Kenpeitai's atrocities, attacked the Kenpeitai's headquarters, situated in front of the former office of the East Java governor. There was fierce fighting. Although the Japanese used machine guns, they were unable to save themselves from the massive crowd that stormed into the building—with some carrying only sharpened bamboo sticks and knives. The Kenpeitai fought to the last man. After this incident the crowd went wild. Quite disorganized, they just attacked and killed any Japanese they saw and even stormed the Japanese military camp without proper weapons. Many in the crowd were killed or mowed down by Japanese machine guns. It took us a week to disarm all the Japanese troops in Surabaya. Some of them surrendered peacefully, and some gave us a hard fight.[13]

---

[12] Upset at the return of the Dutch, the *pemuda* saw the raising of the Dutch flag as a severe provocation. They were successful in using this incident to gain popular support, and the taking down of the flag from the Oranje Hotel remains an important symbol of resistance to the attempt to reimpose colonial rule.

[13] Anderson, *Java*, pp. 128–29.

In the meantime, we managed to organize our own forces, based on our underground boys, plus some students and ex-Indonesian soldiers who had been organized by the Japanese during the Occupation. These forces were already considered the fighting troops of our independence movement. We managed to evacuate and transport the Japanese soldiers to the mountains of East Java, and cleared the city of any anti-Indonesian forces, including anti-independence Dutch Eurasians.

Two weeks after the flag incident at the Oranje Hotel, in early October 1945, we were practically in control of the city of Surabaya and the interior of East Java. Most of the Japanese weapons were in our hands, including coastal batteries, antiaircraft guns, and heavy machine guns. With the people backing the struggle for independence, we became stronger. We opened public kitchens to feed the troops and the population. Youth movements and other political as well as armed groups mushroomed in Surabaya and East Java. Our youth brigade, the PRI, was the strongest and the best-equipped armed organization.

Surabaya came back to life. Trains began to run normally. Hotels and restaurants opened, the streets were lit, and even the oil wells at Wonokromo functioned normally. Those killed during the fighting were buried in Taman Pahlawan, a graveyard for heroes.

Toward the end of October we received news that units of the 49th Indian Infantry (Fighting Cock) Brigade, Indian soldiers with British officers, would be coming to Surabaya to restore law and order, to arrange the evacuation of Japanese troops, and to take care of those who had been prisoners of war during the Occupation. Large troopships landed these units at Tanjung Perak harbor on October 25. The following day they marched from there into the city, occupied the former Japanese military camps, and placed troops at strategic positions. The situation in Surabaya was becoming grave. Any incident could start an open war between our side and the three battalions of the Fighting Cock Brigade. Our combined strength was estimated at around ten thousand troops, plus a large number of armed civilians.

The first incident started when the British military police stopped a jeep of our soldiers. Probably thinking the jeep belonged to them and that we had stolen it, they disarmed our four soldiers and confiscated the jeep. In fact, the jeep was one we got when we disarmed the Japanese garrison at Surabaya. When the British did not release the jeep, the combined armed groups in Surabaya decided to attack the British troops. Street fighting lasted for three days and many of the British troops were killed or taken prisoner. Only the Fighting Cock units that occupied the harbor and the areas around it were untouched.

Because of the jeep incident, on October 29 Sukarno, Hatta, and Amir Sjarifuddin[14] flew from Jakarta to Surabaya in a British plane. Not knowing who was on the plane, our units on the ground shot at it as it was about to land at the Surabaya airport. When the plane landed and Hatta and Sukarno emerged, the three of them rode in a big jeep, which the British called a "power wagon," to our headquarters at the governor's residence. The power wagon was driven by an Indian soldier from the Fighting Cocks, and seated next to him was an armed Indian officer. Behind the three Indonesian leaders were three Indonesian *pemuda* with automatic

---

[14] At that time Amir Sjarifuddin was Minister of Information, and later became Minister of Defense, in the Republican government.

weapons for protection. I jumped into the jeep, standing near the Indian officer, to guide the car to the governor's residence through side streets to avoid the main roads where fighting was occurring, such as Tunjungan and Embong Malang.

After a conference with the commander of the Fighting Cock Brigade, Brigadier General Mallaby, a ceasefire was ordered. However, fighting broke out again, and the following morning, October 30, Sukarno and Hatta met again with Mallaby and the commander of the 23rd Division, General Hawthorn, at the governor's residence. Believing that a truce had been agreed to, Sukarno, Hatta, Amir Sjarifuddin, and General Hawthorn returned to Jakarta that afternoon. Brigadier Mallaby stayed in Surabaya.

A day later, when our units were taking Brigadier Mallaby to the British headquarters at the former Internatio building to implement the ceasefire arrangements, Indian troops opened fire. They mistakenly thought that our troops were about to attack them. Fighting started right in front of the building and Brigadier Mallaby was shot and killed by two *permuda* while he was sitting in a car near the Internatio building.[15]

After Brigadier Mallaby's death the British sent troop reinforcements to Surabaya. They even brought along tanks and Spitfire planes, which were stationed at the former naval air base near the harbor. Suddenly Surabaya skies were filled with fighter planes dropping pamphlets, signed by Major General Mansergh,[16] ordering us to leave Surabaya within twenty-four hours.

We ignored the ultimatum, and then exactly at 6:00 AM on November 10, 1945, British warships and planes started bombarding Surabaya. Then mixed units of British and Indian troops moved up from the harbor with big tanks and smashed our defense along the Perak River. They even occupied the whole of Surabaya's old town, including the Chinatown. We fought back using the heavy weapons we had. Our defense was mostly near the viaduct that separated Surabaya from the old town. The tanks could not overrun us because they could not penetrate the viaduct that barricaded Surabaya. Then the infantry bombarded us with mortars. The effect was disastrous, not so much on the troops as on the population in Surabaya. People were killed everywhere. I had never seen so many dead bodies and wounded on the streets as was the scene in Surabaya. Morale of our troops ran low, and some even started retreating to the outskirts of the city. After three weeks of heavy street fighting, we retreated from Surabaya.

At that time I was radio communication officer of the PRI brigade. As my unit, which consisted of six people and two trucks carrying radio transmitters and equipment, was about to leave Surabaya, a British mortar fell on the first truck, killing the driver and wounding several of us. I was lucky to have been in the second truck, but still I received two fragments in my left leg. We put the dead driver and several of our wounded friends in the other truck and sped south to the town of Sidoarjo, where we were given first aid. I fainted from loss of blood, and was brought to the hill town of Malang, where I spent a week in a hospital. When my wound was healed I returned to Sidoarjo.

---

[15] For a detailed account of the battle of Surabaya and the killing of Brigadier Mallaby, see Richard McMillan, *The British Occupation of Indonesia 1945–1946* (London and New York, NY: Routledge, 2005), pp. 31–58. For a comparison of the Indonesian and British accounts of Mallaby's death, see J. G. A. Parrott, "Who Killed Brigadier Mallaby," *Indonesia* 20 (October 1975): 87–111.

[16] Mansergh was commander of the Fifth Indian Infantry Division.

When Sidoarjo was no longer a safe place to stay, I moved over to Mojokerto, and then to Jogjakarta, which became the capital of the Republic in January 1946. We opened a transmitter there for broadcasting the Voice of Free Indonesia in foreign languages to the outside world. By that time Sjahrir had been appointed as the first Indonesian Prime Minister, but he remained in Jakarta. I was then assigned to Jakarta to obtain ammunition and weapons for our troops in East Java.

During the first year and a half of the Revolution I often traveled between Jakarta, Jogjakarta, and East Java. Twice I was arrested by Dutch troops. The first time I was kept in prison for three days until the British military police released me. The second time, early in 1947, I was arrested near the outskirts of Jakarta, but was released because the Indonesian and Dutch governments had signed the Linggadjati Agreement (March 25, 1947), which recognized the de facto authority of the Republic in parts of Java and Sumatra.[17]

Believing that the Linggadjati Agreement meant that Indonesia was about to receive her independence, I left for Europe to continue my radio studies. After my experiences in Java during the Japanese Occupation and early years of the Revolution, I was no longer a boy from Banda, but a man from Indonesia.

---

[17] For a description of the provisions of the agreement, see Kahin, *Nationalism and Revolution*, pp. 196–99.

POSTSCRIPT

When I first arrived in Europe, I landed at Rotterdam. There I was shocked to see a Dutchman carrying my bag! The world had, indeed, changed. When the first Dutch military action against Indonesia started in July 1947, I went on to London. There I met Sjahrir, who was returning from the United Nations headquarters at Lake Success, where he had put the case for Indonesian independence to the United Nations General Assembly.

Later, an Indonesian-government office was opened in London with Subandrio[18] as head, and I worked there in the information department. At the same time, I took a radio course at the Regent Street Polytechnic, and in 1947 enrolled as a student at the British Institute of Technology in London, receiving some practical work experience at the BBC. I later worked as a technician and a translator for the BBC until Indonesia's independence was recognized on December 27, 1949.

During the previous year, I served as a staff assistant with the Indonesian delegation to the Round Table Conference, which negotiated Indonesia's independence from the Netherlands. In July 1949 I was asked by then-Major M. T. Haryono to help the Indonesian delegation's military committee, and I became the assistant to the head of the committee, Colonel Simatupang, who was the Indonesian armed forces' de facto deputy chief of staff. My tasks included looking after the documents, carrying Simatupang's briefcase to the conference table, and awakening two members of the military committee, Major Haryono and Lieutenant Colonel Daan Yahya, at seven o'clock every morning. My salary was to have been 500 Dutch guilders a month, but Uncle Hatta, who was head of the Indonesian delegation, slashed it to 400 guilders because I was only a clerk.

RETURN TO INDONESIA—REBELLION IN AMBON

In July 1950 I returned to Indonesia, working on a British cargo ship of the Blue Funnel Line to pay for my passage. Then, for the first time in eight years, I was reunited with my mother, who was now staying in Jakarta.

Soon after my arrival in Jakarta, I was assigned by Radio Indonesia to follow the Indonesian national army [Tentara Nasional Indonesia, TNI], which was fighting against the so-called Republic of the South Moluccas [Republik Maluku Selatan, RMS].[19] My mission was to reestablish Radio Ambon, which was in the hands of the

---

[18] Subandrio was a medical doctor who became a diplomat, and later served as Sukarno's last foreign minister.

[19] The Ambonese, many of whom were Christian, had had a privileged position in the colonial period, with many serving in the colonial army, the KNIL. As the Republic moved from a federation structure (which the Dutch had created during the Revolution in an attempt to isolate Java, the heart of the conflict) toward a unitary state, a small group went into revolt in Ambon. That uprising was put down by a TNI expeditionary force, led by a Manadonese Christian, Lt. Col. Alex Kawilarang. For details, see Richard Chauvel, "Ambon: Not a Revolution but a Counterrevolution," in *Regional Dynamics of the Indonesian Revolution: Unity*

RMS. I flew to Makassar aboard an air force plane, and after having obtained three technical assistants, flew to Buru Island, which had just been recaptured from the RMS. That same night we were taken by an Indonesian corvette to Tuleho, a small town on Ambon Island. Our Indonesian troops only occupied half of the island. A week later the TNI occupied the town of Ambon. The transmitters of Radio Ambon were intact, except for two or three broken valves. The town of Ambon was half destroyed, so I used a school building for a radio station. With the assistance of the army, we were able to broadcast from Radio Ambon. We also made use of the buildings as a refugee camp for those who had fled to the hills during the attack; many of them were half-starved.

As soon as some of my relatives and friends knew that I was in Ambon, they all came to see me. In fact, they came to ask for food. One of my visitors was Aunt Willy, my former schoolteacher. I felt sorry for those people who were caught in the political conflict, but who did not know anything about it.

Des Alwi (on left) with Hatta and Mrs. Hatta

BECOMING A DIPLOMAT

I stayed in Ambon for a month, and then went back to Jakarta. I was then assigned as sound engineer for the foreign broadcast section of Radio Indonesia. I also assisted the English section of Radio Indonesia. In 1951 I was sent as a member

from Diversity, ed. Audrey R. Kahin (Honolulu, HI: University of Hawaii Press, 1985), pp. 257–59.

of the Indonesian delegation to an International Telecommunications Union Conference in Geneva. I took part in the conference in the tropical bands section.

In November 1952, I returned to Jakarta and to Radio Indonesia. In 1953 I was married, and that same year I was chosen to join the Indonesian diplomatic service as a press attaché in Bern, Switzerland. Thus I embarked on a diplomatic career.

INDEX

Page numbers in *boldface italics* indicate a photo, map, or illustration

T

SOUTHEAST ASIA PROGRAM PUBLICATIONS

Cornell University

Studies on Southeast Asia

Number 44　*Friends and Exiles: A Memoir of the Nutmeg Isles and the Indonesian Nationalist Movement*, Des Alwi, ed. Barbara S. Harvey. 2008. ISBN 978-0-877277-44-6 (pb).

Number 43　*Early Southeast Asia: Selected Essays*, O. W. Wolters, ed. Craig J. Reynolds. 2008. 255 pp. ISBN 978-0-877277-43-9 (pb).

Number 42　*Thailand: The Politics of Despotic Paternalism* (revised edition), Thak Chaloemtiarana. 2007. 284 pp. ISBN 0-8772-7742-7 (pb).

Number 41　*Views of Seventeenth-Century Vietnam: Christoforo Borri on Cochinchina and Samuel Baron on Tonkin*, ed. Olga Dror and K. W. Taylor. 2006. 290 pp. ISBN 0-8772-7741-9 (pb).

Number 40　*Laskar Jihad: Islam, Militancy, and the Quest for Identity in Post-New Order Indonesia*, Noorhaidi Hasan. 2006. 266 pp. ISBN 0-877277-40-0 (pb).

Number 39　*The Indonesian Supreme Court: A Study of Institutional Collapse*, Sebastiaan Pompe. 2005. 494 pp. ISBN 0-877277-38-9 (pb).

Number 38　*Spirited Politics: Religion and Public Life in Contemporary Southeast Asia*, ed. Andrew C. Willford and Kenneth M. George. 2005. 210 pp. ISBN 0-87727-737-0.

Number 37　*Sumatran Sultanate and Colonial State: Jambi and the Rise of Dutch Imperialism, 1830-1907*, Elsbeth Locher-Scholten, trans. Beverley Jackson. 2004. 332 pp. ISBN 0-87727-736-2.

Number 36　*Southeast Asia over Three Generations: Essays Presented to Benedict R. O'G. Anderson*, ed. James T. Siegel and Audrey R. Kahin. 2003. 398 pp. ISBN 0-87727-735-4.

Number 35　*Nationalism and Revolution in Indonesia*, George McTurnan Kahin, intro. Benedict R. O'G. Anderson (reprinted from 1952 edition, Cornell University Press, with permission). 2003. 530 pp. ISBN 0-87727-734-6.

Number 34　*Golddiggers, Farmers, and Traders in the "Chinese Districts" of West Kalimantan, Indonesia*, Mary Somers Heidhues. 2003. 316 pp. ISBN 0-87727-733-8.

Number 33　*Opusculum de Sectis apud Sinenses et Tunkinenses (A Small Treatise on the Sects among the Chinese and Tonkinese): A Study of Religion in China and North Vietnam in the Eighteenth Century*, Father Adriano de St. Thecla, trans. Olga Dror, with Mariya Berezovska. 2002. 363 pp. ISBN 0-87727-732-X.

Number 32　*Fear and Sanctuary: Burmese Refugees in Thailand*, Hazel J. Lang. 2002. 204 pp. ISBN 0-87727-731-1.

Number 31　*Modern Dreams: An Inquiry into Power, Cultural Production, and the Cityscape in Contemporary Urban Penang, Malaysia*, Beng-Lan Goh. 2002. 225 pp. ISBN 0-87727-730-3.

Number 30　*Violence and the State in Suharto's Indonesia*, ed. Benedict R. O'G. Anderson. 2001. Second printing, 2002. 247 pp. ISBN 0-87727-729-X.

Number 29　*Studies in Southeast Asian Art: Essays in Honor of Stanley J. O'Connor*, ed. Nora A. Taylor. 2000. 243 pp. Illustrations. ISBN 0-87727-728-1.

Number 8	*The Politics of Colonial Exploitation: Java, the Dutch, and the Cultivation System*, Cornelis Fasseur, ed. R. E. Elson, trans. R. E. Elson, Ary Kraal. 1992. 2nd printing 1994. 266 pp. ISBN 0-87727-707-9.
Number 7	*A Malay Frontier: Unity and Duality in a Sumatran Kingdom*, Jane Drakard. 1990. 2nd printing 2003. 215 pp. ISBN 0-87727-706-0.
Number 6	*Trends in Khmer Art*, Jean Boisselier, ed. Natasha Eilenberg, trans. Natasha Eilenberg, Melvin Elliott. 1989. 124 pp., 24 plates. ISBN 0-87727-705-2.
Number 5	*Southeast Asian Ephemeris: Solar and Planetary Positions, A.D. 638–2000*, J. C. Eade. 1989. 175 pp. ISBN 0-87727-704-4.
Number 3	*Thai Radical Discourse: The Real Face of Thai Feudalism Today*, Craig J. Reynolds. 1987. 2nd printing 1994. 186 pp. ISBN 0-87727-702-8.
Number 1	*The Symbolism of the Stupa*, Adrian Snodgrass. 1985. Revised with index, 1988. 3rd printing 1998. 469 pp. ISBN 0-87727-700-1.

SEAP Series

Number 23	*Possessed by the Spirits: Mediumship in Contemporary Vietnamese Communities*. 2006. 186 pp. ISBN 0-877271-41-0 (pb).
Number 22	*The Industry of Marrying Europeans*, Vũ Trọng Phụng, trans. Thúy Tranviet. 2006. 66 pp. ISBN 0-877271-40-2 (pb).
Number 21	*Securing a Place: Small-Scale Artisans in Modern Indonesia*, Elizabeth Morrell. 2005. 220 pp. ISBN 0-877271-39-9.
Number 20	*Southern Vietnam under the Reign of Minh Mạng (1820-1841): Central Policies and Local Response*, Choi Byung Wook. 2004. 226pp. ISBN 0-0-877271-40-2.
Number 19	*Gender, Household, State: Đổi Mới in Việt Nam*, ed. Jayne Werner and Danièle Bélanger. 2002. 151 pp. ISBN 0-87727-137-2.
Number 18	*Culture and Power in Traditional Siamese Government*, Neil A. Englehart. 2001. 130 pp. ISBN 0-87727-135-6.
Number 17	*Gangsters, Democracy, and the State*, ed. Carl A. Trocki. 1998. Second printing, 2002. 94 pp. ISBN 0-87727-134-8.
Number 16	*Cutting across the Lands: An Annotated Bibliography on Natural Resource Management and Community Development in Indonesia, the Philippines, and Malaysia*, ed. Eveline Ferretti. 1997. 329 pp. ISBN 0-87727-133-X.
Number 15	*The Revolution Falters: The Left in Philippine Politics after 1986*, ed. Patricio N. Abinales. 1996. Second printing, 2002. 182 pp. ISBN 0-87727-132-1.
Number 14	*Being Kammu: My Village, My Life*, Damrong Tayanin. 1994. 138 pp., 22 tables, illus., maps. ISBN 0-87727-130-5.
Number 13	*The American War in Vietnam*, ed. Jayne Werner, David Hunt. 1993. 132 pp. ISBN 0-87727-131-3.
Number 12	*The Voice of Young Burma*, Aye Kyaw. 1993. 92 pp. ISBN 0-87727-129-1.
Number 11	*The Political Legacy of Aung San*, ed. Josef Silverstein. Revised edition 1993. 169 pp. ISBN 0-87727-128-3.

Number 10   *Studies on Vietnamese Language and Literature: A Preliminary Bibliography*, Nguyen Dinh Tham. 1992. 227 pp. ISBN 0-87727-127-5.

Number 8   *From PKI to the Comintern, 1924–1941: The Apprenticeship of the Malayan Communist Party*, Cheah Boon Kheng. 1992. 147 pp. ISBN 0-87727-125-9.

Number 7   *Intellectual Property and US Relations with Indonesia, Malaysia, Singapore, and Thailand*, Elisabeth Uphoff. 1991. 67 pp. ISBN 0-87727-124-0.

Number 6   *The Rise and Fall of the Communist Party of Burma (CPB)*, Bertil Lintner. 1990. 124 pp. 26 illus., 14 maps. ISBN 0-87727-123-2.

Number 5   *Japanese Relations with Vietnam: 1951–1987*, Masaya Shiraishi. 1990. 174 pp. ISBN 0-87727-122-4.

Number 3   *Postwar Vietnam: Dilemmas in Socialist Development*, ed. Christine White, David Marr. 1988. 2nd printing 1993. 260 pp. ISBN 0-87727-120-8.

Number 2   *The Dobama Movement in Burma (1930–1938)*, Khin Yi. 1988. 160 pp. ISBN 0-87727-118-6.

Cornell Modern Indonesia Project Publications

Number 75   *A Tour of Duty: Changing Patterns of Military Politics in Indonesia in the 1990s.* Douglas Kammen and Siddharth Chandra. 1999. 99 pp. ISBN 0-87763-049-6.

Number 74   *The Roots of Acehnese Rebellion 1989–1992*, Tim Kell. 1995. 103 pp. ISBN 0-87763-040-2.

Number 73   *"White Book" on the 1992 General Election in Indonesia*, trans. Dwight King. 1994. 72 pp. ISBN 0-87763-039-9.

Number 72   *Popular Indonesian Literature of the Qur'an*, Howard M. Federspiel. 1994. 170 pp. ISBN 0-87763-038-0.

Number 71   *A Javanese Memoir of Sumatra, 1945–1946: Love and Hatred in the Liberation War*, Takao Fusayama. 1993. 150 pp. ISBN 0-87763-037-2.

Number 70   *East Kalimantan: The Decline of a Commercial Aristocracy*, Burhan Magenda. 1991. 120 pp. ISBN 0-87763-036-4.

Number 69   *The Road to Madiun: The Indonesian Communist Uprising of 1948*, Elizabeth Ann Swift. 1989. 120 pp. ISBN 0-87763-035-6.

Number 68   *Intellectuals and Nationalism in Indonesia: A Study of the Following Recruited by Sutan Sjahrir in Occupation Jakarta*, J. D. Legge. 1988. 159 pp. ISBN 0-87763-034-8.

Number 67   *Indonesia Free: A Biography of Mohammad Hatta*, Mavis Rose. 1987. 252 pp. ISBN 0-87763-033-X.

Number 66   *Prisoners at Kota Cane*, Leon Salim, trans. Audrey Kahin. 1986. 112 pp. ISBN 0-87763-032-1.

Number 65   *The Kenpeitai in Java and Sumatra*, trans. Barbara G. Shimer, Guy Hobbs, intro. Theodore Friend. 1986. 80 pp. ISBN 0-87763-031-3.

Number 64   *Suharto and His Generals: Indonesia's Military Politics, 1975–1983*, David Jenkins. 1984. 4th printing 1997. 300 pp. ISBN 0-87763-030-5.

Number 62   *Interpreting Indonesian Politics: Thirteen Contributions to the Debate, 1964–1981*, ed. Benedict Anderson, Audrey Kahin, intro. Daniel S. Lev. 1982. 3rd printing 1991. 172 pp. ISBN 0-87763-028-3.

Number 60   *The Minangkabau Response to Dutch Colonial Rule in the Nineteenth Century*, Elizabeth E. Graves. 1981. 157 pp. ISBN 0-87763-000-3.

Number 59   *Breaking the Chains of Oppression of the Indonesian People: Defense Statement at His Trial on Charges of Insulting the Head of State, Bandung, June 7–10, 1979*, Heri Akhmadi. 1981. 201 pp. ISBN 0-87763-001-1.

Number 57   *Permesta: Half a Rebellion*, Barbara S. Harvey. 1977. 174 pp. ISBN 0-87763-003-8.

Number 55   *Report from Banaran: The Story of the Experiences of a Soldier during the War of Independence*, Maj. Gen. T. B. Simatupang. 1972. 186 pp. ISBN 0-87763-005-4.

Number 52   *A Preliminary Analysis of the October 1 1965, Coup in Indonesia (Prepared in January 1966)*, Benedict R. Anderson, Ruth T. McVey, assist. Frederick P. Bunnell. 1971. 3rd printing 1990. 174 pp. ISBN 0-87763-008-9.

Number 51   *The Putera Reports: Problems in Indonesian-Japanese War-Time Cooperation*, Mohammad Hatta, trans., intro. William H. Frederick. 1971. 114 pp. ISBN 0-87763-009-7.

Number 50   *Schools and Politics: The Kaum Muda Movement in West Sumatra (1927–1933)*, Taufik Abdullah. 1971. 257 pp. ISBN 0-87763-010-0.

Number 49   *The Foundation of the Partai Muslimin Indonesia*, K. E. Ward. 1970. 75 pp. ISBN 0-87763-011-9.

Number 48   *Nationalism, Islam and Marxism*, Soekarno, intro. Ruth T. McVey. 1970. 2nd printing 1984. 62 pp. ISBN 0-87763-012-7.

Number 43   *State and Statecraft in Old Java: A Study of the Later Mataram Period, 16th to 19th Century*, Soemarsaid Moertono. Revised edition 1981. 180 pp. ISBN 0-87763-017-8.

Number 39   Preliminary Checklist of Indonesian Imprints (1945-1949), John M. Echols. 186 pp. ISBN 0-87763-025-9.

Number 37   *Mythology and the Tolerance of the Javanese*, Benedict R. O'G. Anderson. 2nd edition, 1996. Reprinted 2004. 104 pp., 65 illus. ISBN 0-87763-041-0.

Number 25   *The Communist Uprisings of 1926–1927 in Indonesia: Key Documents*, ed., intro. Harry J. Benda, Ruth T. McVey. 1960. 2nd printing 1969. 177 pp. ISBN 0-87763-024-0.

Number 7   *The Soviet View of the Indonesian Revolution*, Ruth T. McVey. 1957. 3rd printing 1969. 90 pp. ISBN 0-87763-018-6.

Number 6   *The Indonesian Elections of 1955*, Herbert Feith. 1957. 2nd printing 1971. 91 pp. ISBN 0-87763-020-8.

Translation Series

Volume 4   *Approaching Suharto's Indonesia from the Margins*, ed. Takashi Shiraishi. 1994. 153 pp. ISBN 0-87727-403-7.

Volume 3   *The Japanese in Colonial Southeast Asia,* ed. Saya Shiraishi, Takashi Shiraishi. 1993. 172 pp. ISBN 0-87727-402-9.

Volume 2   *Indochina in the 1940s and 1950s,* ed. Takashi Shiraishi, Motoo Furuta. 1992. 196 pp. ISBN 0-87727-401-0.

Volume 1   *Reading Southeast Asia,* ed. Takashi Shiraishi. 1990. 188 pp. ISBN 0-87727-400-2.

Language Texts

INDONESIAN

Beginning Indonesian through Self-Instruction, John U. Wolff, Dédé Oetomo, Daniel Fietkiewicz. 3rd revised edition 1992. Vol. 1. 115 pp. ISBN 0-87727-529-7. Vol. 2. 434 pp. ISBN 0-87727-530-0. Vol. 3. 473 pp. ISBN 0-87727-531-9.

Indonesian Readings, John U. Wolff. 1978. 4th printing 1992. 480 pp. ISBN 0-87727-517-3

Indonesian Conversations, John U. Wolff. 1978. 3rd printing 1991. 297 pp. ISBN 0-87727-516-5

Formal Indonesian, John U. Wolff. 2nd revised edition 1986. 446 pp. ISBN 0-87727-515-7

TAGALOG

Pilipino through Self-Instruction, John U. Wolff, Maria Theresa C. Centeno, Der-Hwa V. Rau. 1991. Vol. 1. 342 pp. ISBN 0-87727—525-4. Vol. 2., revised 2005, 378 pp. ISBN 0-87727-526-2. Vol 3., revised 2005, 431 pp. ISBN 0-87727-527-0. Vol. 4. 306 pp. ISBN 0-87727-528-9.

THAI

A. U. A. Language Center Thai Course, J. Marvin Brown. Originally published by the American University Alumni Association Language Center, 1974. Reissued by Cornell Southeast Asia Program, 1991, 1992. Book 1. 267 pp. ISBN 0-87727-506-8. Book 2. 288 pp. ISBN 0-87727-507-6. Book 3. 247 pp. ISBN 0-87727-508-4.

A. U. A. Language Center Thai Course, Reading and Writing Text (mostly reading), 1979. Reissued 1997. 164 pp. ISBN 0-87727-511-4.

A. U. A. Language Center Thai Course, Reading and Writing Workbook (mostly writing), 1979. Reissued 1997. 99 pp. ISBN 0-87727-512-2.

KHMER

Cambodian System of Writing and Beginning Reader, Franklin E. Huffman. Originally published by Yale University Press, 1970. Reissued by Cornell Southeast Asia Program, 4th printing 2002. 365 pp. ISBN 0-300-01314-0.

Modern Spoken Cambodian, Franklin E. Huffman, assist. Charan Promchan, Chhom-Rak Thong Lambert. Originally published by Yale University Press, 1970. Reissued by Cornell Southeast Asia Program, 3rd printing 1991. 451 pp. ISBN 0-300-01316-7.

Intermediate Cambodian Reader, ed. Franklin E. Huffman, assist. Im Proum. Originally published by Yale University Press, 1972. Reissued by Cornell Southeast Asia Program, 1988. 499 pp. ISBN 0-300-01552-6.

Cambodian Literary Reader and Glossary, Franklin E. Huffman, Im Proum. Originally published by Yale University Press, 1977. Reissued by Cornell Southeast Asia Program, 1988. 494 pp. ISBN 0-300-02069-4.

HMONG

White Hmong-English Dictionary, Ernest E. Heimbach. 1969. 8th printing, 2002. 523 pp. ISBN 0-87727-075-9.

VIETNAMESE

Intermediate Spoken Vietnamese, Franklin E. Huffman, Tran Trong Hai. 1980. 3rd printing 1994. ISBN 0-87727-500-9.

* * *

Southeast Asian Studies: Reorientations. Craig J. Reynolds and Ruth McVey. Frank H. Golay Lectures 2 & 3. 70 pp. ISBN 0-87727-301-4.

Javanese Literature in Surakarta Manuscripts, Nancy K. Florida. Vol. 1, *Introduction and Manuscripts of the Karaton Surakarta.* 1993. 410 pp. Frontispiece, illustrations. Hard cover, ISBN 0-87727-602-1, Paperback, ISBN 0-87727-603-X. Vol. 2, *Manuscripts of the Mangkunagaran Palace.* 2000. 576 pp. Frontispiece, illustrations. Paperback, ISBN 0-87727-604-8.

Sbek Thom: Khmer Shadow Theater. Pech Tum Kravel, trans. Sos Kem, ed. Thavro Phim, Sos Kem, Martin Hatch. 1996. 363 pp., 153 photographs. ISBN 0-87727-620-X.

In the Mirror: Literature and Politics in Siam in the American Era, ed. Benedict R. O'G. Anderson, trans. Benedict R. O'G. Anderson, Ruchira Mendiones. 1985. 2nd printing 1991. 303 pp. Paperback. ISBN 974-210-380-1.

To order, please contact:

Cornell University
Southeast Asia Program Publications
95 Brown Road
Box 1004
Ithaca NY 14850

Online: http://www.einaudi.cornell.edu/southeastasia/publications/
Tel: 1-877-865-2432 (Toll free – U.S.)
Fax: (607) 255-7534

E-mail: SEAP-Pubs@cornell.edu
Orders must be prepaid by check or credit card (VISA, MasterCard, Discover).

www.ingramcontent.com/pod-product-compliance
Ingram Content Group UK Ltd.
Pitfield, Milton Keynes, MK11 3LW, UK
UKHW031857120325
456183UK00010B/357